Funerals: a guide

When a death occurs it almost always takes us by surprise and we rarely have more than a very few days in which to arrange a funeral. The result is all too often inadequate, even irrelevant to the occasion. This book gives positive encouragement to the bereaved in enabling them to share in making arrangements for the funeral and, within the framework of what churches and funeral directors may propose, in the planning of the funeral service. This book explains the meaning and significance of the customary funeral service and suggests variations upon it and alternative forms. Throughout it urges the bereaved to play an active part in ensuring that everything in connection with the funeral is appropriate to the person who has died and to the experience of a particular death.

The major part of this book consists of a wide-ranging anthology of prayers, passages from the Bible, hymns and readings drawn from a variety of cultural traditions especially from the Christian heritage. The anthology is arranged in such a way as to reflect different attitudes to death and also to enable those who use this book readily to find material relevant to what is after all a unique and special occasion. The bereaved will find it will help them to make sure that the funeral is a worthy memorial to the person who has died, and an occasion which they will always be glad to remember. They may well want to return to the anthology for inspiration and solace at other times.

The Revd Dr James Bentley graduated in History and Theology at the University of Oxford, and was for many years parish priest at St Mary's, Oldham, Lancs. He then became Maurice Reckitt Research Fellow at the University of Sussex, where his doctoral research resulted in his book *Between Marx and Christ; the Christian-Marxist Dialogue in German-speaking Europe 1870-1970*. He then became Conduct and Senior Chaplain at Eton College, and for the last nearly twenty years he has been a freelance writer. Perhaps best known for his travel books and articles, he has also published *Cry God for England, Ritual and Politics in Victorian Britain, Oberammergau and the Passion Play* and important biographies of Martin Niemöller and of Albert Schweitzer. He has also published *A Calendar of Saints*, *A Children's Bible*, and a volume of selections from the Authorised Version of the Bible.

Andrew Best was born in London and graduated in History and English at the University of Cambridge. After seven years as a schoolteacher, he joined Longman, educational publishers, where he was in charge of publishing schoolbooks in a number of subjects, including Religious Education. He was a literary agent with Curtis Brown for twenty years and is now a freelance consultant. He edited (with M. J. Cohen) an annotated schools edition of Arnold Wesker's *The Wesker Trilogy*, and *The World of the Short Story*, an anthology for schools. He has written on music for *Country Life*, has been a concert reviewer for *The Guardian*, and is an occasional book reviewer for *The Literary Review*.

Jackie Hunt was born in Portsmouth. For several years she worked for a human rights organization, the International Commission of Jurists in Geneva and New York, and later with the London-based International African Institute. In New York she worked with the historian W. L. Katz and co-edited an anthology *Making Our Way: America at the Turn of the Century in the Words of the Poor and Powerless*. For the last few years she has been a freelance writer and editor (and is co-author of *Philip Diamond's Covent Garden Fish Book*). She is married to Andrew Best.

FUNERALS
a guide

Prayers • Readings • Hymns

JAMES BENTLEY
ANDREW BEST
JACKIE HUNT

Hodder & Stoughton
LONDON SYDNEY AUCKLAND

First published in Great Britain 1994
Reprinted with corrections 1995

3 5 7 9 10 8 6 4 2

British Library Cataloguing in Publication Data
A record for this book is available from the British Library

ISBN 0 340 61240 1

Designed and typeset by
Images, Upton-upon-Severn, Worcestershire

Printed and bound in Great Britain by
Clays Ltd, St Ives plc

Hodder and Stoughton Ltd
A Division of Hodder Headline PLC
338 Euston Road
London NW1 3BH

Contents

To

A. M. B.
1907-1987

M. W. F. H.
1906-1987

*In Loving
Memory*

Authors' Preface

We were stimulated to compile this book by Jackie Hunt's and Andrew Best's experience of having to arrange the funerals of parents, a mother and a father. Both were terminally ill, death was expected, yet when each death occurred they were caught napping. As it happened, all went off well, but those few days were hectic. Where is that hymn? Which is that psalm? Who wrote "Ask not for whom the bell tolls . . .", and where can we find it? On both occasions James Bentley helped with suggestions for prayers and hymns.

When the idea of this book began to take hold, the three of us decided to join forces. We have been helped by many others with whom we have talked and who have written to us. Some are friends who have been patient and encouraging in their letters and in conversation; some have responded to a letter that we published in a number of newspapers; yet others we have prevailed upon.

We hope that the readings we have chosen will speak with strength and clarity equally to those who listen and to those who read: many are charged with depth of feeling and numinousness. We have aimed to reach the user and reader on different levels. The numbered passages are suggested for use at the funeral service (or memorial service) and for private reading: these are indexed. The short passages in italics at the foot of the page – often no more than one line – are indexed only by author. They are intended to stimulate and provoke your own thoughts and feelings. The Epitaphs – and there are few of them – are also given in italics, and are indexed by first lines. Overall, our touchstone has been the ring of sincerity and truth.

In particular we would like to thank the Revd Fr. Will Baynes who gave us welcome and help with alacrity; Caroline Belgrave, who has been a tower of strength, lending us her house in the country from time to time for concentrated sessions of uninterrupted work on this book, and allowing us to borrow a number of her books which have proved invaluable sources; Elizabeth Best, who has pointed us towards a whole world of contemporary spirituality and psychological insight which is reflected, however inadequately, in these pages; the Rt Hon. Sir Edward du Cann, who was the first to draw our attention to the pregnant passage on page 256; Judith Eagle, who has responded to the idea of this book with her distinctive enthusiasm backed by practical suggestions; Simon Gay, for his cheerful and ready responses over the telephone to our stop press questions on hymnody; Rabbi Hugo Gryn, who has introduced to us the Jewish tradition which is, we trust, well reflected here; Professor Charles Handy, who gave us much initial encouragement, and whose Thoughts for the Day endure well beyond their five-minute span; Stuart Hughes, erstwhile financial director of Hodder & Stoughton, who first encouraged us to submit the idea for this book to its publishers; Bryan Jones of Kenyons, Funeral Directors, who has given us access to his archive; Eric Major of Hodder Headline who took the baton from Stuart Hughes and sprinted with it; Fr Jude McHugo CJ, Chaplain of St George's College, Addlestone, for his initiative in sending us poems, in particular that by 15-year old Dan Bovington (page 270); Keith Munnings of SAROS for giving us early sight of the Address given at the SAROS 1994 Seminar by Geoffrey Wellens of S. Wellens & Sons, Funeral Directors, Middleton; Ruth Nesfield-Cookson who volunteered the witness of Fr. Andrew Glazewscki; Jeremy Nicholas, who has kindly brought his Tingle Factor to the suggestions for music (page 286); Colin Nicholson, who has also made his special contribution to the music section and who selflessly manned the Camberwell office at the eleventh hour; Mary Oakley, of Bristol, who devotes much of her time to counselling the bereaved and who has published three small books of thoughts, poems and prayers which she has kindly shared with us and who introduced to us prayers by Florence Roe; Canon Michael Perham, Precentor, Norwich Cathedral and member of the Liturgical Commission, who conducted us through the significance (and the shortcomings) of the funeral service at Praxis' one-day conference on The Funeral of the Future at Chichester Theological College one wet day in October 1993 and whose further counsel has been invaluable; Richard Putt, MBIFD, General Manager, Leverton & Sons Ltd., who in his busy year as National President of the British Institute of Funeral Directors and beyond has nevertheless found the time to educate us as to how the best of Funeral Directors works with the bereaved and who has also read this book, at different stages of its making, and helped us keep it on the rails; the Revd Donald Reeves, Rector of St James' Church, Piccadilly; Rosalind Richards and her husband Brian for talks in Yorkshire and for ever-swift responses down the fax; Dr Norman Routledge for entering into the spirit of this book with so much gusto and for his help with suggestions for music; Anita Sherwood of Images, who worked long hours with us in Upton-upon-Severn preparing the camera ready pages of this book; Mike Steer and Deirdre Clancy for their witness on behalf of the Society of Friends; Pauline Webb for her readiness to bring forward prayers, including one of her own; and Dr Landeg White for sharing with us his knowledge of Africa's oral tradition. Finally, special and heartfelt thanks go to Rodney Williams, Vicar-Choral at Westminster Abbey, who has given generously of his lifelong love and experience of the English church music tradition, especially with regard to suggestions for hymns and music, all of which have been made with Rodney's characteristic discrimination and enthusiasm.

There are many others who have helped by writing to us to suggest passages for inclusion in this book. They are too numerous to mention by name, but we thank them all, and a number of them will see evidence in these pages that their contributions have indeed been welcome.

James Bentley · Andrew Best · Jackie Hunt
Camberwell Eye Slough 1994

NON NOBIS DOMINE NON NOBIS SED NOMINI TUO DA GLORIAM ·

Practicalities

As death is inevitable, so is a funeral. The most practical thing you can do is to arrange your own funeral before you die, and so relieve those left behind of the burden. Unfortunately for the bereaved, very few people do this; perhaps a superstitious feeling lingers that to make plans for one's own funeral may invite the approach of death.

The law says that when someone dies we must obtain a death certificate, that the death must be registered, and that arrangements for the 'disposal of the body' must be made. A funeral, therefore, is necessary. But it need not be a chore. Over hundreds of years funerals have been found not only to be necessary, but needful. They are necessary for the dead, and at the same time are needful for the living.

A funeral presents a unique opportunity to bring together a gathering fitting for the dead and mutually supportive for those left behind, and to share our memories, our grief, and our celebration of the departed. Of course we want to pay our last respects, but we also need to express – or have expressed for us – our grief, our sorrow, and even our guilt and anger. In short, we *need* a funeral. It is one of the few occasions where we are allowed outwardly to show our emotions.

The person to turn to in this need is a funeral director. Funeral directors, or undertakers, may seem at a distance impersonal, gloomy and forbidding. For most of us, only death brings the opportunity to meet one. In fact, most funeral directors will be found to be ready with advice, sympathy and practical help. You have one obligation, which is to obtain the certificate of registration of death. Armed with that, you can engage the funeral director as one who, in consultation with you, will organise the funeral. He should be a member of the British Institute of Funeral Directors and his firm or company should belong to a nationally recognised organisation. Specifically, he can and will

- take care of the deceased
- deal with the paperwork (except registration of the death)
- liaise and make arrangements with church, cemetery, and/or crematorium
- liaise with others, for example when a body needs to be brought home for the funeral
- arrange for the disposal of ashes
- help to cover day-to-day expenses, such costs being charged in the funeral director's final account
- arrange for individual service sheets to be printed
- advise and help on matters such as announcements, flowers, the choice of coffin, a gathering after the service, etc.

Here are some examples of the various circumstances which may apply to a death, and where the funeral director should be qualified to help you:

If you were close to the deceased, you are likely to know the cause of death, whether or no the deceased was a churchgoer, whether the deceased was ill, and so you may already be in touch with the minister of religion, doctor, psychiatrist or counsellor who knew the deceased and to whom it would be natural for you to turn. If not, the funeral director can introduce you to the appropriate person.

If the deceased died from natural causes, which include disease and other ills such as drugs, neglect or even suicide, there may already be a helper. This helper may be a minister of religion, a counsellor, or a friend. The next of kin may already know that person, or may meet him or her only when death is imminent or has occurred. Such a person can be enormously helpful: not so much in the practical duties already summarised, but in opening doors towards rites of passage which will be comforting and memorable to those left behind. If there is no such helper, the funeral director can advise.

Was the deceased a churchgoer? Seek out the parish priest or minister, and enlist his or her help in planning the funeral service. Even if the deceased was not a churchgoer, there may be a religious tradition to which he or she belonged: the funeral director can introduce you to the appropriate person. Many non-churchgoers feel very reluctant to become involved with their local church after a long period of non-attendance. Such people, and they are in a majority, will find that the church understands this, and welcomes the opportunity to help even if only during the time of bereavement. The church combines hundreds of years of experience in seeing people come and go, and its long-established framework is always ready to offer help and encouragement. The churches are reserves of strength which are there for you to use.

Was the deceased ill, lonely, or neglected? Seek out the doctor, counsellor, social worker and/or neighbour who might have been involved with the deceased. You'll be surprised at the support you may get. Again, the funeral director can help.

You may be spouse, parent, offspring, or a more distant relation to the deceased. Even if you are the spouse you may not have known – or known well – the deceased's friends or colleagues. Again, seek them out: you will learn about aspects of the deceased you'd never known, in a way that will be as enriching as it may be surprising.

If the deceased has made her/his funeral arrangements during her/his lifetime, you may have reason to be thankful. You will then have clear guidelines which you can follow with confidence. Even so, the wishes of the deceased may need to be interpreted in the light of circumstances that prevail at the time of death. The funeral director can advise.

All of these, funeral director, parish priest, counsellor, social worker, home help, friends, colleagues will be ready to help: when death approaches, when death occurs, and in preparing the funeral.

You, the next of kin, have – with or without the support of an executor – legal and practical obligations. But you – next of kin and the bereaved – have rights as well as duties, and these rights are far greater and more wide-ranging than many people think, and belong to non-churchgoers as well as churchgoers. These rights include:

Before death

You may if you wish invite the parish priest or other counsellor to visit the dying person and to share that experience with you. The parish priest may administer the last rites to the dying, if that is part of the family tradition.

After death

In many cases the wishes of the deceased will be known and wherever possible should be respected. Indeed, executors have a duty to ensure that this is so. Unless these wishes are known or specified otherwise:

- you may if you wish arrange for the laying out at the deceased's home, and for a gathering of family and friends in the presence of the body who together may pray, grieve and reflect – with or without the guidance of the parish priest

- you may if you wish arrange for the body to be received in the church prior to the funeral, and to hold a night vigil there

- you have every right to contribute to the content of the funeral and/or memorial service: to suggest hymns, psalms, readings, music and to seek the help of funeral director and celebrant in this

- you have the right to choose the means of committal

- you have the right to determine whether or no there shall be:
    flowers
    formal dress
    children present

personal motifs
a reception afterwards
notices in the press
invitations

These are examined in more detail below

- you have the right to hold a memorial service

- you have the right to celebrate the anniversary of the death

- you have the right to join in larger annual thanksgivings, such as All Souls Day and Easter Day.

Church or Cemetery or Crematorium?

Together with the choice of a funeral director, the question of whether a funeral should take place in church, at a cemetery or at a crematorium will be uppermost in the minds of the bereaved. The funeral director will of course advise, but he will need to know what religious persuasion the deceased held, and, if there was little or no religion in the life of the deceased, what underlying religious tradition there may be. A member of, for example, the Muslim or Orthodox Jewish faith will have no doubt about where to apply for the funeral ceremony. But for those with little or no religion, there are options to consider and a decision to be made very quickly. If, for example, the deceased was a lapsed Roman Catholic, then the inclination will be to engage the services of the Roman Catholic parish priest. If there is a Church of England tradition in the family, then the inclination will be towards the Anglican parish priest. Again, the funeral director will advise.

Simultaneously the question of burial or cremation arises. Burial in a church is very rare nowadays, and certainly cannot take place without prior arrangements having been made, so in practical terms, this is not an option. Burial in a churchyard nay be an option if the deceased was a churchgoer or lived in the vicinity of a church, and especially if the deceased had made arrangements prior to death or the circumstances are exceptional such as the death of a child. Burial in a cemetery is open to all by arrangement with those who administer the cemetery, often the local authority.

The option of cremation has one major social advantage: the deceased will not occupy valuable land-space. Even so, because of the pressure on the crematorium, again often administered by the local authority, a funeral held in the crematorium chapel may not last for much longer than twenty minutes, and this is a lamentably short space of time in which to grieve for and commemorate the deceased. Also, unless those arranging the funeral express a wish, the crematorium chapel service will be conducted by a minister of religion who knows neither the deceased nor the family (the same will be true of the cemetery chaplain). But most crematoria are able to accept bookings for a longer time for the service in the crematorium chapel, at extra cost, and the bereaved have the right to introduce a speaker at the funeral service who does know the deceased, the next of kin and friends.

The shock of a death needs to be absorbed over time, and as much room as possible should be allowed for the expression of feeling on the part of the bereaved. This means that time needs to be taken to express the often conflicting feelings that surround a death. As we have indicated, these may include grief, regret, guilt, even anger. They may also include relief, gratitude and pride in a life lived well. Time – time before the funeral, during the funeral service itself, and after the funeral – is needed if the full range of emotions are to be felt and expressed by the bereaved, and such time is well-spent, for it will to a great extent dilute the onslaught of delayed shock. We shall come later to the funeral service itself, but you may be assured that the Church of England, Roman Catholic and a number of Non-Conformist churches all share the same underlying pattern which gives room for emotions to be expressed.

If a tablet or a headstone is required, there are regulations that must be observed, and there are certain restrictions on the scattering or burial of ashes. The funeral director will be able to tell you about these.

When the choice is for cremation, it is increasingly customary that the first part of the funeral takes place in church, and the last, shorter, part in the crematorium chapel. This has the advantage of allowing more time for the ceremony, at least an hour if so wished. It is also possible for cremation to take place first, the ashes enclosed in a casket being brought into the church for the funeral service.

It may be that where the deceased was unsure as to belief (agnostic), was a professed unbeliever (atheist), or was a member of a Humanist or Ethical association a non-religious funeral service will be appropriate. Such a service is allowable in the crematorium chapel, and elsewhere such as a public meeting place.

Be assured that funeral directors and ministers of religion will be pleased to know the wishes of the bereaved where the choice of hymns, prayers, psalms, readings and music is concerned, and also if the bereaved would like a particular person or members of the family to contribute their own personal reminiscences.

There are options that lie beyond church, cemetery or crematorium. The funeral director can help with all of these. One of the options is woodland burial, now being actively promoted in various parts of the country. The body may be shrouded in a decomposable material before burial and thereafter a tree or bush planted at the spot. Burial at sea is possible but arrangements are somewhat complex and contact should be made with local fisheries District Inspectors or the Marine Environmental Protection department at the Ministry of Agriculture, Fisheries and Food. For those wishing to be more personally involved in all aspects of burial rites – making the coffin, dealing with the paperwork, as well as composing the funeral service – it is recommended that contact be made with The Natural Death Centre or the British Humanist Association.

Where a tablet or headstone is desired, this need not be left to the funeral director or monumental mason. The next of kin or executor can have a hand in the wording of the inscription and in the design of and material used for such a memorial, though there will be restrictions, for example of size and design, in churchyard, cemetery or the crematorium's garden of remembrance. You may wish to contact the

National Association of Master Masons or the Memorials Advisory
Bureau. Harriet Frazer founded the Memorials by Artists movement
which puts the bereaved in touch with artists who will design
headstones or other memorials to individual specifications. Remember
that a memorial lasts a long time and may need to be maintained.

The following are notes on certain aspects of arranging funerals which
often trouble people:

Announcement of the Death

A notice in the press of a death is a way to alert distant friends and
family who might not otherwise have means of knowing that someone
has died. It is particularly appropriate where a person has been well-
known in the local or wider community and an obituary or
appreciation might be welcomed in the local press.

If all would be welcome to attend the ceremony, the notice should
include details of the funeral arrangements – date, time, place – or the
name and telephone number of the funeral director or organizer. If it is
wished that the funeral ceremony be private and restricted to family
and/or close friends, that too should be indicated.

Because of the normally short time between the occurrence of
death and the funeral, it is not usual to circulate formal invitations;
information is most often given by telephone. However, if time permits
and you wish to invite specific people to the ceremony, there is no
reason why you should not issue formal invitations.

Viewing the body/Lying-in

For many, it is a great help to see the body of the person who has died.
It is a way to say goodbye. This is a personal matter and one which can
only be decided by the individual. No pressure should be brought on
either adult or child on whether or no to make this gesture. Most often
what is imagined is much worse than the reality. Clearly, if a young
child wants to see a parent or grandparent for the last time, a trusted
adult should be in attendance to reassure.

The funeral director will, if requested, make arrangements for viewing. We were fortunate to know the West Indian philosopher C. L. R. James. Because we were unable to go to his funeral, we went to pay our last respects at the funeral parlour where his body lay. The funeral director greeted us with a warm smile, and said: "He must have been a wonderful person." Her feeling was richly confirmed when we saw him for the last time: he looked radiant and at peace.

Some may wish the body to remain at or to be returned to the family home in order that viewing may take place there, and/or a vigil maintained. These are options for decision by the family.

The Service Sheet

This need not be elaborate – a photocopy will suffice – but a printed order of service is very helpful for all who attend the funeral. It will give them indications of what is to be read, what is to be sung and where they are asked to participate. Give the words of hymns or songs in full where they are to be sung by all; if readings are to be included, give the title and author of each piece and who will read it; if a solo singer or choir will perform, give the title and composer. It is usual to give the name of the deceased in full with dates of birth and death. Copies of the service sheet can be handed to people as they enter the place of service, or they can be put on the seats before the service. They may also be sent to those who were not able to attend the funeral.

Children

Some people feel that children are not able to cope with the rigours and stresses of a funeral. Largely, this is not so. But the matter of their attendance should, where possible, be their decision. They should be neither excluded from the occasion nor forced to attend. Too often one has heard of the resentment of young persons at having been excluded from all or part of the funeral rites when they would have wished to be able to participate and make their own gesture of farewell.

Dress

The matter of dress is one which troubles a number of people. Should black be worn? If you feel it is appropriate for you and what the deceased would want, then yes. But others may wish to dress as the deceased always saw them; or incorporate a favourite colour or piece of clothing. William Leith told the story of a young student who was to attend his grandfather's funeral, could not bring himself to wear a borrowed suit that his mother wished him to wear, but finally wore his usual clothing with a borrowed, though shabby, jacket and felt 'I think Grandpa would want me to wear this.' At the funeral of a woman who was always to be seen in her favourite blue, many of her friends wore something of that colour in remembrance of her. Again, friends of a young man killed in an incident in Cyprus wore the T-shirts they had bought on the last occasion they were all together as a token of remembrance.

Flowers

Some feel that money is wasted on provision of formal flower arrangements or wreaths and would prefer donations to be made to a favoured charity or other organization. This preference should be made clear to the funeral director and in any announcement or invitation. If uncertain, those who wish to attend a funeral should contact the family, friends, or the funeral director. Bunches of cut flowers and garden posies may be preferred which could later be given to a local hospital or home. Cards accompanying flowers are usually collected by the funeral director and handed to the person who has been most involved in organizing the funeral in order that they might be acknowledged. They can also form an important part of one's record of the occasion and memory of the person who has died.

After the Funeral

This can be a very bleak time if the participants simply depart and go their own way. If resources permit it is preferable to invite those who have attended the funeral to the deceased's home, to the family home, or to some other convenient gathering place for whatever refreshment is thought suitable, and to enjoy the opportunity to meet and talk to one another and to pay personal respects to the bereaved. On two occasions we have returned from the funeral to the home of our departed friend, to meet and talk with friends and family, surrounded by the furnishings, pictures and objects with which we had been familiar during the lifetime. To meet in this way after a funeral is particularly comforting, because the departed remains so near. A 'wake' can be a wonderful way to relieve emotions and to allow memories of the dead – often humorous – to be recalled.

The invitation is most conveniently made by printing it on the service sheet if provided, or by asking the person conducting the service to make an announcement at the end.

A custom which is not often observed, and which requires much from the bereaved, is to stand at the door of the church, crematorium, or meeting-place after the ceremony to greet and thank people for their attendance. We were very moved to see this done by a mother who had lost her child.

It is often the case that the bereaved are overwhelmed by the response to a death, and while it is always preferable to write personal notes of thanks for letters of condolence and attendance at funerals, you can have cards or letters printed with your own form of words of thanks.

The bereaved and all those who attend a funeral should not later feel cheated of an occasion which should mark and celebrate the life of the person who has died. Members of the deceased's circle of family and friends may also be bereaved if they are not encouraged and enabled to share in the experience by those closest to the deceased. They should be given jobs to do: one should be asked to make the catering arrangements, others should be asked to hand out the service sheets and act as ushers; another can deal with the announcement of the death; another can order the flowers. Remember also to thank the hearse driver, the pall bearers, the gravediggers and others, for they too are helpers and their gain comes from being able to help you. In short, the care taken in arranging an appropriate ceremony will be rewarded by warm memories and shared appreciation. We are all one family.

How to use this book

Who has died, and how? This book is arranged so as to enable you to find prayers, hymns, and readings – from the Bible and other sources – which are appropriate to the person who has died and to the manner of death. The indexes will help you do this. Bold numbers in the indexes refer you to the numbered prayers, psalms, extracts from the bible and other readings. Ordinary numbers refer you to page numbers. Let us suppose that a husband, who was a keen golfer, has died while away from home. Index 1 (page 297) gives Husband and also Golfer. Index 2 (page 298) gives Away from home.

Next you should consider *What messages do you want the funeral to bring to those present, and what feelings do you want the funeral to express?* The funeral 'messages' are indicated by the section headings used for the readings, especially:

Faith, Hope, Love   **Celebration and Thanks**
Consolation   **Continuing Presence**
Reconciliation   **Eternal Life**

Of course these include feelings, but as well as these, more specific feelings, themes and attitudes to life and death are given in Index 3 (page 298). These indexes are linked by number to the individual prayers and readings. Let us also suppose that the user of this book believes in **Eternal Life**, requires **Consolation**, and hopes to experience the **Continuing Presence** of the departed: let us further suppose that the departed was of Scottish descent, and that he died suddenly on holiday at sea. Index 3 (page 298) gives **Consolation, Continuing Presence, Eternal Life, Scottish,** and **Sea.**

In this way you will be guided to – for example – *My Heart's in the Highlands*, by Robert Burns (No. 405), *Now finalè to the shore*, by Walt Whitman (No. 488), and *Seaside Golf* by John Betjeman (No. 406), as well as to many other prayers and readings from which you may choose, in consultation with family and friends and with the celebrant and the funeral director.

Yet these indexes are themselves only indications. You may, in browsing through this book, come across pieces which you feel are right for the departed and right for you. We hope that you will.

Preparing for your own funeral We hope that this is where this book may be especially helpful. To leave, as part of your Will, a plan and content for your own funeral service is to lift a load from the shoulders of the bereaved for which they will be always grateful. They will continue to have a voice, but you will have led them and helped them towards an appropriate memorial and farewell. The sections **Preparing for Death** and **In the Midst of Life** should be found especially valuable to the living who are preparing for their own deaths, while equally relevant to the bereaved who themselves must perforce look death in the face as the end or as the dawn of a new beginning.

For months, even for years after a death, the process of grief continues. To read and re-read *your* chosen passages in this book will be part of the healing process, and will help you to recognise your pain, to come to terms with it and to turn sorrow into joy.

The funeral service

The underlying form of the religious funeral service is common to many different churches, including the Roman Catholic Church, the Church of England, the Church in Wales, the Methodist Church, the Baptist Union of England and Wales, and the United Reformed Church.

A typical funeral service consists of the following elements:

- **The Bidding** (prayers)

- **The Word** (the Bible)

- **Prayer** (general prayers)

- **The Commendation and Farewell** (prayers)

- **The Committal** (prayers)

Readings may be appropriate to all the above.

The Bidding: This first part of the service consists of the gathering together of the bereaved, their being made welcome by the celebrant, and their being invited to remember the personality of the deceased, to give thanks for her/his life and to grieve for their immediate loss.

The Word: Essentially this is what the Bible and the churches say about death. The Word is expressed variously in prayer, in readings from the Bible, in psalms and hymns, and in the address in which the celebrant (or another) sums up the life, work and personality of the deceased, often in relation to the Christian belief in the mercy of God and in eternal life.

Prayer: Obviously this will be expressed in the form of prayers, and in readings. These will invite the bereaved to remember the deceased, and to express in their hearts a range of feelings, including penitence for what may have been their own shortcomings in their relationship with the deceased. This aspect of the service is also an opportunity for the bereaved to search their hearts for shortcomings in their own lives, to be sorry for these and to resolve to do better. Fully-fledged Christian funerals will often celebrate the Eucharist (Communion service) at this point, for the Christian finds that this great prayer, celebrating the death and resurrection of Our Lord, lies at the heart of the faith, expressing as it does grief, penitence, remembrance, thanksgiving and triumph over death.

The Commendation and Farewell: Here the celebrant combines with those present to urge that the soul of the deceased will find rest, peace and the life hereafter. It is also the opportunity for the bereaved, in the presence of the deceased, to say their last goodbyes.

The Committal: This is that part of the service during which the body in its coffin is lowered into the earth for burial or, at the crematorium, passes into the crematory to be consumed by fire.

Relevant quotations from the Bible – **The Word** – will be found immediately after this section. **Readings** which, as we have said, have their place in every element of the funeral service, will again be found below and we have already offered guidance to the readings given in this book in the section "How to Use this Book", and further guidance will be found in the indexes.

To return to the **Funeral Service**: this is at the same time a bringing together of the living with the deceased, and a parting. The spirit of the service is to help the soul of the deceased on its way, as it were to speed the parting guest, and to reaffirm our relationships with the deceased including our wishes for the soul's peace and happiness in the hereafter.

The **Bidding** provides a great opportunity for the bereaved to tell the celebrant before the service about the deceased: what sort of a person she/he was at work, at play, in relationships, in all manifestations of humanity. The Bidding prayers can then become personally relevant to the deceased and also relevant to the perception and appreciation of the bereaved, who will be helped by the Bidding prayers to share remembrance of the departed.

We have seen many examples of Bidding prayers. One gives thanks for the work of a hard-working rancher who died young; who was happily married, who was proud of his children, who loved his fishing holidays, and who enjoyed close family ties. Another gives thanks and praise to God for the life and work of a writer who died at the age of nearly 80, who loved beauty, who was brave, witty, who did not suffer fools gladly, and who loved cats. Yet another celebrates the life of a woman who died from cancer relatively young, and draws the congregation together in remembrance of her wit, beauty, kindness, sense of humour and love of spectacle. Another thanks the Lord for a woman's life of piety and patience, cheerfulness and endurance; for her unstinting work for old people, the lonely and the sick. The **Bidding**, then, can only be effective if you, the bereaved, enable the celebrant to give thanks and to remember the person who has died. Otherwise, you may be disappointed by generalities. Even so, this part of the service may be introduced by more formal sentences or prayers, for example:

> I am the resurrection and the life, saith the Lord: he that believeth in me, though he were dead, yet shall he live: and whosever liveth and believeth in me shall never die.
>
> St John 11: 25, 26

> We brought nothing into this world, and it is certain we can carry nothing out. The Lord gave, and the Lord hath taken away; blessed be the name of the Lord.
>
> 1 Timothy 6: 7; Job 1: 21

It may be summed up by a more formal prayer, such as:

O Almighty God, we praise and magnify Thy holy Name for all Thy servants who, having fought the good fight, have finished their course in Thy faith and fear; and especially for [N] and we beseech Thee that, encouraged by her/his example and strengthened by her/his fellowship, we may with her/him be found meet to be partakers of the inheritance of the saints in light, through Jesus Christ our Lord.

Before moving on to specific prayers, here is a quotation which defines prayer:

Surely the 'tender bridge' that joins the living and the dead in Christ is prayer. Mutual intercession is the life-blood of the fellowship, and what is there in a Christian's death that can possibly check its flow? To ask for the prayers of others in this life, and to know that they rely on mine, does not show any lack of faith in the all-sufficiency of God. Then, in the same faith, let me ask for their prayers still, and offer mine for them, even when death has divided us. They pray for me, I believe, with clearer understanding, but I for them in ignorance, though still with love. And love, not knowledge, is the substance of prayer.

J. TAYLOR from *The Primal Vision*

Prayer at the funeral service, as we have said, invites remembrance, and also may invoke a wide range of feelings in the hearts of those present. Here are some prayers – and there are many, many more – from which you may like to choose. But first, there is one short prayer which was made by Sir Jacob Astley on the eve of the Battle of Edgehill in England's Civil War which has special relevance to the bustle of arranging a funeral:

Lord, Thou knowest that I must be very busie this day.
If I forget Thee, yet do not Thou forget mee.

Many psalms (see pages 49 to 63) may also be said or sung as prayers: all may join in. The same applies to hymns (see pages 275 to 285).

Prayers

The prayers that follow come from many different sources, and wherever possible these have been given. Where no source is given, this is because we have found such prayers in books or on funeral service sheets where no source has been given or author credited. The authors and publishers would welcome information which would enable them to credit such prayers appropriately in later editions of this book.

GENERAL

1   Our Father, which art in heaven, Hallowed be thy Name. Thy kingdom come. Thy will be done, in earth as it is in heaven. Give us this day our daily bread. And forgive us our trespasses, As we forgive them that trespass against us. And lead us not into temptation; But deliver us from evil: For thine is the kingdom, The power, and the glory, For ever and ever.

THE LORD'S PRAYER

2   Dear God, may we look backward with gratitude, forward with courage, upwards with confidence.

3   In the presence of death let us not fear. We share it with all who have ever lived and with all who will ever be. For it is only the dust which returns to the dust as it was, but the spirit returns to God who gave it, and in His hand is the care of

every soul. The world we inhabit is a corridor to the world beyond. We prepare ourselves in the corridor to enter His presence. He is our employer who knows our sorrows and our labour. Faithful is He to give us the reward of our good deeds. He redeems us from destruction and leads us in the way of everlasting life.

JEWISH FUNERAL SERVICE

4   O God, give me the serenity to accept the things I cannot change; the courage to change the things I can; and the wisdom to know the difference.

REINHOLD NIEBUHR

5   O Lord God, when Thou givest to Thy servants to endeavour any great matter, grant us also to know that it is not the beginning but the continuing of the same unto the end, until it be thoroughly finished, which yieldeth the true glory; through him who for the finishing of Thy work laid down his Life, our Redeemer Jesus Christ.

SIR FRANCIS DRAKE

6   Lord, make me a channel of Thy peace; where there is hatred may I bring love; where there is injury, pardon; where there is doubt, faith; where there is despair, hope; where there is darkness, light; and where there is sadness, joy. O Divine Lover, grant that we may not so much seek to be consoled as to console; to be understood as to understand; to be loved as to love; for it is in giving that we receive, it is in pardoning that we are pardoned, and it is in dying that we are born to eternal life.

ST FRANCIS OF ASSISI

7   O Lord, support us all the day long of this troublous life, until the shades lengthen, and the evening comes, and the busy world is hushed, the fever of life is over, and our work is

done. Then, Lord, in Thy mercy, grant us safe lodging, a holy rest, and peace at the last; through our Lord Jesus Christ.

JOHN HENRY NEWMAN

8   Bring us O Lord God at our last awakening into the house and gate of Heaven, to enter into that house where there shall be no darkness nor dazzling, but one equal light; no noise nor silence but one equal music; no fears or hopes but one equal possession: no ends or beginnings but one equal eternity in the habitations of Thy Glory and Dominion, world without end.

JOHN DONNE

9   Father in heaven, you gave your Son Jesus Christ to suffering and to death on the cross, and raised him to life in glory. Grant us a patient faith in time of darkness, and strengthen our hearts with the knowledge of your love; through Jesus Christ our Lord.

ALTERNATIVE SERVICE BOOK

10   O Father of all, we pray to thee for those whom we love, but see no longer. Grant them thy peace; let light perpetual shine upon them; and in thy loving wisdom and almighty power, work in them the good purpose of thy perfect will; through Jesus Christ our Lord.

PROPOSED PRAYER BOOK, 1928

11   O God, forasmuch as without thee we are not able to please thee; Mercifully grant, that thy Holy Spirit may in all things direct and rule our hearts; through Jesus Christ our Lord.

BOOK OF COMMON PRAYER

12   Almighty and everlasting God, mercifully look upon our infirmities, and in all our dangers and necessities stretch forth thy right hand to help and defend us; through Jesus Christ our Lord.

BOOK OF COMMON PRAYER

13   Almighty God, who seest that we have no power of ourselves
to help ourselves; Keep us both outwardly in our bodies, and
inwardly in our souls; that we may be defended from all
adversities which may happen to the body, and from all evil
thoughts which may assault and hurt the soul; through Jesus
Christ our Lord.

BOOK OF COMMON PRAYER

GRIEF AND MOURNING

14   O God, the Strength of the weak, the Comfort of the
sorrowful, the Friend of the lonely: let not sorrow overwhelm
Thy children, nor anguish of heart turn them from Thee.
Grant that in the patience of hope and the fellowship of Christ
they may continue in Thy service and in all godly living, until
at length they also attain unto fullness of life before Thy face,
through Jesus Christ our Lord.

METHODIST BOOK OF OFFICES

15   O God, who healest the broken-hearted and bindest up their
wounds, to Thee I turn in trust and submission in this dark
hour . . . Send forth Thy light so that amid this shadow of
death . . . I may see the path to Thee, to a better use of my
powers, to a better understanding of life. I do not ask Thee to
take this sorrow from me altogether, but to aid me in purging
it from all taint of selfishness . . . May my own pain make me
more heedful of human woe, more responsive to it, more
resolute in my endeavour to assuage it! Fix my thoughts not
only on this lower life, but on life with Thee; not only on the
things of Time, but on the joyous promise of Eternity . . .
Strengthen my faith in my higher self . . . in my soul which
. . . will unite me to Thee hereafter in blissful and endless
communion . . . . Then will the veil that hides Thee from me
be torn away, and I shall see Thee clearly . . . Then shall love

come by its own – my dear one's which has been my joy in the bygone years, Thine which has blessed me all my life long.

MORRIS JOSEPH

16   Support us, Lord, when we are silent through grief! Comfort us when we are bent down with sorrow! Help us as we bear the weight of our loss! Lord, our Rock and our Redeemer, give us strength!

JEWISH FUNERAL SERVICE

17   Almighty God, Father of all mercies and giver of all comfort: Deal graciously, we pray thee, with those who mourn, that casting every care on thee, they may know the consolation of thy love; through Jesus Christ our Lord

PROPOSED PRAYER BOOK, 1928

BEREAVEMENT

18   Lord we pray for the bereaved, asking that their heartbreak may be healed by the balm of God's comfort, and that beyond the dreadful silence of death they may hear the songs of the angels bringing the hope of heaven. Through Jesus Christ our Lord.

PAULINE WEBB

19   O Lord, God of the spirits of all flesh, You are with us at all times: in joy and in sorrow, in light and in darkness, in life and in death. Open our hearts, that we may feel Your presence even at this hour of bereavement. Let the knowledge of Your nearness soothe our spirits and heal our wounds. Teach us to trust You. We do not always understand Your ways, but even as we grieve, make us grateful for the

blessings we have received, and give us the faith to declare:
The Lord gave, and the Lord has taken away; praised be the
name of the Lord.

JEWISH PRAYER

20   Lord, we remember with gratitude all those people whom we
have loved – and those who have loved us. May that love be a
link between this world and the next, and may their souls rest
in peace.

MARJORIE BEREZA

CONSOLATION

21   To complete the work of God in this world is not given to
anyone, for even if we work with all our strength, the result is
in the hands of God. May those who mourn be comforted, for
the Lord is faithful to all His creatures, and His love is
constant for all eternity.

JEWISH PRAYER

22   Eternal God, in Your hands are the souls of the living and the
spirits of all creatures. We turn to You in grief as well as in
joy, for Your mercy is always with us, and Your love and
truth support us at all times. Though we walk through the
valley of the shadow of death, we fear no harm, for You are
beside us; Your rod and staff they comfort us. Lord, you have
taken from us [N]. In Your mercy bear *her/him* to life
everlasting.

     May the memory of *her/his* life and *her/his* good deeds
bring blessing and comfort to those who mourn for *her/him*.
May it give them the courage and strength to continue bravely
in their daily life, trusting You in their hearts.

     God of mercy, help those who mourn, and comfort them
in their grief. Lighten their darkness, and console them in
their sorrow. It is said: 'As a mother comforts her child so

will I myself comfort you. Never again shall your sun set, nor your moon withdraw its light, because the Lord shall be your everlasting light, and the days of your mourning shall be ended.'

JEWISH FUNERAL SERVICE

23   O God the King of glory, who has exalted thine only Son Jesus Christ with great triumph unto thy kingdom in heaven; We beseech thee, leave us not comfortless; but send to us thine Holy Ghost to comfort us, and exalt us unto the same place whither our Saviour Christ is gone before, who liveth and reigneth with thee and the Holy Ghost, one God, world without end.

BOOK OF COMMON PRAYER

PENITENCE

24   Have mercy upon him, pardon all his transgressions, for there is not a just man upon earth who does good and does not sin.

JEWISH PRAYER

25   Almighty and everlasting God, who hatest nothing that thou hast made, and dost forgive the sins of all them that are penitent; Create and make in us new and contrite hearts, that we worthily lamenting our sins, and acknowledging our wretchedness, may obtain of thee, the God of all mercy, perfect remission and forgiveness; through Jesus Christ our Lord.

BOOK OF COMMON PRAYER

26   The everlasting God has in His wisdom foreseen from eternity the cross that He now presents to you as a gift from His inmost heart. This cross He now sends you He has considered with His all-knowing eyes, understood with His Divine mind, tested with His wise justice, warmed with loving arms and weighed with His own hands, to see that it be not one inch too large and not one ounce too heavy for you. He has blessed it with His holy name, anointed it with His grace, perfumed it with His consolation, taken one last glance at you and your courage, and then sends it to you from Heaven, a special greeting of God to you, an alms of the all-merciful God.

ST FRANCIS DE SALES

27   Forgiving God, in the face of death we discover how many things are still undone, how much might have been done otherwise. Redeem our failure. Bind up the wounds of past mistakes. Transform our guilt to active love, and by your forgiveness make us whole.

Lord, in your mercy
hear our prayer

SCOTTISH EPISCOPAL FUNERAL RITE

28   God our Redeemer, you love all that you have made, you are merciful beyond our deserving. Pardon your servant's sins, acknowledged or unperceived. Help us also to forgive as we pray to be forgiven, through him who on the cross asked forgiveness for those who wounded him.

Lord, in your mercy
Hear our prayer

SCOTTISH EPISCOPAL FUNERAL RITE

GOD'S MERCY

29   O Lord, the first and the last, the beginning and the end: You who were with us at our birth be with us through our life; You who are with us through our life, be with us at our death; and because your mercy will not leave us then, grant that we die not, but rise to the life everlasting.

30 Lord, without our consent we are born, without our consent we live, without our consent we die, without our consent our bodies return to the grave and our spirit goes forward to life everlasting. We cannot always understand Your plans and we do not see Your ways, for our minds are overwhelmed and our eyes are too weak. Yet to comfort us and give us hope You lift the veil of eternity, and we are permitted to know that the world is a corridor, and we are on a journey, that the end is perfection, and the reward is peace.

For a short time You gave into our care a child whom we loved. Our hearts would be broken if we did not know that You are love itself, which makes good all that is lost. The tears would never leave our eyes if we did not know that at the end You bring all together, with mercy and tenderness, in the gathering of life. Therefore with sadness and with hope we commend the soul of [N] into your care. You are with *her/him*, we cannot fear.

JEWISH FUNERAL SERVICE

31 Almighty and everlasting God, who art always more ready to hear than we to pray, and art wont to give more than either we desire or deserve; Pour down upon us the abundance of thy mercy; forgiving us those things whereof our conscience is afraid, and giving us those good things which we are not worthy to ask, but through the merits and mediation of Jesus Christ, thy Son, our Lord.

BOOK OF COMMON PRAYER

32 O God, the protector of all that trust in Thee, without whom nothing is strong, nothing is holy: Increase upon us Thy mercy that Thou being our ruler and guide, we may pass through things temporal, that we finally lose not the things eternal; Grant this for Jesus Christ's sake our Lord.

BOOK OF COMMON PRAYER

33   Father of all, have mercy on those who have taken their own lives. We do not know what tensions or what deprivations led them to this act. Help us to become more understanding and more loving to the lonely, the hurt and unlovely of this world so they will not take the same way out. Wrap those who have killed themselves in your love so that they will live anew with you in your kingdom and come to glorify you, world without end.

FLORENCE ROE *For those bereaved through suicide*

34   Grant that this life, so troubled here, may unfold itself in Thy sight, and find sweet employment in the spacious fields of Eternity.

FLORENCE ROE *For a suicide*

PEACE

35   Give them rest with the devout and the just, in the place of the pasture of rest and of refreshment, of waters in the paradise of delight; whence grief and pain and sighing have fled away.

EARLY CHRISTIAN PRAYER

36   O Father, give the spirit power to climb
To the fountain of all light, and be purified.
Break through the mists of earth, the weight of the clod,
Shine forth in splendour, thou that art calm weather
And quiet resting place for faithful souls.
To see Thee is the end and the beginning,
Thou carriest us, and Thou dost go before,
Thou art the journey and the journey's end.

HELEN WADDELL from *the Latin*

37   God full of compassion whose presence is over us, grant perfect rest beneath the shelter of Your presence to [N] who has gone to *her/his* everlasting home. Master of mercy, cover

her/him in the shelter of Your wings forever, and bind *her/his* soul into the gathering of life. It is the Lord who is *her/his* heritage. May *he/she* be at peace in *her/his* place of rest.

JEWISH PRAYER

38   Lead me from death to life,
            From falsehood to truth;
        Lead me from despair to hope,
            From fear to trust;
        Lead me from hate to love,
            From war to peace;
        Let peace fill our hearts,
            Our world,
            Our universe

SATISH KUMAR from *the Upanishads*

39   Lord Jesus Christ, you care for little children in this present life and have prepared for them in the life to come a home where they behold your Father's face. Make us assuredly to know that you have received [N] in peace. For you have said, Let the children come to me, for to such belongs the kingdom of heaven. To you, with the Father and the Holy Spirit, be all glory, honour and worship, now and ever, world without end.

REMEMBRANCE

40   Grant, O Lord, that keeping in glad remembrance those who have gone before, who have stood by us and helped us, who have cheered us by their sympathy and strengthened us by their example, we may seize every opportunity of life and rejoice in the promise of a glorious resurrection with them, through Jesus Christ our Lord.

41   O Eternal God, before whose face the generations rise and pass away, thyself unchanged abiding, we bless thy holy Name for all who have completed their earthly course in thy faith and fear and are now at rest. We remember before thee this day [N] rendering thanks to thee for *her/his* life of devoted service and ready friendship. To *her/him*, with all the faithful departed, grant thy peace; and in thy loving wisdom and almighty power, work in them the good purpose of thy perfect will: through Jesus Christ our Lord.

42   Father of all, by whose mercy and grace your saints remain in everlasting light and peace, we remember with thanksgiving those whom we love but see no longer and we pray that in them your perfect will may be fulfilled. Through Jesus Christ our Lord.

43   Almighty God, we remember this day before thee thy faithful servant [N], and we pray that, having opened to *her/him* the gates of life, thou wilt receive *her/him* more and more into thy joyful service; that, with all who have faithfully served thee in times past, *she/he* may share in the eternal victory of Jesus Christ our Lord; who liveth and reigneth with thee, in the unity of the Holy Spirit, one God, world without end.

JOY AND THANKS

44   Father of spirits, we have joy at this time in all who have faithfully lived, and in all who have peacefully died. We thank Thee for all fair memories and all lively hopes; for the sacred ties that bind us to the unseen world; for the dear and holy dead who compass us as a cloud of witnesses and make the distant heaven a home to our hearts. May we be followers of those who now inherit the promises, through Jesus Christ our Lord.

METHODIST BOOK OF OFFICES

45   Almighty God, Father of all mercies, we thine unworthy
           servants do give thee most humble and hearty thanks for all
           thy goodness and loving-kindness to us, and to all men; We
           bless thee for our creation, preservation, and all the blessings
           of this life; but above all, for thine inestimable love in the
           redemption of the world by our Lord Jesus Christ; for the
           means of grace, and for the hope of glory. And, we beseech
           thee, give us that due sense of all thy mercies, that our hearts
           may be unfeignedly thankful, and that we shew forth thy
           praise, not only with our lips, but in our lives; by giving up
           ourselves to thy service, and by walking before thee in
           holiness and righteousness all our days; through Jesus Christ
           our Lord, to whom with thee and the Holy Ghost be all
           honour and glory, world without end.

                                       BOOK OF COMMON PRAYER

46   Almighty God, giver of every good and perfect gift, we thank
           you for the happiness and love this child has brought and for
           the assurance we have that *she/he* is in your care. Strengthen
           us to commit ourselves to your gracious providence, so that
           we may live our lives here in the peace and joy of faith, until
           at the last we are united with all the children of God in the
           brightness of your glory, through Jesus Christ our Lord.

47   Eternal God, whose love is stronger than death, we rejoice
           that the dead as well as the living are held in your love and
           care. As we remember with thanksgiving those we have loved
           who have gone on before us, we pray that we may look
           forward with confidence to the day when we shall be reunited
           in the joy and peace of your everlasting kingdom.

ETERNAL LIFE

48   Lord, we turn to You in our grief and our bewilderment, for a
           mystery surrounds the birth and death of man. Your will

summons us into this world and then calls us to depart, but Your plan is so vast and Your purposes so deep that our understanding fails, and our reason cannot follow. Yet You have taught us that time and space are not the measure of all things. Beyond them is the life of eternity. We do not die into the grave but into the love of God.

It has been Your will to receive the soul of [N], to bring *her/him* to life everlasting, and *she/he* is beyond the tragedies of this world. We find our comfort in Your teaching. Beyond the grave we shall meet together in the life that has no end.

JEWISH FUNERAL SERVICE

49 You, O Lord, are the endless power that renews life beyond death; you are the greatness that saves. You care for the living with love. You renew life beyond death with unending mercy. You support the falling, and heal the sick. You free prisoners, and keep faith with those who sleep in the dust. Who can perform such mighty deeds, and who can compare with You, a king who brings death and life, and renews salvation? You are faithful to renew life beyond death.

JEWISH FUNERAL SERVICE

50 Almighty God, give us grace that we may cast away the works of darkness, and put upon us the armour of light, now in the time of this mortal life, in which thy Son Jesus Christ came to visit us in great humility; that in the last day, when he shall come again in his glorious Majesty to judge both the quick and the dead, we may rise to the life immortal, through him who liveth and reigneth with thee and the Holy Ghost, now and ever.

BOOK OF COMMON PRAYER

51 O Almighty God, who has knit together thine elect in one communion and fellowship, in the mystical body of thy Son Christ our Lord; Grant us grace so to follow thy blessed

Saints in all virtuous and godly living, that we may come to those unspeakable joys, which thou hast prepared for them that unfeignedly love thee; through Jesus Christ our Lord.

BOOK OF COMMON PRAYER

52   Almighty and everlasting God, who, of thy tender love towards mankind, hast sent thy Son, our Saviour Jesus Christ, to take upon him our flesh, and to suffer death upon the cross, that all mankind should follow the example of his great humility; Mercifully grant, that we may both follow the example of his patience, and also be made partakers of his resurrection; through the same Jesus Christ our Lord.

BOOK OF COMMON PRAYER

53   Grant, we beseech thee, Almighty God, that like as we do believe thy only-begotten Son our Lord Jesus Christ to have ascended into the heavens; so we may also in heart and mind thither ascend, and with him continually dwell, who liveth and reigneth with thee and the Holy Ghost, one God, world without end.

BOOK OF COMMON PRAYER

54   O God, the maker and redeemer of all mankind; grant us, with our loved one and all the faithful departed, the sure benefits of your Son's saving passion and glorious resurrection, that in the last day, when you gather up all things in Christ, we may with them enjoy the fullness of your promises; through Jesus Christ our Lord.

adapted from ALTERNATIVE SERVICE BOOK

55   We remember, Lord, the slenderness of the thread which separates life from death, and the suddenness with which it can be broken. Help us also to remember that on both sides of that division we are surrounded by your love. Persuade our hearts that when our dear ones die neither we nor they are parted from you. In you may we find our peace and in you be united with them in the glorious body of Christ, who has burst the bonds of death and is alive for evermore, our Saviour and theirs for ever and ever.

DICK WILLIAMS

56   May he give us all the courage that we need to go the way he shepherds us.

That when he calls we may go unfrightened.

If he bids us come to him across the waters, that unfrightened we may go.

And if he bids us climb a hill, may we not notice that it is a hill, mindful only of the happiness of his company.

He made us for himself, that we should travel with him and see him at the last in his unveiled beauty in the abiding city where he is light and happiness and endless home.

FR. BEDE JARRETT O.M.

COMMENDATION AND FAREWELL

57   We seem to give them back to Thee, O God, who gavest them to us. Yet, as Thou didst not lose them in giving, so do we not lose them by their return. Not as the world giveth, givest Thou, O Lover of souls. What Thou givest, Thou takest not away, for what is Thine is ours also if we are Thine. And life is eternal and love is immortal, and death is only an horizon, and an horizon is nothing save the limit of our sight. Lift us up, strong Son of God, that we may see further; cleanse our eyes that we may see more clearly; draw us closer to Thyself that we may know ourselves to be nearer to our loved ones who are with Thee. And while Thou dost prepare a place for us, prepare us also for that happy place, that where Thou art we may be also for evermore.

WILLIAM PENN

58　　May the Angels lead thee into paradise, may the martyrs
receive thee at thy coming and take thee to Jerusalem, the
holy city. May the choirs of the angels receive thee and
mayest thou with the once poor Lazarus have rest everlasting.

ROMAN MISSAL

59　　Go forth upon thy journey, Christian soul!
Go from this world! Go, in the Name of God
The Omnipotent Father, who created thee!
Go, in the Name of Jesus Christ, our Lord,
Son of the Living God, who bled for thee!
Go, in the Name of the Holy Spirit, who
Hath been poured out on thee! Go, in the name
Of Angels and Archangels; in the name
Of Thrones and Dominations; in the name
Of Princedoms and of Powers; and in the name
Of Cherubim and Seraphim, go forth!
Go, in the name of Patriarchs and Prophets;
And of Apostles and Evangelists,
Of Martyrs and Confessors; in the name
Of holy Monks and Hermits; in the name
Of holy Virgins; and all Saints of God,
Both men and women, go! Go on thy course;
And may thy place to-day be found in peace,
And may thy dwelling be the Holy Mount
Of Sion: – through the Same, through Christ, our Lord.

JOHN HENRY NEWMAN

60　　Give rest, O Christ, to Thy servant with Thy saints where
sorrow and pain are no more; neither sighing but life
everlasting. Thou only art immortal, the Creator and Maker
of man: and we are mortal, formed of the earth, and unto
earth shall we return: for so Thou didst ordain, when Thou
createdst me, saying, Dust thou art, and unto dust shalt thou

return. All we go down to the dust; and, weeping o'er the
grave, we make our song: Alleluya.

RUSSIAN CONTAKION OF THE DEPARTED
trans. W. J. Birkbeck

61   Let us commend [N] into the hands of God, our Maker and
Redeemer. O God our heavenly Father, who by thy mighty
power, has given us life, and by thy loving kindness has
bestowed upon us new life in Christ Jesus. We commend to
thy merciful keeping thy servant [N] our *brother/sister* here
departed; through Jesus Christ thy son our Lord, who died
and rose again to save us, now liveth and reigneth in glory for
ever.

62   O Almighty Lord, the God of the spirits of all flesh, fulfil we
beseech Thee the purpose of Thy love in those who are now
at rest, that the good work which Thou didst begin in them
may be perfected unto the day of Jesus Christ, who lives and
reigns with Thee and the Holy Spirit, one God, world without
end.

63   Merciful Father and Lord of all life, we praise thee that men
are made in thine image and reflect thy truth and light. We
thank thee for the life of [N], for the love and mercy *she/he*
received from you and showed amongst us. Above all we
rejoice at your gracious promise to all your servants, living
and departed, that we shall rise again at the coming of Christ.
And we ask that in due time we may share with [N] that
clearer vision, when we shall see your face, in the same Christ
our Lord.

64   You shared life with us: God give eternal life to you.
You gave your love to us: God give his deep love to you.
You gave your time to us: God give his eternity to you.

You gave your light to us: God give everlasting light to you.
Go upon your journey dear soul to love, light and life eternal.

DAVID ADAM *For a Loved One*

65   It is now time for us to take our leave of [N] whom we shall
always remember with a great warmth of appreciation. We
return to our daily lives resolved to follow *her/his* example of
courage and of sharing: to live our lives more fully and with
the same integrity of purpose, cheerfulness and love. From
the midst of our proud mourning, we leave this service
knowing love is never changed by death: that nothing is ever
lost through death: that in the end is the harvest of a new
beginning.

COMMITTAL

*The celebrant will have prayers specific to this solemn moment in the
service, but here are two from the Elizabethan prayer book.*

66   Thou knowest Lord the secrets of our hearts; shut not thy
merciful ears unto our prayer; but spare us, Lord most Holy,
O Lord most Mighty, O Holy and Merciful Saviour, Thou
most worthy Judge eternal, suffer us not, at our last hour, for
any pains of death, to fall from Thee.

BOOK OF COMMON PRAYER

67   Forasmuch as it hath pleased Almighty God of His great
mercy to take unto Himself the soul of our dear *brother* we
therefore commit *his* body to the ground; earth to earth, ashes
to ashes, dust to dust; in sure and certain hope of the
resurrection to eternal life, through our Lord Jesus Christ;
who shall change our vile body, that it may be like unto his
glorious body, according to the mighty working, whereby he
is able to subdue all things to himself.

BOOK OF COMMON PRAYER

BLESSING

68   God be in my head, and in my understanding;
        God be in mine eyes, and in my looking;
    God be in my mouth, and in my speaking;
        God be in my heart, and in my thinking;
    God be at mine end, and at my departing.

SARUM PRAYER

69   May the road rise to meet you,
    May the wind be always at your back,
    May the sun shine warm upon your face,
    May the rains fall softly upon your fields.
    Until we meet again,
    May God hold you in the hollow of his hand.

GAELIC PRAYER

70   Grant, O Lord, that we may walk in your presence, with your love in our hearts, your trust in our minds, your strength in our wills: that when we finally stand before you, it may be with the assurance of your welcome and the joy of our homecoming. And the blessing of God Almighty, the Father, the Son and the Holy Spirit rest upon you and be with you, now and always.

71   Though I am dead, grieve not for me with tears,
    Think not of death with sorrowing and fears,
    I am so near that every tear you shed
    Touches and tortures me, though you think me dead . . .
    But when you laugh and sing in glad delight,
    My soul is lifted upwards to the Light:
    Laugh and be glad for all that Life is giving,
    And I though dead will share your joy of living.

72   Deep peace of the running wave to you
      Deep peace of the flowing air to you
      Deep peace of the quiet earth to you
      Deep peace of the shining stars to you
      Deep peace of the Son of peace to you

                                    IONA COMMUNITY PRAYER

73   The Lord bless you, and keep you: the Lord make his face to
      shine upon you, and be gracious unto you: the Lord lift up the
      light of his countenance upon you, and give you peace.

                                          NUMBERS 6: 24-26

74   We leave this service knowing Love is never changed by
      death; that nothing of Love is ever lost through death; that in
      the end is the harvest of a new beginning.

75   As you were before us at our life's beginning, be you so again
          at our journey's end.
      As you were beside us at our soul's shaping, God be also
          at our journey's close.

Psalms

The following psalms are taken from the
Book of Common Prayer by permission (see page 83)

76   Lord, who shall dwell in thy tabernacle: or who shall rest upon thy holy hill?

Even he, that leadeth an uncorrupt life: and doeth the thing which is right, and speaketh the truth from his heart.

He that hath used no deceit in his tongue, nor done evil to his neighbour: and hath not slandered his neighbour.

He that setteth not by himself, but is lowly in his own eyes: and maketh much of them that fear the Lord.

He that sweareth unto his neighbour, and disappointeth him not: though it were to his own hindrance.

He that hath not given his money upon usury: nor taken reward against the innocent.

Whoso doeth these things: shall never fall.

PSALM 15

77   The Lord is my shepherd: therefore can I lack nothing.

He shall feed me in a green pasture: and lead me forth beside the waters of comfort.

He shall convert my soul: and bring me forth in the paths of righteousness, for his Name's sake.

Yea, though I walk through the valley of the shadow of death, I will fear no evil: for thou art with me; thy rod and staff comfort me.

Thou shalt prepare a table before me against them that trouble me: thou hast anointed my head with oil, and my cup shall be full.

But thy loving-kindness and mercy shall follow me all the days of my life: and I will dwell in the house of the Lord for ever.

PSALM 23

78 The Lord is my light, and my salvation; whom then shall I fear: the Lord is the strength of my life; of whom then shall I be afraid?

When the wicked, even mine enemies, and my foes, came upon me to eat up my flesh: they stumbled and fell.

Though an host of men were laid against me, yet shall not my heart be afraid: and though there rose up war against me, yet will I put my trust in him.

One thing have I desired of the Lord, which I will require: even that I may dwell in the house of the Lord all the days of my life, to behold the fair beauty of the Lord, and to visit his temple.

For in the time of trouble he shall hide me in his tabernacle: yea, in the secret place of his dwelling shall he hide me, and set me up upon a rock of stone.

And now shall he lift up mine head: above mine enemies round about me.

Therefore will I offer in his dwelling an oblation with great gladness: I will sing, and speak praises unto the Lord.

Hearken unto my voice, O Lord, when I cry unto thee: have mercy upon me, and hear me.

My heart hath talked of thee, Seek ye my face: Thy face, Lord, will I seek.

O hide not thou thy face from me: nor cast thy servant away in displeasure.

Thou hast been my succour: leave me not, neither forsake me, O God of my salvation.

When my father and my mother forsake me: the Lord taketh me up.

Teach me thy way, O Lord: and lead me in the right way,

because of mine enemies.

Deliver me not over into the will of mine adversaries: for there are false witnesses risen up against me, and such as speak wrong.

I should utterly have fainted: but that I believe verily to see the goodness of the Lord in the land of the living.

O tarry thou the Lord's leisure: be strong, and he shall comfort thine heart; and put thou thy trust in the Lord.

PSALM 27

79 I said, I will take heed to my ways: that I offend not in my tongue.

I will keep my mouth as it were with a bridle: while the ungodly is in my sight.

I held my tongue, and spake nothing: I kept silence, yea, even from good words; but it was pain and grief to me.

My heart was hot within me, and while I was thus musing the fire kindled: and at the last I spake with my tongue;

Lord, let me know mine end, and the number of my days: that I may be certified how long I have to live.

Behold, thou hast made my days as it were a span long: and mine age is even as nothing in respect of thee; and verily every man living is altogether vanity.

For man walketh in a vain shadow, and disquieteth himself in vain: he heapeth up riches, and cannot tell who shall gather them.

And now, Lord, what is my hope: truly my hope is even in thee.

Deliver me from all mine offences: and make me not a rebuke unto the foolish.

I became dumb, and opened not my mouth: for it was thy doing.

Take thy plague away from me: I am even consumed by the means of thy heavy hand.

When thou with rebukes dost chasten man for sin, thou

makest his beauty to consume away, like as it were a moth fretting a garment: every man therefore is but vanity.

Hear my prayer, O Lord, and with thine ears consider my calling: hold not thy peace at my tears.

For I am a stranger with thee: and a sojourner, as all my fathers were.

O spare me a little, that I may recover my strength: before I go hence, and be no more seen.

PSALM 39

80   Like as the hart desireth the water-brooks: so longeth my soul after thee, O God.

My soul is athirst for God, yea, even for the living God: when shall I come to appear before the presence of God?

My tears have been my meat day and night: while they daily say unto me, Where is now thy God?

Now when I think thereupon, I pour out my heart by myself: for I went with the multitude, and brought them forth into the house of God;

In the voice of praise and thanksgiving: among such as keep holy-day.

Why art thou so full of heaviness, O my soul: and why art thou so disquieted within me?

Put thy trust in God: for I will yet give him thanks for the help of his countenance.

My God, my soul is vexed within me: therefore will I remember thee concerning the land of Jordan, and the little hill of Hermon.

One deep calleth another, because of the noise of the water-pipes: all thy waves and storms are gone over me.

The Lord hath granted his loving-kindness in the day-time: and in the night-season did I sing of him, and made my prayer unto the God of my life.

I will say unto the God of my strength, Why hast thou forgotten me: why go I thus heavily, while the enemy oppresseth me?

My bones are smitten asunder as with a sword: while mine enemies that trouble me cast me in the teeth:

Namely, while they say daily unto me: Where is now thy God?

Why art thou so vexed, O my soul: and why art thou so disquieted within me?

O put thy trust in God: for I will yet thank him, which is the help of my countenance, and my God.

PSALM 42

81 God is our hope and strength: a very present help in trouble.

Therefore will we not fear, though the earth be moved: and though the hills be carried into the midst of the sea.

Though the waters thereof rage and swell: and though the mountains shake at the tempest of the same.

The rivers of the flood thereof shall make glad the city of God: the holy place of the tabernacle of the most Highest.

God is in the midst of her, therefore shall she not be removed: God shall help her, and that right early.

The heathen make much ado, and the kingdoms are moved: but God hath shewed his voice, and the earth shall melt away.

The Lord of hosts is with us: the God of Jacob is our refuge.

O come hither, and behold the works of the Lord: what destruction he hath brought upon the earth.

He maketh wars to cease in all the world: he breaketh the bow, and knappeth the spear in sunder, and burneth the chariots in the fire.

Be still then, and know that I am God: I will be exalted among the heathen, and I will be exalted in the earth.

The Lord of hosts is with us: the God of Jacob is our refuge.

PSALM 46

82   Hear my crying, O God: give ear unto my prayer.

From the ends of the earth will I call upon thee: when my heart is in heaviness.

O set me up upon the rock that is higher than I: for thou hast been my hope, and a strong tower for me against the enemy.

I will dwell in thy tabernacle for ever: and my trust shall be under the covering of thy wings.

For thou, O Lord, hast heard my desires: and hast given an heritage unto those that fear thy Name.

Thou shalt grant the King a long life: that his years may endure throughout all generations.

He shall dwell before God for ever: O prepare thy loving mercy and faithfulness, that they may preserve him.

So will I always sing praise unto thy Name: that I may daily perform my vows.

PSALM 61

83   God be merciful unto us, and bless us: and shew us the light of his countenance, and be merciful unto us.

That thy way may be known upon earth: thy saving health among all nations.

Let the people praise thee, O God: yea, let all the people praise thee.

O let the nations rejoice and be glad: for thou shalt judge the folk righteously, and govern the nations upon earth.

Let the people praise thee, O God: let all the people praise thee.

Then shall the earth bring forth her increase: and God, even our own God, shall give us his blessing.

God shall bless us: and all the ends of the world shall fear him.

PSALM 67

84   O how amiable are thy dwellings: thou Lord of hosts!

My soul hath a desire and longing to enter into the courts of the Lord: my heart and my flesh rejoice in the living God.

Yea, the sparrow hath found her an house, and the swallow a nest where she may lay her young: even thy altars, O Lord of hosts, my King and my God.

Blessed are they that dwell in thy house: they will be alway praising thee.

Blessed is the man whose strength is in thee: in whose heart are thy ways.

Who going through the vale of misery use it for a well: and the pools are filled with water.

They will go from strength to strength: and unto the God of gods appeareth everyone of them in Sion.

O Lord God of hosts, hear my prayer: hearken, O God of Jacob.

Behold, O God our defender: and look upon the face of thine Anointed.

For one day in thy courts: is better than a thousand.

I had rather be a door-keeper in the house of my God: than to dwell in the tents of ungodliness.

For the lord God is a light and defence: the Lord will give grace and worship, and no good thing shall he withhold from them that live a godly life.

O Lord God of hosts: blessed is the man that putteth his trust in thee.

PSALM 84

85   Lord, thou hast been our refuge: from one generation to another.

Before the mountains were brought forth, or ever the earth and the world were made: thou art God from everlasting, and world without end.

Thou turnest man to destruction: again thou sayest, Come again, ye children of men.

For a thousand years in thy sight are but as yesterday: seeing that is past as a watch in the night.

As soon as thou scatterest them thcy are even as a sleep: and fade away suddenly like the grass.

In the morning it is green, and groweth up: but in the evening it is cut down, dried up, and withered.

For we consume away in thy displeasure: and are afraid at thy wrathful indignation.

Thou hast set our misdeeds before thee: and our secret sins in the light of thy countenance.

For when thou art angry all our days are gone: we bring our years to an end, as it were a tale that is told.

The days of our age are threescore years and ten, and though men be so strong that they come to fourscore years: yet is their strength then but labour and sorrow; so soon passeth it away, and we are gone.

But who regardeth the power of thy wrath:; for even thereafter as a man feareth, so is thy displeasure.

So teach us to number our days: that we may apply our hearts unto wisdom.

Turn thee again, O Lord, at the last: and be gracious unto thy servants.

O satisfy us with thy mercy, and that soon: so shall we rejoice and be glad all the days of our life.

Comfort us again now after the time that thou hast plagued us: and for the years wherein we have suffered adversity.

Shew thy servants thy work: and their children thy glory.

And the glorious Majesty of the Lord our God be upon us: prosper thou the work of our hands upon us, O prosper thou our handy-work.

PSALM 90

86 Whoso dwelleth under the defence of the most High: shall abide under the shadow of the Almighty.

I will say unto the Lord, Thou art my hope, and my stronghold: my God, in him will I trust.

For he shall deliver thee from the snare of the hunter: and from the noisome pestilence.

He shall defend thee under his wings, and thou shalt be safe under his feathers: his faithfulness and truth shall be thy shield and buckler.

Thou shalt not be afraid for any terror by night: nor for the arrow that flieth by day;

For the pestilence that walketh in darkness: nor for the sickness that destroyeth in the noon-day.

A thousand shall fall beside thee, and ten thousand at thy right hand: but it shall not come nigh thee.

Yea, with thine eyes shalt thou behold: and see the reward of the ungodly.

For thou, Lord, art my hope: thou hast set thine house of defence very high.

There shall no evil happen unto thee: neither shall any plague come nigh thy dwelling.

For he shall give his angels charge over thee: to keep thee in all thy ways.

They shall bear thee in their hands: that thou hurt not thy foot against a stone.

Thou shalt go upon the lion and adder: the young lion and the dragon shalt thou tread under thy foot.

Because he hath set his love upon me, therefore will I deliver him: I will set him up, because he hath known my Name.

He shall call upon me, and I will hear him: yea, I am with him in trouble; I will deliver him, and bring him to honour.

With long life will I satisfy him: and shew him my salvation.

PSALM 91

87   Praise the Lord, O my soul: and all that is within me praise his holy Name.

Praise the Lord, O my soul: and forget not all his benefits.

Who forgiveth all thy sin: and healeth all thine infirmities;

Who saveth thy life from destruction: and crowneth thee with mercy and loving-kindness;

Who satisfieth thy mouth with good things: making thee young and lusty as an eagle.

The Lord executeth righteousness and judgement: for all them that are oppressed with wrong.

He shewed his ways unto Moses: his works unto the children of Israel.

The Lord is full of compassion and mercy: long-suffering, and of great goodness.

He will not alway be chiding: neither keepeth he his anger for ever.

He hath not dealt with us after our sins: nor rewarded us according to our wickednesses.

For look how high the heaven is in comparison of the earth: so great is his mercy also toward them that fear him.

Look how wide also the east is from the west: so far hath he set our sins from us.

Yea, like as a father pitieth his own children: even so is the Lord merciful unto them that fear him.

For he knoweth whereof we are made: he remembereth that we are but dust.

The days of man are but as grass: for he flourisheth as a flower of the field.

For as soon as the wind goeth over it, it is gone: and the place thereof shall know it no more.

But the merciful goodness of the Lord endureth for ever and ever upon them that fear him: and his righteousness upon children's children.

Even upon such as keep his covenant: and think upon his commandments to do them.

The Lord hath prepared his seat in heaven: and his kingdom ruleth over all.

O praise the Lord, ye angels of his, ye that excel in strength: ye that fulfil his commandment, and hearken unto the voice of his words.

O praise the Lord, all ye his hosts: ye servants of his that do his pleasure.

O speak good of the Lord, all ye works of his, in all places of his dominion: praise thou the Lord, O my soul.

PSALM 103

88 I am well pleased: that the Lord hath heard the voice of my prayer.

That he hath inclined his ear unto me: therefore will I call upon him as long as I live.

The snares of death compassed me round about: and the pains of hell gat hold upon me.

I shall find trouble and heaviness, and I will call upon the Name of the Lord: O Lord, I beseech thee, deliver my soul.

Gracious is the Lord, and righteous: yea, our God is merciful.

The Lord preserveth the simple: I was in misery, and he helped me.

Turn again then unto thy rest, O my soul: for the Lord hath rewarded thee.

And why? thou hast delivered my soul from death: mine eyes from tears, and my feet from falling.

I will walk before the Lord: in the land of the living.

I believed, and therefore will I speak; but I was sore troubled: I said in my haste, All men are liars.

What reward shall I give unto the Lord: for all the benefits that he hath done unto me?

I will receive the cup of salvation: and call upon the Name of the Lord.

I will pay my vows now in the presence of all his people:

right dear in the sight of the Lord is the death of his saints.

Behold, O Lord, how that I am thy servant: I am thy servant, and the son of thine handmaid; thou hast broken my bonds in sunder.

I will offer to thee the sacrifice of thanksgiving: and will call upon the Name of the Lord.

I will pay my vows unto the Lord, in the sight of all his people: in the courts of the Lord's house, even in the midst of thee, O Jerusalem. Praise the Lord.

PSALM 116

89   I will lift up mine eyes unto the hills: from whence cometh my help.

My help cometh even from the Lord: who hath made heaven and earth.

He will not suffer thy foot to be moved: and he that keepeth thee will not sleep.

Behold, he that keepeth Israel: shall neither slumber nor sleep.

The Lord himself is thy keeper: the Lord is thy defence upon thy right hand.

So that the sun shall not burn thee by day: neither the moon by night.

The Lord shall preserve thee from all evil: yea, it is even he that shall keep thy soul.

The Lord shall preserve thy going out, and thy coming in: from this time forth for evermore.

PSALM 121

90   When the Lord turned again the captivity of Sion: then were we like unto them that dream.

Then was our mouth filled with laughter: and our tongue with joy.

Then said they among the heathen: The Lord hath done great things for them.

Yea, the Lord hath done great things for us already: whereof we rejoice.

Turn our captivity, O Lord: as the rivers in the south.

They that sow in tears: shall reap in joy.

He that now goeth on his way weeping, and beareth forth good seed: shall doubtless come again with joy, and bring his sheaves with him.

PSALM 126

91 Out of the deep have I called unto thee, O Lord: Lord, hear my voice.

O let thine ears consider well: the voice of my complaint.

If thou, Lord, wilt be extreme to mark what is done amiss: O Lord, who may abide it?

For there is mercy with thee: therefore shalt thou be feared.

I look for the Lord; my soul doth wait for him: in his word is my trust.

My soul fleeth unto the Lord: before the morning watch, I say, before the morning watch.

O Israel, trust the Lord, for with the Lord there is mercy: and with him is plenteous redemption.

And he shall redeem Israel: from all his sins.

PSALM 130

92 O Lord, thou hast searched me out, and known me: thou knowest my down-sitting, and mine up-rising; thou understandest my thoughts long before.

Thou art about my path, and about my bed: and spiest out all my ways.

For lo, there is not a word in my tongue: but thou, O Lord, knowest it altogether.

Thou hast fashioned me behind and before: and laid thine hand upon me.

Such knowledge is too wonderful and excellent for me: I

cannot attain unto it.

Whither shall I go then from thy Spirit: or whither shall I go then from thy presence?

If I climb up into heaven, thou art there: if I go down to hell, thou art there also.

If I take the wings of the morning: and remain in the uttermost part of the sea;

Even there also shall thy hand lead me: and thy right hand shall hold me.

If I say, Peradventure the darkness shall cover me: then shall my night be turned to day.

Yea, the darkness is no darkness with thee, but the night is as clear as the day: the darkness and light to thee are both alike.

For my reins are thine: thou hast covered me in my mother's womb.

I will give thanks unto thee, for I am fearfully and wonderfully made: marvellous are thy works, and that my soul knoweth right well.

My bones are not hid from thee: though I be made secretly, and fashioned beneath in the earth.

Thine eyes did see my substance, yet being imperfect: and in thy book were all my members written;

Which day by day were fashioned: when as yet there was none of them.

How dear are thy counsels unto me, O God: O how great is the sum of them!

If I tell them, they are more in number than the sand: when I wake up I am present with thee.

Wilt thou not slay the wicked, O God: depart from me, ye blood-thirsty men.

For they speak unrighteously against thee: and thine enemies take thy Name in vain.

Do not I hate them, O Lord, that hate thee: and am not I grieved with those that rise up against thee?

Yea, I hate them right sore: even as though they were mine enemies.

Try me, O God, and seek the ground of my heart; prove me, and examine my thoughts.

Look well if there be any way of wickedness in me: and lead me in the way everlasting.

PSALM 139

The Word

The following passages from the Holy Bible are taken from the Authorized Version of the Bible (the King James Bible) and from the Holy Bible, New International Version, by permission (see page 83). The source of each passage is indicated AV and NIV respectively. The passages from the Apocrypha are all from the Authorized Version.

OLD TESTAMENT

93   I have set my rainbow in the clouds, and it will be the sign of the covenant between me and the earth.

GENESIS 9: 13 NIV

94   The eternal God is your refuge,
       and underneath are the everlasting arms.

DEUTERONOMY 33: 27 NIV

95   Naked I came from my mother's womb,
       and naked I shall depart.
The Lord gave and the Lord has taken away;
       may the name of the Lord be praised.

JOB 1: 21 NIV

96   I know that my Redeemer lives,
       and that in the end he will stand upon the earth.
And after my skin has been destroyed,
       yet in my flesh I will see God;
I myself will see him

with my own eyes – I, and not another.
How my heart yearns within me!

JOB 19: 25-27 NIV

97 Who can find a virtuous woman? for her price is far above rubies.

The heart of her husband doth safely trust in her, so that he shall have no need of spoil.

She will do him good and not evil all the days of her life.

Her children arise up, and call her blessed; her husband also, and he praiseth her.

Give her of the fruit of her hands; and let her own works praise her in the gates.

PROVERBS 31: 10-12, 28, 31 AV

98 To every thing there is a season, and a time to every purpose under the heaven: a time to be born, and a time to die; a time to plant, and a time to pluck up that which is planted; a time to kill, and a time to heal; a time to break down, and a time to build up; a time to weep, and a time to laugh; a time to mourn, and a time to dance; a time to cast away stones, and a time to gather stones together; a time to embrace, and a time to refrain from embracing; a time to get, and a time to lose; a time to keep, and a time to cast away; a time to rend, and a time to sew; a time to keep silence, and a time to speak; a time to love, and a time to hate; a time of war, and a time of peace.

That which hath been is now; and that which is to be hath already been; and God requireth that which is past.

For that which befalleth the sons of men befalleth beasts; even one thing befalleth them: as the one dieth, so dieth the other; yea, they have all one breath; so that a man hath no preeminence above a beast: for all is vanity. All go unto one place; all are of the dust, and all turn to dust again.

ECCLESIASTES 3: 1-8, 15, 19-20 AV

99   Remember now thy Creator in the days of thy youth, while
           the evil days come not, nor the years draw nigh, when thou
           shalt say, I have no pleasure in them.

           While the sun, or the light, or the moon, or the stars, be
           not darkened, nor the clouds return after the rain:

           In the day when the keepers of the house shall tremble,
           and the strong men shall bow themselves, and the grinders
           cease because they are few, and those that look out of the
           windows be darkened.

           And the doors shall be shut in the streets, when the sound
           of the grinding is low, and he shall rise up at the voice of the
           bird, and all the daughters of musick shall be brought low;

           Also when they shall be afraid of that which is high, and
           fears shall be in the way, and the almond tree shall flourish,
           and the grasshopper shall be a burden, and desire shall fail:
           because man goeth to his long home, and the mourners go
           about the streets:

           Or ever the silver cord be loosed, or the golden bowl be
           broken, or the pitcher be broken at the fountain, or the wheel
           broken at the cistern.

           Then shall the dust return to the earth as it was: and the
           spirit shall return unto God who gave it.

                                           ECCLESIASTES 12: 1-7 AV

100   Set me as a seal upon thine heart, as a seal upon thine arm: for
           love is strong as death; jealousy is cruel as the grave: the
           coals thereof are coals of fire, which hath a most vehement
           flame. Many waters cannot quench love, neither can the
           floods drown it.

                                           SONG OF SOLOMON 8: 6-7 AV

101   The voice said, Cry. And he said, What shall I cry? All flesh
           is grass, and all the goodliness thereof is as the flower of the
           field:

           The grass withereth, the flower fadeth: because the spirit

of the Lord bloweth upon it: surely the people is grass.

The grass withereth, the flower fadeth: but the word of our God shall stand for ever.

ISAIAH 40: 6-8 AV

102   Hast thou not known? hast thou not heard, that the everlasting God, the Lord, the Creator of the ends of the earth, fainteth not, neither is weary? there is no searching of his understanding.

He giveth power to the faint; and to them that have no might he increaseth strength.

Even the youths shall faint and be weary, and the young men shall utterly fall.

But they that wait upon the Lord shall renew their strength; they shall mount up with wings as eagles; they shall run, and not be weary; and they shall walk, and not faint.

ISAIAH 40: 28-31 AV

103   It is of the Lord's mercies that we are not consumed, because his compassions fail not. They are new every morning: great is thy faithfulness. The Lord is my portion, saith my soul; therefore will I hope in him. The Lord is good unto them that wait for him, to the soul that seeketh him. It is good that a man should both hope and quietly wait for the salvation of the Lord.

LAMENTATIONS 3: 22-26 AV

NEW TESTAMENT

104   Now when he saw the crowds, he went up on a mountainside and sat down. His disciples came to him, and he began to teach them, saying:

Blessed are the poor in spirit
    for theirs is the kingdom of heaven.
Blessed are those who mourn,

> for they will be comforted.
> Blessed are the meek,
> > for they will inherit the earth.
> Blessed are those who hunger and thirst for
> righteousness,
> > for they will be filled.
> Blessed are the merciful,
> > for they will be shown mercy.
> Blessed are the pure in heart,
> > for they will see God.
> Blessed are the peacemakers,
> > for they will be called sons of God.
> Blessed are those who are persecuted because of
> righteousness,
> > for theirs is the kingdom of heaven.

Blessed are you when people insult you, persecute you and falsely say all kinds of evil against you because of me.

Rejoice and be glad because great is your reward in heaven, for in the same way they persecuted the prophets who were before you.

You are the salt of the earth. But if the salt loses its saltiness, how can it be made salty again? It is no longer good for anything, except to be thrown out and trampled by men.

You are the light of the world. A city on a hill cannot be hidden. Neither do people light a lamp and put it under a bowl. Instead they put it on its stand, and it gives light to everyone in the house. In the same way, let your light shine before men, that they may see your good deeds and praise your Father in heaven.

ST MATTHEW 5: 1-16 NIV

105   And they brought young children to him, that he should touch them: and his disciples rebuked those that brought them.

But when Jesus saw it, he was much displeased, and said unto them, Suffer the little children to come unto me, and forbid them not: for of such is the kingdom of God.

Verily I say unto you, Whosoever shall not receive the kingdom of God as a little child, he shall not enter therein.

And he took them up in his arms, put his hands upon them, and blessed them.

ST MARK 10: 13-16 AV

106 Lord, now lettest thou thy servant depart in peace, according to thy word:

For mine eyes have seen thy salvation,

Which thou hast prepared before the face of all people;

A light to lighten the Gentiles, and the glory of thy people Israel.

ST LUKE 2: 29-32 AV

107 My sheep listen to my voice; I know them, and they follow me. I give them eternal life, and they shall never perish; no-one can snatch them out of my hand. My Father, who has given them to me, is greater than all; no-one can snatch them out of my Father's hand.

ST JOHN 10: 27-29 NIV

108 Now a man named Lazarus was sick. He was from Bethany, the village of Mary and her sister Martha. This Mary, whose brother Lazarus now lay sick, was the same one who poured perfume on the Lord and wiped his feet with her hair. So the sisters sent word to Jesus, "Lord, the one you love is sick."

When he heard this, Jesus said, "This sickness will not end in death. No, it is for God's glory so that God's Son may be glorified through it."

ST JOHN 11: 1-4 NIV

109 When Martha heard that Jesus was coming, she went out to meet him, but Mary stayed at home.

"Lord," Martha said to Jesus, "if you had been here, my

brother would not have died. But I know that even now God
will give you whatever you ask."

Jesus said to her, "Your brother will rise again."

Martha answered, "I know he will rise again in the
resurrection at the last day."

Jesus said to her, "I am the resurrection and the life. He
who believes in me will live, even though he dies; and
whoever lives and believes in me will never die. Do you
believe this?"

ST JOHN 11: 20-26 NIV

110   Jesus, once more deeply moved, came to the tomb. It was a
cave with a stone laid across the entrance. "Take away the
stone," he said.

"But, Lord," said Martha, the sister of the dead man, "by
this time there is a bad odour, for he has been there four
days."

Then Jesus said, "Did I not tell you that if you believed,
you would see the glory of God?"

So they took away the stone. Then Jesus looked up and
said, "Father, I thank you that you have heard me. I knew that
you always hear me, but I said this for the benefit of the
people standing here, that they may believe that you sent me."

When he had said this, Jesus called in a loud voice,
"Lazarus, come out!" The dead man came out, his hands and
feet wrapped with strips of linen, and a cloth around his face.

Jesus said to them, "Take off the grave clothes and let him
go."

ST JOHN 11: 38-44 NIV

111   Let not your heart be troubled: ye believe in God, believe also
in me. In my Father's house are many mansions: if it were not
so, I would have told you. I go to prepare a place for you.
And if I go and prepare a place for you, I will come again,
and receive you unto myself; that where I am, there ye may

be also. And whither I go ye know, and the way ye know. Thomas saith unto him, Lord, we know not whither thou goest; and how can we know the way? Jesus saith unto him, I am the way, the truth, and the life: no man cometh unto the Father, but by me. If ye had known me, ye should have known my Father also: and from henceforth ye know him, and have seen him.

ST JOHN 14: 1-7 AV

112   If ye love me, keep my commandments. And I will pray the Father, and he shall give you another Comforter, that he may abide with you for ever; even the Spirit of truth; whom the world cannot receive, because it seeth him not, neither knoweth him: but ye know him; for he dwelleth with you, and shall be in you. I will not leave you comfortless: I will come to you. Yet a little while, and the world seeth me no more; but ye see me: because I live, ye shall live also. At that day ye shall know that I am in my Father, and ye in me, and I in you.

ST JOHN 14: 15-20 AV

113   If a man love me, he will keep my words: and my Father will love him, and we will come unto him, and make our abode with him.

ST JOHN 14: 23 AV

114   I have told you these things, so that in me you may have peace. In this world you will have trouble. But take heart! I have overcome the world.

ST JOHN 16: 33 NIV

115   For I reckon that the sufferings of this present time are not worthy to be compared with the glory which shall be revealed in us.

PAUL THE APOSTLE TO THE ROMANS 8: 18 AV

116   And we know that all things work together for good to them
            that love God, to them who are called according to his
            purpose.

                              PAUL THE APOSTLE TO THE ROMANS 8: 28 AV

117   Who shall separate us from the love of Christ? shall
            tribulation, or distress, or persecution, or famine, or
            nakedness, or peril, or sword?

                              PAUL THE APOSTLE TO THE ROMANS 8: 35 AV

118   For I am persuaded, that neither death, nor life, nor angels,
            nor principalities, nor powers, nor things present, nor things
            to come, nor height, nor depth, nor any other creature, shall
            be able to separate us from the love of God, which is in Christ
            Jesus our Lord.

                           PAUL THE APOSTLE TO THE ROMANS 8: 38-39 AV

119   If I speak in the tongues of men and of angels, but have not
            love, I am only a resounding gong or a clanging cymbal. If I
            have the gift of prophecy and can fathom all mysteries and all
            knowledge, and if I have a faith that can move mountains, but
            have not love, I am nothing. If I give all I possess to the poor
            and surrender my body to the flames, but have not love, I
            gain nothing.

            Love is patient, love is kind. It does not envy, it does not
            boast, it is not proud. It is not rude, it is not self-seeking, it is
            not easily angered, it keeps no record of wrongs. Love does
            not delight in evil but rejoices with the truth. It always
            protects, always trusts, always hopes, always perseveres.

            Love never fails. But where there are prophecies, they will
            cease; where there are tongues, they will be stilled; where
            there is knowledge, it will pass away. For we know in part
            and we prophesy in part, but when perfection comes, the
            imperfect disappears. When I was a child, I talked like a
            child, I thought like a child, I reasoned like a child. When I

became a man, I put childish ways behind me. Now we see but a poor reflection as in a mirror; then we shall see face to face. Now I know in part; then I shall know fully, even as I am fully known.

And now these three remain: faith, hope and love. But the greatest of these is love.

PAUL THE APOSTLE TO THE CORINTHIANS 1, 13: 1-13 NIV

120   But now is Christ risen from the dead, and become the firstfruits of them that slept. For since by man came death, by man came also the resurrection of the dead. For as in Adam all die, even so in Christ shall all be made alive.

PAUL THE APOSTLE TO THE CORINTHIANS 1, 15: 20-22 AV

121   And so it is written. The first man Adam was made a living soul; the last Adam was made a quickening spirit. Howbeit that was not first which is spiritual, but that which is natural; and afterward that which is spiritual. The first man is of the earth, earthy: the second man is the Lord from heaven.

As is the earthy, such are they also that are earthy: and as is the heavenly, such are they also that are heavenly. And as we have borne the image of the earthy, we shall also bear the image of the heavenly. Now this I say, brethren, that flesh and blood cannot inherit the kingdom of God; neither doth corruption inherit incorruption.

Behold, I shew you a mystery; We shall not all sleep, but we shall all be changed. In a moment, in the twinkling of an eye, at the last trump: for the trumpet shall sound, and the dead shall be raised incorruptible, and we shall be changed. For this corruptible must put on incorruption, and this mortal must put on immortality. So when this corruptible shall have put on incorruption, and this mortal shall have put on immortality, then shall be brought to pass the saying that is written, Death is swallowed up in victory.

O death, where is thy sting? O grave, where is thy victory?

The sting of death is sin; and the strength of sin is the law. But thanks be to God, which giveth us the victory through our Lord Jesus Christ. Therefore. my beloved brethren, be ye stedfast, unmoveable, always abounding in the work of the Lord, forasmuch as ye know that your labour is not in vain in the Lord.

PAUL THE APOSTLE TO THE CORINTHIANS 1, 15: 45-58 AV

122   For our conversation is in heaven; from whence also we look for the Saviour, the Lord Jesus Christ: who shall change our vile body, that it may be fashioned like unto his glorious body, according to the working whereby he is able even to subdue all things unto himself.

PAUL THE APOSTLE TO THE PHILIPPIANS 3: 20-21 AV

123   But I would not have you to be ignorant, brethren, concerning them which are asleep, that ye sorrow not, even as others which have no hope. For if we believe that Jesus died and rose again, even so them also which sleep in Jesus will God bring with him. For this we say unto you by the word of the Lord, that we which are alive and remain unto the coming of the Lord shall not prevent them which are asleep. For the Lord himself shall descend from heaven with a shout, with the voice of the archangel, and with the trump of God: and the dead in Christ shall rise first. Then we which are alive and remain shall be caught up together with them in the clouds, to meet the Lord in the air: and so shall we ever be with the Lord. Wherefore comfort one another with these words.

PAUL THE APOSTLE TO THE THESSALONIANS 1, 4: 13-18 AV

124   Blessed be the God and Father of our Lord Jesus Christ, which according to his abundant mercy hath begotten us again unto a lively hope by the resurrection of Jesus Christ from the dead. To an inheritance incorruptible, and undefiled, and that fadeth not away, reserved in heaven for you. Who

are kept by the power of God through faith unto salvation ready to be revealed in the last time. Wherein ye greatly rejoice, though now for a season, if need be, ye are in heaviness through manifold temptations: that the trial of your faith, being much more precious than of gold that perisheth, though it be tried with fire, might be found unto praise and honour and glory at the appearing of Jesus Christ: whom having not seen, ye love; in whom, though now ye see him not, yet believing, ye rejoice with joy unspeakable and full of glory.

FIRST LETTER GENERAL OF PETER 1: 3-9 AV

125 I was in the Spirit on the Lord's day, and heard behind me a great voice, as of a trumpet, saying, I am Alpha and Omega, the first and the last . . . And I turned to see the voice that spake with me. And being turned, I saw seven golden candlesticks; and in the midst of the seven candlesticks one like unto the Son of man, clothed with a garment down to the foot, and girt about the breasts with a golden girdle. His head and his hairs were white like wool, as white as snow; and his eyes were as a flame of fire; and his feet like unto fine brass, as if they burned in a furnace; and his voice as the sound of many waters. And he had in his right hand seven stars: and out of his mouth went a sharp twoedged sword: and his countenance was as the sun shineth in his strength.

And when I saw him, I fell at his feet as dead. And he laid his right hand upon me, saying unto me, Fear not; I am the first and the last: I am he that liveth, and was dead; and, behold, I am alive for evermore, Amen; and have the keys of hell and of death.

THE REVELATION OF ST JOHN THE DIVINE 1: 10-18 AV

126 And I heard a voice from heaven saying unto me, Write, Blessed are the dead which die in the Lord from henceforth:

Yea, saith the Spirit, that they may rest from their labours; and their works do follow them.

THE REVELATION OF ST JOHN THE DIVINE 14: 13 AV

127   And I saw a new heaven and a new earth: for the first heaven and the first earth were passed away; and there was no more sea. And I John saw the holy city, new Jerusalem, coming down from God out of heaven, prepared as a bride adorned for her husband. And I heard a great voice out of heaven saying, Behold, the tabernacle of God is with men, and he will dwell with them, and they shall be his people, and God himself shall be with them, and be their God.

And God shall wipe away all tears from their eyes; and there shall be no more death, neither sorrow, nor crying, neither shall there be any more pain: for the former things are passed away. And he that sat upon the throne said, Behold, I make all things new. And he said unto me, Write: for these words are true and faithful. And he said unto me, It is done. I am Alpha and Omega, the beginning and the end. I will give unto him that is athirst of the fountain of the water of life freely. He that overcometh shall inherit all things; and I will be his God, and he shall be my son.

THE REVELATION OF ST JOHN THE DIVINE 21: 1-7 AV

128   And I saw no temple therein: for the Lord God Almighty and the Lamb are the temple of it. And the city had no need of the sun, neither of the moon, to shine in it: for the glory of God did lighten it, and the Lamb is the light thereof. And the nations of them which are saved shall walk in the light of it: and the kings of the earth do bring their glory and honour into it. And the gates of it shall not be shut at all by day: for there shall be no night there. And they shall bring the glory and honour of the nations into it. And there shall in no wise enter into . . . but they which are written in the Lamb's book of life.

THE REVELATION OF ST JOHN THE DIVINE 21: 22-27 AV

129 And there shall be no night there: and they need no candle, neither light of the sun: for the Lord God giveth them light: and they shall reign for ever and ever.

THE REVELATION OF ST JOHN THE DIVINE 22: 5 AV

APOCRYPHA

130 I Esdras saw upon the mount Sion a great people, whom I could not number, and they all praised the Lord with songs.

And in the midst of them there was a young man of a high stature, taller than all the rest, and upon every one of their heads he set crowns, and was more exalted; which I marvelled at greatly.

So I asked the angel, and said, Sir, what are these? He answered and said unto me, These be they that have put off the mortal clothing, and put on the immortal, and have confessed the name of God: now are they crowned, and receive palms.

Then said I unto the angel, What young person is it that crowneth them, and giveth them palms in their hands?

So he answered and said unto me, It is the Son of God, whom they have confessed in the world. Then began I greatly to commend them that stood so stiffly for the name of the Lord.

Then the angel said unto me, Go thy way, and tell my people what manner of things, and how great wonders of the Lord thy God, thou hast seen.

2 ESDRAS 2: 42-48

131 But the souls of the righteous are in the hand of God, and there shall no torment touch them.

In the sight of the unwise they seemed to die: and their departure is taken for misery,

And their going from us to be utter destruction: but they are in peace.

For though they be punished in the sight of men, yet is their hope full of immortality.

And having been a little chastised, they shall be greatly rewarded: for God proved them, and found them worthy for himself.

They that put their trust in him shall understand the truth: and such as be faithful in love shall abide with him: for grace and mercy is to his saints, and he hath care for his elect.

WISDOM OF SOLOMON 3: 1-5; 9

132   But though the righteous be prevented with death, yet shall he be in rest.

For honourable age is not that which standeth in length of time, nor that which is measured by number of years.

But wisdom is the gray hair unto men, and an unspotted life is old age.

He pleased God, and was beloved of him . . . .

He, being made perfect in a short time, fulfilled a long time:

For his soul pleased the Lord: therefore hasted he to take him away from among the wicked.

WISDOM OF SOLOMON, 4: 7-10, 13-14

133   Therefore have we erred from the way of truth, and the light of righteousness hath not shined unto us, and the sun of righteousness rose not upon us.

We wearied ourselves in the way of wickedness and destruction: yea, we have gone through deserts, where there lay no way: but as for the way of the Lord, we have not known it.

What hath pride profited us? or what good hath riches with our vaunting brought us?

All those things are passed away like a shadow, and as a post that hasted by;

And as a ship that passeth over the waves of the water, which when it is gone by, the trace thereof cannot be found, neither the pathway of the keel in the waves;

Or as when a bird hath flown through the air, there is no token of her way to be found, but the light air being beaten with the stroke of her wings, and parted with the violent noise and motion of them, is passed through, and therein afterwards no sign where she went is to be found . . . .

But the righteous live for evermore; their reward also is with the Lord, and the care of them is with the most High.

Therefore shall they receive a glorious kingdom, and a beautiful crown from the Lord's hand: for with his right hand shall he cover them, and with his arm shall he protect them.

WISDOM OF SOLOMON, 5: 6-11, 15-16

134   For wisdom, which is the worker of all things, taught me: for in her is an understanding spirit, holy, one only, manifold, subtil, lively, clear, undefiled, plain, not subject to hurt, loving the thing that is good, quick, which cannot be letted, ready to do good.

Kind to man, stedfast, sure, free from care, having all power, overseeing all things, and going through all understanding, pure, and most subtil, spirits.

For wisdom is more moving than any motion: she passeth and goeth through all things by reason of her pureness.

For she is the breath of the power of God, and a pure influence flowing from the glory of the Almighty: therefore can no defiled thing fall into her.

For she is the brightness of the everlasting light, the unspotted mirror of the power of God, and the image of his goodness.

And being but one, she can do all things: and remaining in herself, she maketh all things new: and in all ages entering into holy souls, she maketh them friends of God, and prophets.

For God loveth none but him that dwelleth with wisdom.

For she is more beautiful than the sun, and above all the order of stars: being compared with the light, she is found before it.

For after this cometh night: but vice shall not prevail against wisdom.

WISDOM OF SOLOMON 7: 22-30

135   The fear of the Lord is honour, and glory, and gladness, and a crown of rejoicing.

The fear of the Lord maketh a merry heart, and giveth joy, and gladness, and a long life.

Whoso feareth the Lord, it shall go well with him at the last, and he shall find favour in the day of his death.

ECCLESIASTICUS 1: 11-13

136   As for the wondrous works of the Lord, there may nothing be taken from them, neither may any thing be put unto them, neither can the ground of them be found out.

When a man hath done, then he beginneth; and when he leaveth off, then he shall be doubtful.

What is man, and whereto serveth he? what is his good, and what is his evil?

The number of a man's days at the most are an hundred years.

As a drop of water unto the sea, and a gravel stone in comparison of the sand; so are a thousand years to the days of eternity.

Therefore is God patient with them, and poureth forth his mercy upon them.

He saw and perceived their end to be evil; therefore he multiplied his compassion.

The mercy of man is toward his neighbour; but the mercy of the Lord is upon all flesh: he reproveth, and nurtureth, and teacheth, and bringeth again, as a shepherd his flock.

ECCLESIASTICUS 18: 6-13

137   Give not over thy mind to heaviness, and afflict not thyself in
thine own counsel.

The gladness of the heart is the life of man, and the
joyfulness of a man prolongeth his days.

Love thine own soul, and comfort thy heart, remove
sorrow far from thee: for sorrow hath killed many, and there
is no profit therein.

ECCLESIASTICUS 30: 21-23

138   . . . Let tears fall down over the dead, and begin to lament, as
if thou hadst suffered great harm thyself; and then cover his
body according to the custom, and neglect not his burial.

Weep bitterly, and make great moan, and use lamentation,
as he is worthy, and that a day or two, lest thou be evil spoken
of: and then comfort thyself for thy heaviness.

For of heaviness cometh death, and the heaviness of the
heart breaketh strength.

In affliction also sorrow remaineth . . .

Take no heaviness to heart: drive it away, and remember
the last end.

ECCLESIASTICUS 38: 16-20

139   He that giveth his mind to the law of the most High, and is
occupied in the meditation thereof, will seek out the wisdom
of all the ancient, and be occupied in prophecies.

He will keep the sayings of the renowned men: and where
subtil parables are, he will be there also.

He shall shew forth that which he hath learned, and shall
glory in the law of the covenant of the Lord.

Many shall commend his understanding; and so long as
the world endureth, it shall not be blotted out; his memorial
shall not depart away, and his name shall live from generation
to generation.

ECCLESIASTICUS 39: 1-2, 8-9

140   O death, acceptable is thy sentence unto the needy, and unto him whose strength faileth, that is now in the last age, and is vexed with all things, and to him that despaireth, and hath lost patience!

Fear not the sentence of death, remember them that have been before thee, and that come after; for this is the sentence of the Lord over all flesh.

There is no inquisition in the grave, whether thou have lived ten, or an hundred, or a thousand years.

ECCLESIASTICUS 41: 2-4

141   Let us now praise famous men, and our fathers that begat us.
The Lord hath wrought great glory by them through his great power from the beginning.

Such as did bear rule in their kingdoms, men renowned for their power, giving counsel by their understanding, and declaring prophecies:

Leaders of the people by their counsels, and by their knowledge of learning meet for the people, wise and eloquent in their instructions:

Such as found out musical tunes, and recited verses in writing:

Rich men furnished with ability, living peaceably in their habitations:

All these were honoured in their generations, and were the glory of their times.

There be of them, that have left a name behind them, that their praises might be reported.

And some there be, which have no memorial; who are perished, as though they had never been; and are become as though they had never been born; and their children after them.

But these were merciful men, whose righteousness hath not been forgotten.

With their seed shall continually remain a good inheritance, and their children are within the covenant.

Their seed standeth fast, and their children for their sakes.

Their seed shall remain for ever, and their glory shall not be blotted out.

Their bodies are buried in peace; but their name liveth for evermore.

The people will tell of their wisdom, and the congregation will shew forth their praise.

ECCLESIASTICUS 44: 1-15

142 And here will I make an end. And if I have done well, and as is fitting the story, it is that which I desired: but if slenderly and meanly, it is that which I could attain unto.

For as it is hurtful to drink wine or water alone; and as wine mingled with water is pleasant, and delighteth the taste: even so speech finely framed delighteth the ears of them that read the story. And here shall be an end.

2 MACCABEES 15: 38-39

Extracts from the Authorized Version of the Bible (the King James Bible) and from the Book of Common Prayer, the rights in which are vested in the Crown, are reproduced by permission of the Crown's patentee, Cambridge University Press (and see page 316).

Scripture quotations taken from the HOLY BIBLE, NEW INTERNATIONAL VERSION. Copyright © 1973, 1978, 1984 by International Bible Society. Used by permission of Hodder & Stoughton Limited and Zondervan Publishing House. All rights reserved. "NIV" is a registered trademark of International Bible Society. UK trademark number 1448790 (and see page 318).

Readings

And almost everyone when age,
Disease, or sorrows strike him,
Inclines to think there is a God,
Or something very like him.

Arthur Hugh Clough

While preparing this book, we have become deeply impressed by the way in which the largest part of what we have read from different times and cultures points in the same direction.

Love and death are humanity's great themes, and the overwhelmingly prevalent attitude to death is the life hereafter. From the Gilgamesh epic of c.3,300 BC to D. J. Enright's poem *Guest* (p.246) life after death is proposed continually. Few will categorically deny it in conversation or in writing. It underpins the religions of India and Africa, of ancient Egypt, of the Far East, of Greece and Rome and of the Christian tradition. The readings in this book continually recall the life to come.

Responses to death can vary greatly. Stephen Levine, in his book *Healing into Life and Death* explores grief, anger and guilt as feelings that are often provoked by death:

"I am not grieving, I am not sad about the death of my father. I am angry as hell."
"I am not feeling grief. I am feeling anxiety."

"Well I don't know if it's grief, but I sure feel kind of lost."

"What I am feeling isn't grief, it's guilt."

Such states of mind are aspects of grief, says Levine, and they need to be explored and understood. His book helps with techniques of acceptance and letting go.

Geoffrey Wellens, of S. Wellens & Sons, Funeral Directors, raised another profound question in his talk at the SAROS seminar (1994):

> Life without faith is like a ship without a rudder. Having faith certainly helps the healing process . . . What happens today? Are we not guilty of chasing our tails; darting from one thing to another; never satisfied; never having enough money? I feel sure that many people go to their final resting-place unfulfilled. Shall we ever rest in peace?

The readings in this book are as much about life and love as about death and grief. While some may be somewhat melancholy – for grief is likely to be uppermost at a funeral – others will be found to hint at or to express different feelings and a wide range of aspects of human existence. After all, we have lived and laughed and shared our life with the person who has died. While we need to purge the grief of loss, we need also to remember past happiness and to look to the future.

We have looked at many funeral service sheets and we have been struck by how often the same pieces appear. For example, Henry Scott Holland's 'Death is nothing at all . . .'; 'To every thing there is a season . . .' from Ecclesiastes; Joyce Grenfell's 'If I should go before the rest of you . . .'; 'Abide with me'; the Crimond setting of Psalm 23: all are frequently used.

We started where we began, many years ago, with our own reading, re-acquainting ourselves with old friends from our own bookshelves. At the same time we continued to read new things and to get to know the literature of funeral and memorial. We became increasingly struck by the resonance of poetry, as well as by its sheer practicality. A poem is so often more clear, more simple and shorter than its equivalent in prose. It is also memorable. Only later did we turn to the anthologies. Then we found many of our early choices confirmed, and made many new and happy choices with the help of the anthologists. In this context we would mention June Benn's *Memorials* (Ravette, 1986), Walter Oakeshott's *The Sword of the Spirit* (Faber and Faber, 1950), John Wain's *Everyman's Book of English Verse* (Dent, 1981), and *The London Book of English Verse* selected by Herbert Read and Bonamy Dobrée (Eyre & Spottiswoode 1949, 1952). Of the many texts that we have examined dedicated to aspects of grief and bereavement, an outstanding book is *All in the End is Harvest: An Anthology for Those who Grieve*, published by Darton, Longman & Todd in association with CRUSE, The National Organization for the Widowed and Their Children.

We made a rule for ourselves. This was that every reading in this book should be capable of getting its message across by being read aloud once only, and that it should be short. We have succumbed to temptation and have broken this rule on more than one occasion. A few readings are long, some would say very long, but these could not be reduced without loss, and have been found by us to have overwhelming value for meditation as well as in their immediacy. Also, it seemed right to give the psalms that we have chosen in their entirety – the user of this book can, after all, choose from within them, and to give certain passages from the Bible in full from which, again, the user may select.

While we have tried to give as broad a selection as possible, we shall have failed if this book does not encourage you to bring forward your own favourites for reading at the funerals in which you are involved.

We do not grieve alone: the sharing of grief can itself bring comfort. And others' words so often express our feelings better than our own.

Music brings infinite possibilities. Besides the hymns and other music suggested later on, you may know of recordings of music that have special memories. A friend of ours who died after a brave fight against cancer was mourned and celebrated by a tape consisting of her favourite jazz pieces; an actor, who died with AIDS, planned his own funeral and chose music from 'Cabaret' and 'No Business Like Show Business'. Any favourite song or piece of music could be chosen to recall joyful times and shared happiness.

In his Address to a conference of the World Spiritual Council (1968) Sir George Trevelyan said:

> We live in a fear-ridden age . . . the overcoming of fear is the greatest challenge to any individual. In a civilization based on the materialistic world view, fear is inevitable. If matter is all there is, then loss of "things" is a disaster. If death is extinction, then it is the great bogey before which we shudder. But if we take the alternative world view, which recognises the spiritual in man and matter, then everything is seen in a new proportion. This view enables us to believe that we are, in core, spiritual beings belonging to an eternal realm of wider experience.

Sir George continues by referring to the spiritual being, entering at birth into life as we know it and leaving this life by the doorway of death. This introduces themes which may not be explicity addressed in this book, but which are certainly implicit in many of the readings we have found, and which flit in and out of the minds of most of us. Some believe that each one of us is a new creation, sown in the womb, and for whom death is the gateway to eternal life. Another belief is that life goes on through reincarnation, that through successive lives we may accumulate experience which may bring us reward or punishment in further lives depending on how we have performed previously. Yet another is that death comes as the end. Interwoven with much of this is the idea – and sometimes the recorded experience – that the living and the dead may communicate, and that only a veil or a low wall separates us from the departed.

Death is the one single issue about which we are condemned to ignorance, and yet it is the one issue about which we most long for knowledge. This is the great paradox of life.

PREPARING FOR DEATH

143   Have you built your ship of death, oh have you?
Oh build your ship of death, for you will need it.

Now in the twilight, sit by the invisible sea
Of peace, and build your little ship
Of death, that will carry the soul
On its last journey, on and on, so still
So beautiful, over the last of seas.

When the day comes, that will come.
Oh think of it in the twilight peacefully!
The last day, and the setting forth
On the longest journey, over the hidden sea
To the last wonder of oblivion

Oblivion, the last wonder!
When we have trusted ourselves entirely
To the unknown, and are taken up
Out of our little ships of death
Into pure oblivion.

Oh build your ship of death, be building it now
With dim, calm thoughts and quiet hands
Putting its timbers together in the dusk,
Rigging its mast with the silent, invisible sail
That will spread in death to the breeze
Of the kindness of the cosmos, that will waft
The little ship with its soul to the wonder-goal.

Ah, if you want to live in peace on the face of the earth
Then build your ship of death, in readiness
For the longest journey, over the last of seas.

                                            D. H. LAWRENCE from *The Ship of Death*

For all that has been – thanks; To all that will be – yes.

                                                Dag Hammarskjold

144   I am convinced it is a great art to know how to grow old
gracefully, and I am determined to practise it . . . I always
thought I should love to grow old, and I find it is even more
delightful than I thought. It is so delicious to be *done* with
things, and to feel no need any longer to concern myself
much about early affairs . . . I am tremendously content to let
one activity after another go, and to await quietly and happily
the opening of the door at the end of the passage way, that
will let me in to my real abiding place.

HANNAH WHITALL SMITH

145   That time of year thou mayst in me behold
When yellow leaves, or none, or few, do hang
Upon those boughs which shake against the cold,
Bare ruined choirs, where late the sweet birds sang.
In me thou seest the twilight of such day
As after sunset fadeth in the west;
Which by and by black night doth take away,
Death's second self, that seals up all in rest.
In me thou seest the glowing of such fire,
That on the ashes of his youth doth lie,
As the death-bed whereon it must expire,
Consumed with that which it was nourished by.
This thou perceiv'st, which makes thy love more strong,
To love that well which thou must leave ere long.

WILLIAM SHAKESPEARE *Sonnet LXXIII*

*Is there not a certain satisfaction in the fact that natural limits are set
to the life of the individual, so that at its conclusion it may appear as a
work of art?*   Albert Einstein

146   Oh, Son of Man, if Thee and not another
            I here have known,
      If I may see Thee then, our First-born Brother,
            Upon Thy Throne;

      How stern soe'er, how terrible in brightness
            That dawn shall break,
      I shall be satisfied with Thy dear likeness
            When I awake.

                                    THOMAS HODGKIN

147   Whatever pains we may take for our nourishment, for the care of the body, we cannot prolong life by a single hour. Is it not folly to trouble ourselves about a thing that we cannot possibly accomplish?

                      LEO TOLSTOY from *My Religion*

148   When we are dead, and people weep for us and grieve, let it be because we touched their lives with beauty and simplicity. Let it not be said that life was good to us, but, rather, that we were good to life.

                                JACOB P. RUDIN

149   The various miseries of life which lie before us wherever we turn our eyes, the frailty of this mortal state we are passing through, may put us in mind that the present world is not our home; that we are merely strangers and travellers in it, as all our fathers were. It is therefore to be considered as a foreign country . . .

                JOSEPH BUTLER from *Fifteen Sermons*

God shall wipe away all tears from their eyes, and there shall be no more death, neither sorrow, nor crying, neither shall there be any more pain; for the former things are passed away.

                The Revelation of St John the Divine

150   When I lie where shades of darkness
       Shall no more assail mine eyes,
       Nor the rain make lamentation
           When the wind sighs;
       How will fare the world whose wonder
       Was the very proof of me?
       Memory fades, must the remembered
           Perishing be?

       Oh, when this my dust surrenders
       Hand, foot, lip, to dust again,
       May these loved and loving faces
           Please other men!
       May the rusting harvest hedgerow
       Still the Traveller's Joy entwine,
       And as happy children gather
           Posies once mine.

       Look thy last on all things lovely,
       Every hour. Let no night
       Seal thy sense in deathly slumber
           Till to delight
       Thou have paid thy utmost blessing;
       Since that all things thou wouldst praise
       Beauty took from those who loved them
           In other days.

                          WALTER DE LA MARE *Fare Well*

151   One wears his mind out in study, and yet has more mind with
       which to study. One gives away his heart in love, and yet has
       more heart to give away. One perishes out of pity for a suf-
       fering world, and is the stronger therefore. So, too, it is
       possible at one and the same time to hold on to life and let it
       go . . .   MILTON STEINBERG

*The call of God that both challenges us and sets us free is to be heard
in the voices of all who suffer.*   The Right Rev. Rowan Williams

152   O, have you seen the leper healed,
            And fixed your eyes upon his look?
            There is the book of God revealed,
            And God has made no other book.

            The withered hand which time interred
            Grasps in a moment the unseen.
            The word we had not heard, is heard.
            What we are then, we had not been.

            Plotinus, preaching on heaven's floor,
            Could not give praise like that loud cry
            Bursting the bondage of death's door;
            For we die once; indeed we die.

            What Sandro Botticelli found
            Rose from the river where we bathe:
            Music the air, the stream, the ground;
            Music the dove, the rock, the faith.

            And all that music whirled upon
            The eyes' deep-sighted, burning rays,
            Where all the prayers of labours done
            Are resurrected into praise.

            But look: his face is like a mask
            Surrounded by the beat of wings.
            Because he knows that ancient task
            His true transfiguration springs.

            All fires the prophets' words contained
            Fly to those eyes, transfixed above.
            Their awful precept has remained:
            'Be nothing, first; and then, be love.'

                           VERNON WATKINS *The Healing of the Leper*

Why should we fear death who welcome the repose of sleep? Josephus

153   Pain, anxiety, distress, slip away from us like a torn and bleeding skin. We are alive, and yet on the edge of something else. We are conscious, and yet on the edge of something else. It is now nothing to us that in our mortal life we have made no mark among men; that we shall perish unknown, unregarded, even as we have lived! It is now nothing to us that we are but one solitary consciousness among uncountable millions of consciousnesses, dead, living, and as yet unborn.

Something has stirred within us that transvalues all our values, transcends all our personal cravings. The impersonality of the Inanimate, which has been sharing our vigil all our days from its sublime patience, seems at last on the edge of whispering to us the lost clue.

The 'Wait! wait!' of Matter's eternal reiteration, the 'How long? how long?' of the tragic expectancy of the whole astronomical universe, are rendered the more prophetic of some tremendous issue in proportion as each individual spirit abdicates its human tenure, retreats into the elements, and shares, incognito, its fate with the Inanimate.

JOHN COWPER POWYS from *A Philosophy of Solitude*

154   Good by, my dear. Whenever you think of me do not forget to think how much happiness your loving kindness has given me and how you have helped my last, long months. I really think the door will open soon now and I may be able to scurry through at last. But I shall remember you wherever I wake.

E. NESBIT *postscript to a letter, March 1924*

A man must take with him into the next world an adamantine faith in truth and right   Plato

155   Naked we came here, naked of Natural things, & naked we
        shall return; but while cloth'd with the Divine Mercy, we are
        richly cloth'd in Spiritual & suffer all the rest gladly.

                                                        WILLIAM BLAKE

156   When I have fears that I may cease to be
        Before my pen has glean'd my teeming brain,
        Before high-pilèd books, in charact'ry,
        Hold like rich garners the full-ripened grain;
        When I behold, upon the night's starr'd face,
        Huge cloudy symbols of a high romance,
        And think that I may never live to trace
        Their shadows, with the magic hand of chance;
        And when I feel, fair creature of an hour!
        That I shall never look upon thee more,
        Never have relish in the faery power
        Of unreflecting love! – then on the shore
        Of the wide world I stand alone, and think,
        Till Love and Fame to nothingness do sink.

                                                        JOHN KEATS

157   We do not die wholly at our deaths: we have mouldered away
        gradually long before. Faculty after faculty, interest after
        interest, attachment after attachment disappear: we are torn
        from ourselves while living, year after year sees us no longer
        the same, and death only consigns the last fragment of what
        we were to the grave. That we should wear out by slow
        stages, and dwindle at last into nothing, is not wonderful,
        when even in our prime our strongest impressions leave little
        trace for the moment, and we are the creatures of petty
        circumstance.

                                                        WILLIAM HAZLITT

158 During each life period, a new measure of the Word of God must be built, living stone by stone, into the very structure of the growing personality, just as the energy of the sun is built into the plants of the earth. Childhood, adolescence, maturity, middle age and old age, each and every phase of life calls for the discovery of new potentialities within the eternal self . . . Thus, by a process of growth, the healthy spirit is prepared for the last crisis, death, when the body returns to the earth, and the spirit to God who gave it. If the spirit be in health, the fate of its tabernacle becomes of slight concern . . .

STEPHEN GRELLET

159 Of all the evils of the world which are reproached with an evil character, death is the most innocent of its accusation. For when it is present, it hurts nobody; and when it is absent, it is indeed troublesome, but the trouble is owing to our fears, not the affrighting and mistaken object: and besides this, if it were an evil, it is so transient, that it passes like the instant or undiscerned portion of the present time; and either it is past, or it is not yet; for just when it is, no man hath reason to complain of so insensible, so sudden, so undiscerned a change.

BISHOP JEREMY TAYLOR from *Holy Dying*

The woods are lovely, dark and deep.
But I have promises to keep,
And miles to go before I sleep,
And miles to go before I sleep.

Robert Frost

160   To regret one's own experience is to arrest one's own
            development. To deny one's own experiences is to put a lie
            into the lips of one's own life. It is no less than a denial of the
            soul . . . .

            The important thing, the thing that lies before me, the
            thing that I have to do, if the brief remainder of my days is
            not to be maimed, marred, and incomplete, is to absorb into
            my nature all that has been done to me, to make it part of me,
            to accept it without complaint, fear, or reluctance.

                                    OSCAR WILDE from *De Profundis*

161   Look to this day! For it is life, the very life of life. In its brief
            course lie all the varieties and realities of your existence: the
            bliss of growth, the glory of action, the splendour of beauty.
            For yesterday is already a dream, and tomorrow is only a
            vision, but today, well-lived, makes every yesterday a dream
            of happiness, and every tomorrow a vision of hope.

            Look well, therefore, to this day! Such is the salutation of
            the dawn.

                                    ANON *Sanskrit*

162   To venerate the simple days
                Which lead the seasons by,
                Needs but to remember
                That from you or I
                They may take the trifle
                Termed mortality !

                                    EMILY DICKINSON

*Why do you weep? All my life has been given to me merely that I
might learn to die.*   Rabbi Bunam *to his wife on his deathbed*

163   Leave me, O love, which reachest but to dust,
        And thou, my mind, aspire to higher things!
    Grow rich in that which never taketh rust:
        Whatever fades, but fading pleasure brings.
    Draw in thy beams, and humble all thy might
        To that sweet yoke where lasting freedoms be;
    Which breaks the clouds and opens forth the light
        That doth both shine and give us sight to see.
    O take fast hold! let that light be thy guide
        In this small course which birth draws out to death,
    And think how evil becometh him to slide
        Who seeketh Heaven, and comes of heavenly breath.
           Then farewell, world! thy uttermost I see:
           Eternal Love, maintain thy life in me!
             Sir Philip Sidney *Splendidis Longum Valedico Nugis*

164   I believe it is of real value to our earthly life to have the next
life in mind, because if we shut it out of our thoughts we are
starving part of our spiritual nature – we are like children who
fail to grow up – none the finer children for that. Not only do
we miss much joy in the earth life if we imagine it to be the
whole of our existence, but we arrive on the further shore
with no knowledge of the language of the new country where
we shall find ourselves unfitted for the larger life of the spirit.

        Joan Mary Fry from *her last letter to her friends*

165   As for myself, I am content with the conviction that God's
eyes are forever upon me, that His providence and justice will
follow me into the future life as it has protected me in this,
and that my true happiness consists in the devleopment of the
powers of my soul. It is such felicity that awaits me in the life
to come. More I do not desire to know.

        Moses Mendelssohn

166   The gay will laugh
         When thou art gone, the solemn brood of care
         Plod on, and each one as before will chase
         His favourite phantom; yet all these shall leave
         Their mirth and their employments, and shall come,
         And make their bed with thee.
                                    WILLIAM CULLEN BRYANT from *Thanatopsis*

167   The sunlicht still on me, you row'd in clood,
         We look upon each ither noo like hills
         Across a valley. I'm nae mair your son.
         It is my mind, nae son o yours, that looks,
         And the great darkness o your death comes up
         And equals it across the way.
         A livin man upon a deid man thinks
         And ony sma'er thocht's impossible.
                                    HUGH MACDIARMID from *At My Father's Grave*

168   She had been shaken out of sorrow. She had looked into the
         clear face of death and known her lover. She would fear no
         longer . . . She would live out her time and finish the task
         before her, because she knew that even the burden of living
         was not endless. Comforted by death, she faced the future.
                                    WINIFRED HOLTBY from *South Riding*

*We are comrades of those who are gone; though death separate us,
their work, their fortitude, their love shall be ours.*
                                    John Wilhelm Rowntree

169 From all that terror teaches,
  From lies of tongue and pen,
  From all the easy speeches
  That comfort cruel men,
  From sale and profanation
  Of honour and the sword,
  From sleep and from damnation,
  Deliver us, good Lord!

G. K. CHESTERTON from A Hymn

170 My prime of youth is but a frost of cares,
  My feast of joy is but a dish of pain,
  My crop of corn is but a field of tares,
  And all my good is but vain hope of gain;
  My life is fled, and yet I saw no sun;
  And now I live, and now my life is done.

  My tale was heard, and yet it was not told;
  My fruit is fallen, and yet my leaves are green;
  My youth is spent, and yet I am not old;
  I saw the world, and yet I was not seen;
  My thread is cut, and yet it is not spun;
  And now I live, and now my life is done.

  I sought my death, and found it in the womb,
  I looked for life and saw it was a shade;
  I trod the earth and knew it was my tomb,
  And now I die, and now I was but made;
  My glass is full, and now my glass is run,
  And now I live, and now my life is done.

CHIDIOCK TICHBOURNE

What is this land where our friends go and do not return?

Traditional, Zaire

171   Even such is Time, which takes in trust
       Our youth, our joys, and all we have,
       And pays us but with age and dust;
       Who in the dark and silent grave,
       When we have wandered all our ways,
       Shuts up the story of our days:
       And from which earth, and grave, and dust,
       The Lord shall raise me up, I trust.

                                        SIR WALTER RALEIGH

172   I learned very early on in my life that nothing was for ever; so
       I should have been aware of disillusion in early middle age:
       but, somehow, we try to obliterate early warnings and go
       cantering along hopefully, idiotically . . .

       No matter that the tide will turn once again and destroy all
       that you build (and in the depths of your soul you know that
       this will happen), you thrust the spade in the hard-packed
       rippled sand, outline the beginning of a moat. Soon the fort
       will arise, decorated all about, once again, with shells and
       weed, with towers and turrets, arches and a drawbridge, each
       turret capped with a conical limpet shell. As glorious as the
       first one ever was, probably even better from the experience
       gained by its destruction, and every bit as impermanent . . .

       How odd it is that one is not prepared for the "dissolving
       of the fort" one has constructed with such care in later life.
       But we do not learn. We always believe that it'll be all right
       for us. That our fort will stand, the tide will never turn. But,
       of course, it does.

                       DIRK BOGARDE from *A Short Walk from Harrods*

Men fear death as children fear to go into the dark.   Francis Bacon

173 I remember my youth and the feeling that will never come back any more – the feeling that I could last for ever, outlast the sea, the earth, and all men; the deceitful feeling that lures us on to joys, to perils, to love, to vain effort – to death; the triumphant conviction of strength, the heat of life in the handful of dust, the glow in the heart that with every year grows dim, grows cold, grows small, and expires – and expires, too soon, too soon – before life itself.

JOSEPH CONRAD from *Youth*

174 Return me, oh sun,
to my wild destiny,
rain of the ancient wood,
bring me back the aroma and the swords
that fall from the sky,
the solitary peace of pasture and rock,
the damp at the river-margins,
the smell of the larch tree,
the wind alive like a heart
beating in the crowded restlessness
of the towering araucaria.

Earth, give me back your pure gifts,
the towers of silence which rose
from the solemnity of their roots.
I want to go back to being what I have not been,
and learn to go back from such deeps
that amongst all natural things
I could live or not live; it does not matter
to be one stone more, the dark stone,
the pure stone which the river bears away.

PABLO NERUDA *Oh Earth, Wait for Me*
trans. Alastair Reid

I've hoped to live, and am prepared to die.   William Shakespeare

175   There's a long, long trail awinding
        Into the land of my dreams,
        Where the nightingales are singing
        And a white moon beams;
        There's a long, long night of waiting
        Until my dreams all come true,
        Till the day when I'll be going down
        That long, long trail with you.

                                        STODDARD KING *Song*

176   Keep right on to the end of the road,
        Keep right on to the end.
        Tho' the way be long, let your heart be strong,
        Keep right on round the bend.
        Tho' you're tired and weary,
        Still journey on
        Till you come to your happy abode,
        Where all you love you've been dreaming of
        Will be there at the end of the road.

                                        SIR HARRY LAUDER *Song*

177   One thing alone I charge you. As you live, believe in life!
        Always human beings will live and progress to greater,
        broader and fuller life.
            The only possible death is to lose belief in this truth
        simply because the great end comes slowly, because time is
        long.

                                        W. E. B. DuBOIS *His last message*

Death destroys a man: the idea of Death saves him.   E. M. Forster

178   I have a rendezvous with Death
At some disputed barricade,
When Spring comes round with rustling shade
And apple blossoms fill the air.
I have a rendezvous with Death
When Spring brings back blue days and fair.

ALAN SEEGER

179   For every year of life we light
A candle on your cake
To make the simple sort of progress
Anyone can make,
And then, to test your nerve or give
A proper view of death,
You're asked to blow each light, each year,
Out with your own breath.

JAMES SIMMONS *A Birthday Poem*

180   Let him not cease that seeketh Wisdom until
He find, and when he has found let him marvel, and
Having marvelled he shall reign, and reigning
He shall rest.

JESUS from *Oxyrhynchus Sayings*
trans. Rev. Charles Taylor

181   I wake to sleep, and take my waking slow.
I feel my fate in what I cannot fear.
I learn by going where I have to go.

THEODORE ROETHKE from *The Waking*

Death, like birth, is a secret of Nature.   Marcus Aurelius

182   I would know whether after the parting of the body and the
soul I shall ever know more than I now know of all that which
I have long wished to know; for I cannot find anything better
in man than that he know, and nothing worse than that he be
ignorant.

KING ALFRED THE GREAT

183   When God at first made man,
Having a glass of blessings standing by;
Let us (said He) pour on him all we can:
Let the world's riches, which dispersèd lie,
     Contract into a span.

     So strength first made a way,
Then beauty flow'd, then wisdom, honour, pleasure;
When almost all was out, God made a stay,
Perceiving that alone of all His treasure
     Rest in the bottom lay.

     For if I should (said He)
Bestow this jewel also on My creature,
He would adore My gifts instead of Me,
And rest in Nature, not the God of Nature:
     So both should losers be.

     Yet let him keep the rest,
But keep them with repining restlessness:
Let him be rich and weary, that at least,
If goodness lead him not, yet weariness
     May toss him to My breast.

GEORGE HERBERT *The Pulley*

God is never sought in vain, even when we do not find him.

St Bernard

184   O crooked ways of mine! Woe be to my audacious soul,
which hoped that, had it forsaken thee, it might find
something else which was better. Though it turn and toss,
upon the back and side and breast, it hath found all things
hard; and that thou alone art Rest. And behold, thou art near
at hand, thou deliverest us from our wretched errrors, thou
dost place us in thy right way, and dost comfort us, saying,
"Run on, and I will carry you. I will conduct you to the end,
and even there will I uphold you."

ST AUGUSTINE

185   I must go down to the seas again, to the lonely sea and the
sky,
And all I ask is a tall ship and a star to steer her by;
And the wheel's kick and the wind's song and the white sail's
shaking,
And a grey mist on the sea's face, and a grey dawn breaking.

I must go down to the seas again, for the call of the running
tide
Is a wild call and a clear call that may not be denied;
And all I ask is a windy day with the white clouds flying,
And the flung spray and the blown spume, and the sea-gulls
crying.

I must go down to the seas again, to the vagrant gypsy
life,
To the gull's way and the whale's way where the wind's like a
whetted knife;
And all I ask is a merry yarn from a laughing fellow-rover,
And quiet sleep and a sweet dream when the long trick's over.

JOHN MASEFIELD *Sea Fever*

186   Now I saw in my dream, that the highway up which Christian
was to go, was fenced on either side with a wall, and that wall
was called Salvation. Up this way, therefore, did burdened
Christian run, but not without great difficulty, because of the
load on his back.

He ran thus till he came to a place somewhat ascending,
and upon that place stood a Cross, and a little below, in the
bottom, a sepulchre. So I saw in my dream, that just as
Christian came up with the Cross, his burden loosed from off
his shoulders, and fell from off his back, and began to tumble,
and to continue to do, till it came to the mouth of the
sepulchre, where it fell in, and I saw it no more.

Then was Christian glad and lightsome, and said, with a
merry heart, 'He hath given me rest by his sorrow, and life by
his death'. Then he stood still a while to look and wonder; for
it was very surprising to him, that the sight of the Cross
should thus ease his burden. He looked, therefore, and looked
again, even till the springs that were in his head sent the
waters down his cheeks. Now, as he stood looking and
weeping, behold three shining ones came to him, and saluted
him with 'Peace be to thee'; so the first said to him, 'Thy sins
be forgiven thee'; the second stripped him of his rags, and
clothed him with a change of raiment; the third also set a
mark on his forehead, and gave him a roll with a seal upon it,
which he bade him look on as he ran, and that he should give
it in at the Celestial Gate; so they went their way. Then
Christian gave three leaps for joy, and went on singing.

JOHN BUNYAN from *The Pilgrim's Progress*

He who laughs, lasts.   Mary Poole

187   I said to my soul, be still, and wait without hope
For hope would be hope for the wrong thing; wait without
    love
For love would be love of the wrong thing; there is yet faith
But the faith and the love and the hope are all in the waiting.
Wait without thought, for you are not ready for thought:
So the darkness shall be the light, and the stillness the
    dancing.
Whisper of running streams, and winter lightning.
The wild thyme unseen and wild strawberry,
The laughter in the garden, echoed ecstasy
Not lost, but requiring, pointing to the agony
Of death and birth.

    You say I am repeating
Something I have said before. I shall say it again.
Shall I say it again? In order to arrive there,
To arrive where you are, to get from where you are not,
    You must go by a way wherein there is no ecstasy.
In order to arrive at what you do not know
    You must go by a way which is the way of ignorance.
In order to possess what you do not possess
    You must go by the way of dispossession.
In order to arrive at what you are not
    You must go through the way in which you are not.
And what you do not know is the only thing you know
And what you own is what you do not own
And where you are is where you are not.

                T. S. ELIOT from *East Coker*

188   I know that I shall meet my fate
            Somewhere among the clouds above;
            Those that I fight I do not hate,
            Those that I guard I do not love;
            My country is Kiltartan Cross,
            My countrymen Kiltartan's poor,
            No likely end could bring them loss
            Or leave them happier than before.
            Nor law, nor duty bade me fight,
            Nor public men, nor cheering crowds,
            A lonely impulse of delight
            Drove to this tumult in the clouds;
            I balanced all, brought all to mind,
            The years to come seemed waste of breath,
            A waste of breath the years behind
            In balance with this life, this death.
                      W. B. YEATS *An Irish Airman Foresees His Death*

189   Jesu, Maria – I am near to death,
                And Thou art calling me; I know it now.
            Not by the token of this faltering breath,
                This chill at heart, this dampness on my brow, –
            (Jesu, have mercy! Mary, pray for me!)
                'Tis this new feeling, never felt before,
            (Be with me, Lord, in my extremity!)
                That I am going, that I am no more.
            'Tis this strange innermost abandonment,
                (Lover of souls! great God! I look to Thee)
            This emptying out of each constituent
                And natural force, by which I come to be.
                      JOHN HENRY NEWMAN from *The Dream of Gerontius*

Those who know the art of true living also know that of true dying.
                                        Gobind Singh Mansukhani

190   Rouse thee, my fainting soul, and play the man;
          And through such waning span
Of life and thought as still has to be trod,
          Prepare to meet thy God.
And while the storm of that bewilderment
          Is for a season spent,
And, ere afresh the ruin on thee fall,
          Use well the interval.

          JOHN HENRY NEWMAN from *The Dream of Gerontius*

191   The soul's dark cottage, battered and decayed,
Lets in new light through chinks that Time has made:
Stronger by weakness, wiser men become
As they draw near to their eternal home.
Leaving the old, both worlds at once they view
That stand upon the threshold of the new.

          EDMUND WALLER from *Old Age*

192   Enough, if something from our hands have power
          To live, and act, and serve the future hour;
And if, as toward the silent tomb we go,
          Through love, through hope, and faith's transcendent
dower,
We feel that we are greater than we know.

    WILLIAM WORDSWORTH from *Valediction to the River Duddon*

193   I believe we can be in unbroken touch with whatever the
Beyond may be *in our hearts*, and receive inspiration,
guidance and protection from those who pass into it, while, in
our prayers, we can also perhaps sustain and encourage them
in their work. Death is really the goal and triumph of Life,
and it is only a little bit dark in the doorway.

          ROLF GARDINER from *a letter*

With mirth and laughter let old wrinkles come.   William Shakespeare

194   Thou hast made me, and shall thy work decay ?
                Repair me now, for now mine end doth haste;
                I run to death, and death meets me as fast,
        And all my pleasures are like yesterday.
        I dare not move my dim eyes any way;
                Despair behind, and death before doth cast
                Such terror, and my feebled flesh doth waste
        By sin in it, which it towards hell doth weigh.
        Only thou art above, and when towards thee
                By thy leave I can look, I rise again;
        But our old subtle foe so tempteth me
                That not one hour I can myself sustain.
                Thy grace may wing me to prevent his art,
                And thou like adamant draw mine iron heart.

                                        JOHN DONNE from *Holy Sonnets*

195   Riches I hold in light esteem,
                And Love I laugh to scorn;
                And lust of Fame was but a dream
                That vanished with the morn –

                And if I pray, the only prayer
                That moves my lips for me
                Is – 'Leave the heart that now I bear,
                And give me liberty.'

                Yes, as my swift days near their goal,
                'Tis all that I implore
                Through life and death, a chainless soul,
                With courage to endure!

                                        EMILY BRONTË *The Old Stoic*

*Since it is possible that you may depart from this life at this very
moment, regulate every act and thought accordingly.*

                                        Marcus Aurelius

196   The sunlight on the garden
        Hardens and grows cold,
        We cannot cage the minute
        Within its nets of gold,
        When all is told
        We cannot beg for pardon.

        Our freedom as free lances
        Advances towards its end;
        The earth compels, upon it
        Sonnets and birds descend;
        And soon, my friend,
        We shall have no time for dances.

        The sky was good for flying
        Defying the church bells
        And every evil iron
        Siren and what it tells:
        The earth compels,
        We are dying, Egypt, dying

        And not expecting pardon,
        Hardened in heart anew,
        But glad to have sat under
        Thunder and rain with you,
        And grateful too
        For sunlight on the garden.

                                                LOUIS MACNEICE

197   God give me work
            Till my life shall end
        And life
            Till my work is done.

                                                ANON

*Certain, 'tis certain; very sure, very sure: death as the Psalmist saith,
is certain to all; all shall die.*   William Shakespeare

198   Where lies the land to which the ship would go?
Far, far ahead, is all her seamen know.
And where the land she travels from? Away,
Far, far behind, is all that they can say.
                    ARTHUR HUGH CLOUGH *Where lies the land?*

199   I am – yet what I am none cares or knows;
My friends forsake me like a memory lost: –
I am the self-consumer of my woes; –
They rise and vanish in oblivions host,
Like shadows in love's frenzied stifled throes: –
And yet I am, and live – like vapours tost

Into the nothingness of scorn and noise, –
Into the living sea of waking dreams,
Where there is neither sense of life or joys,
But the vast shipwreck of my life's esteems;
Even the dearest, that I love the best
Are strange – nay, rather stranger than the rest.

I long for scenes where man has never trod
A place where woman never smiled or wept
There to abide with my Creator, God;
And sleep as I in childhood, sweetly slept,
Untroubling, and untroubled where I lie,
The grass below – above the vaulted sky.
                    JOHN CLARE '*I Am*'

The cradle rocks above an abyss, and common sense tells us that our existence is but a brief crack of light between two eternities of darkness.   Vladimir Nabokov

200   From darkness
Into the path of darkness
Must I enter:
Shine upon me from afar,
O moon above the mountain crest

IZUMI SHIKIBU
from *After the death of her daughter in childbirth*
trans. Edwin A. Cranston

201   Behind Me – dips Eternity –
Before Me – Immortality –
Myself – the Term between –
Death but the Drift of Eastern Gray,
Dissolving into Dawn away,
Before the West begin –

EMILY DICKINSON

202   The first brown leaf has fluttered from the trees along the
lane; the signal has been given – and the year is on the wane;
the swallows have departed, and the house is cloaked in red –
of clinging creepers, certain sign that Summer days have fled
. . . This is no time for idle tears – Look up! – for who dare
weep? This is a preparation for a long and happy sleep, in
which God's hidden hand can re-create new life again – and
form within this seeming death, green buds for April's rain.

And even Death in Nature's world, is lovely to behold – a
carnival of beauty lit by fires of burning gold . . . A mighty
beech in russet robes flames out against the sky; the trees that
teach us how to live, can teach us how to die – magnificently,
gloriously – expressing to the end – the beautiful, with arms
outstretched to Death, as to a friend.

PATIENCE STRONG *Autumn Gold*

Why fear death? It is the most beautiful adventure in life.

Charles Frohman

203   I strove with none, for none was worth my strife:
              Nature I loved, and next to Nature, Art:
            I warmed both hands before the fire of Life;
              It sinks; and I am ready to depart.
                    WALTER SAVAGE LANDOR *On His Seventy-fifth Birthday*

204   Darkling I listen; and for many a time
              I have been half in love with easeful Death,
            Called him soft names in many a musèd rhyme,
              To take into the air my quiet breath;
            Now more than ever seems it rich to die,
              To cease upon the midnight with no pain,
              While thou art pouring forth thy soul abroad
              In such an ecstasy!
            Still wouldst thou sing, and I have ears in vain –
              To thy high requiem become a sod.
                    JOHN KEATS from *Ode to a Nightingale*

205   There are tears of happiness – and there are tears of pain –
            There are tears of sweet relief, when hope revives again –
            There are tears born of compassion – burning tears that come
            – When the heart is torn with pity and the lips are dumb . . .
            Then there are the tears that flow too swiftly to be real –
            Sentiment that simulates a love it cannot feel – Tears that
            spring from sheer self-pity, or a fancied slight – Tears of self-
            inflicted pain – God help us all to fight – our false emotions –
            Make us strong to face what is to be – And may our tears be
            those of selfless love – and sympathy.
                    PATIENCE STRONG *Tears*

We are all serving a life-sentence in the dungeon of self.
                                                    Cyril Connolly

206   I have no fear of death – but I shall welcome a helping hand to see me through.

For it is said that just as everyone has a guardian angel, so to each one comes somebody to help us over the stile.

Once I am over, I know a door will open on a new loveliness and freshness of colour, form and light which is far more beautiful than anything I have ever seen or imagined.

OLIVER HALL from *The Wind in the Oak*

207   Father, before this sparrow's earthly flight
Ends in the darkness of a winter's night;
Father, without whose word no sparrow falls,
Hear this, Thy weary sparrow, when he calls.
Mercy, not justice, is his contrite prayer,
Cancel his guilt, and drive away despair;
Speak but the word, and make his spirit whole,
Cleanse the dark places of his heart and soul,
Speak but the word, and set his spirit free;
Mercy, not justice, still his constant plea.
So shall Thy sparrow, crumpled wings restored,
Soar like the lark, and glorify his Lord.

LORD HAILSHAM *The Sparrow's Prayer*

208   . . . there's a special providence in the fall of a sparrow. If it be now, 'tis not to come; if it be not to come, it will be now; if it be not now, yet it will come: the readiness is all.

WILLIAM SHAKESPEARE from *Hamlet*

Death opens unknown doors. It is most grand to die.   John Masefield

IN THE MIDST OF LIFE

209   In all times and in all places is Creation.
In all times and in all places is Death.
Man is a Gateway.

           C. G. JUNG from *Sermons to the Dead*

210   If I should go before the rest of you
Break not a flower or inscribe a stone,
Nor when I'm gone speak in a Sunday voice
But be the usual selves that I have known.
    Weep if you must,
    Parting is hell,
    But life goes on
    So sing as well.

           JOYCE GRENFELL from *Joyce by Herself and Friends*

211   Some walk with Death as to a leper tied,
and some hold hands as with a summer bride,
and her warm presence serves to red the cheek:
some know her not, nor knowing, fear her state;
some grow too fond impatiently to wait,
and distraught, perfect consummation seek . . .

           JIM BAILEY from *Death in the Aircrew Mess, Debriefing*

The Angels keep their ancient places
Turn but a stone and start a wing
'Tis ye, 'tis your estrangèd faces
That miss the many-splendour'd thing.   Francis Thompson

212   I know my body's of so frail a kind,
        As force without, fevers within, can kill;
    I know the heavenly nature of my mind,
        But 'tis corrupted both in wit and will.

    I know my soul hath power to know all things,
        Yet is she blind and ignorant in all;
    I know I am one of nature's little kings,
        Yet to the least and vilest things am thrall.

    I know my life's a pain, and but a span;
        I know my sense is mocked with everything;
    And, to conclude, I know myself a man,
        Which is a proud, and yet a wretched thing.

SIR JOHN DAVIES

213   O age! Blessed time of life, I salute you even now! Men are afraid of you, but they should love you as the most happy time of life because you are its end. I shall love you as the dawning of the eternal day. I can already see my temples growing white under the touch of your harbingers, and a smile rises to my lips.

LUCIE CHRISTINE

214   The man has vanished like the morning dew,
    The woman in the frost of night remains,
    The river in its endless flow runs on,
    The lone-left bird laments eternally.

CONFUCIUS

I would have written of me on my stone:
I had a lover's quarrel with the world.   Robert Frost

215   I trod on the heels of Death,
               who turned and said:
               Young man, you are in a bit of a hurry.
               I replied: You will find
               it is not I who hurries,
               they are pushing from behind.

                                JIM BAILEY *War-Pilot, 1940*

216   I wish I could translate the things about the dead
               young men and women,
           And the hints about old men and mothers, and the offspring
               taken soon out of their laps.

           What do you think has become of the young and old men?
           And what do you think has become of the women and
               children?

           They are alive and well somewhere,
           The smallest sprout shows there is really no death,
           And if ever there was it led forward life, and does
               not wait at the end to arrest it,
           And ceas'd the moment life appear'd.

           All goes onward and outward, nothing collapses,
           And to die is different from what anyone supposed,
               and luckier.

                            WALT WHITMAN from *Song of Myself*

Ah, what a dusty answer gets the soul
When hot for certainties in this our life!   George Meredith

217   Do not go gentle into that good night,
Old age should burn and rave at close of day;
Rage, rage against the dying of the light.

Though wise men at their end know dark is right,
Because their words had forked no lightning they
Do not go gentle into that good night.

Good men, the last wave by, crying how bright
Their frail deeds might have danced in a green bay,
Rage, rage against the dying of the light.

Wild men who caught and sang the sun in flight,
And learn, too late, they grieved it on its way,
Do not go gentle into that good night.

Grave men, near death, who see with blinding sight
Blind eyes could blaze like meteors and be gay,
Rage, rage against the dying of the light.

And you, my father, there on the sad height,
Curse, bless, me now with your fierce tears, I pray.
Do not go gentle into that good night.
Rage, rage against the dying of the light.

                                                DYLAN THOMAS

Beneath this stone, in hope of Zion,
Doth lie the landlord of the 'Lion'.
His son keeps on the business still,
Resign'd unto the Heavenly will.
                    Epitaph in the Churchyard of Upton upon Severn

Like as the waves make towards the pebbled shore,
So do our minutes hasten to their end.   William Shakespeare

218   I determined that *tomorrow*, and not today, would mark the
start of my sixtieth year.

I was not to know that tomorrow would also bring me the
news that Ma had died.

When the two great tent-poles fall, which have, for so
long, supported the fabric above the circus of one's life, the
guy-ropes fly away, the canvas billows down, and there is
nothing left to do but crawl out from under, and go on one's
way alone.

"A Show For All The Family!" is over.

DIRK BOGARDE from *An Orderly Man*

219   What passing-bells for these who die as cattle?
Only the monstrous anger of the guns.
Only the stuttering rifles' rapid rattle
Can patter out their hasty orisons.
No mockeries for them; no prayers nor bells,
    Nor any voice of mourning save the choirs, –
The shrill, demented choirs of wailing shells;
    And bugles calling for them from sad shires.

What candles may be held to speed them all?
    Not in the hands of boys, but in their eyes
Shall shine the holy glimmer of good-byes.
    The pallor of girls' brows shall be their pall;
Their flowers the tenderness of patient minds,
And each slow dusk a drawing-down of blinds.

WILFRED OWEN *Anthem for Doomed Youth*

O, withered is the garland of the war, The soldier's pole is fallen.

William Shakespeare

220   Into my heart an air that kills
      From yon far country blows:
    What are those blue remembered hills,
      What spires, what farms are those?

    That is the land of lost content,
      I see it shining plain,
    The happy highways where I went
      And cannot come again.

A. E. HOUSMAN

221   O Rose, thou art sick!
    The invisible worm
    That flies in the night,
    In the howling storm,

    Has found out thy bed
    Of crimson joy,
    And his dark secret love
    Does thy life destroy.

WILLIAM BLAKE The Sick Rose

222   Seek Love in the Pity of others' Woe,
    In the gentle relief of another's care,
    In the darkness of night & the winter's snow,
    In the naked & outcast, Seek Love there!

WILLIAM BLAKE from William Bond

In the midst of life we are in death.   Book of Common Prayer

223   Before the beginning of years
              There came to the making of man
        Time, with a gift of tears;
              Grief, with a glass that ran;
        Pleasure, with pain for leaven;
              Summer, with flowers that fell;
        Remembrance fallen from heaven,
              And madness risen from hell;
        Strength without hands to smite;
              Love that endures for a breath;
        Night, the shadow of light,
              And life, the shadow of death.

        And the high gods took in hand
              Fire, and the falling of tears,
        And a measure of sliding sand
              From under the feet of the years,
        And froth and drift of the sea;
              And dust of the labouring earth;
        And bodies of things to be
              In the houses of death and of birth;
        And wrought with weeping and laughter,
              And fashioned with loathing and love,
        With life before and after
              And death beneath and above,
        For a day and a night and a morrow,
              That his strength might endure for a span
        With travail and heavy sorrow,
              The holy spirit of man.

Life is perhaps most wisely regarded as a bad dream between two awakenings, and every day is a life in miniature.

                                        Eugene O'Neill

From the winds of the north and the south
    They gathered as unto strife;
They breathed upon his mouth,
    They filled his body with life;
Eyesight and speech they wrought
    For the veils of the soul therein,
A time for labour and thought,
    A time to serve and to sin;
They gave him light in his ways,
    And love, and a space for delight,
And beauty and length of days,
    And night, and sleep in the night.
His speech is a burning fire;
    With his lips he travaileth;
In his heart is a blind desire,
    In his eyes foreknowledge of death;
He weaves, and is clothed with derision;
    Sows, and he shall not reap;
His life is a watch or a vision
    Between a sleep and a sleep.

A. C. SWINBURNE *Chorus*

224   You who read this fickle page
        Illustrated by the sun,
        Scribbled by the showers' rage,
        Altering as the minutes run;
        Think how alteration must
        All endeavours bring to dust,
        All that's mortal, man and house,
        And of mercy pray for us.

LAURENCE WHISTLER
engraved by him on a window pane at Campion Hall,
Oxford, 1936: given by Lutyens, who designed the college

There is no cure for birth and death save to enjoy the interval.
George Santayana

225   Fair daffodils, we weep to see
              You haste away so soon;
         As yet the early-rising sun
              Has not attained his noon.
                  Stay, stay
              Until the hasting day
                  Has run
              But to the evensong;
         And, having prayed together, we
              Will go with you along.

         We have short time to stay as you,
              We have as short a spring;
         As quick a growth to meet decay,
              As you, or anything.
                  We die
              As your hours do, and dry
                  Away
              Like to the summer's rain;
         Or as the pearls of morning's dew,
              Ne'er to be found again.

ROBERT HERRICK *To Daffodils*

226   I knew, and shall know again, the name of God, closer
              than close;
         But now I know a stranger thing,
         That never can I study too closely, for never will it
              come again, –
         Distractions and the human crowd.

STEVIE SMITH from *Distractions and the Human Crowd*

The time of life is short! To spend that shortness basely were too long.
William Shakespeare

227   Sooner or later in life everyone discovers that perfect happiness is unrealisable, but there are few who pause to consider the antithesis: that perfect unhappiness is equally unattainable. The obstacles preventing the realization of both these extreme states are of the same nature: they derive from our human condition which is opposed to everything infinite. Our ever-sufficient knowledge of the future opposes it: and this is called, in the one instance, hope, and in the other, uncertainty of the following day. The certainty of death opposes it: for it places a limit on every joy, but also on every grief.

PRIMO LEVI from *If This Is A Man*

228   What are days for?
Days are where we live.
They come, they wake us
Time and time over.
They are to be happy in:
Where can we live but days?

Ah, solving that question
Brings the priest and the doctor
In their long coats
Running over the fields.

PHILIP LARKIN *Days*

229   Oh could I believe the living and dead inhabit one house
         under the sky
and you my child run into your future for ever.

FRANCES HOROVITZ from *In Painswick Churchyard*

Life is doubt, And faith without doubt is nothing but death.

Miguel du Unamuno

230   Where art thou friend, whom I shall never see,
Conceiving whom I must conceive amiss?
Or sunder'd from my sight in the age that is
Or far-off promise of a time to be;
Thou who canst best accept the certainty
That thou hadst borne proportion in my bliss,
That likest in me either that or this, –
Oh! even for the weakness of the plea
That I have taken to plead with, – if the sound
Of God's dear pleadings have as yet not moved thee, –
And for those virtues I in thee have found,
Who say that had I known I had approved thee, –
For these, make all the virtues to abound, –
No, but for Christ who hath foreknown and loved thee.

GERARD MANLEY HOPKINS

231   We must make the most of them
we say – these skies of pale
unclouded blue. (Our lives
move in and out of focus too.)

We tread through blankets
of bright leaves like children
playing games – now warm,
now cold and getting colder.

VICKI FEAVER from *Autumn*

The souls of all our brethren are ever hovering about us, craving for a caress, and only waiting for the signal.   Maurice Maeterlinck

232   No one makes any great mention of the horrors of peace, yet I
am told by those who ought to know that more people have
been killed in traffic accidents since the Great War than the
total casualties there amounted to.

That is a horrible affair. In War at least one goes forth
prepared. One has a weapon and the expectation that
something may happen, and one's affairs consequently in
good order. And if one dies, at least the death is an
honourable one, and calls afterwards for kind thoughts, and
calico poppies to be sold on one's behalf in memory of it.

Consider those who fall in Peace.

They are a small and unbelligerent people, perhaps armed
with nothing but the umbrella, the shopping list, when of a
sudden they are mown down from behind or before. There is
also no glory in their death, and many people write letters to
the papers, saying they have no one but themselves to blame.
Unsung they remain. No one retails their gallant effort of
crossing the road with the lights against them. No memorial is
there, only a notice in the paper, for which the relations must
pay.

ANON

from *Letters of an Indian Judge to an English Gentlewoman*

233   I would be true for there are those who trust me
I would be pure for there are those who care
I would be strong for there is much to suffer
I would be brave for there is much to dare
I would be friend of all, the foe, the friendless
I would be giving and forget the gift
I would be humble for I know my weakness
I would look up and laugh and love and live.

ANON

234   He has gone down into the dark cellar
            To talk with the bright-faced Spirit with silver hair;
            But I shall never know what word was spoken there.

            . . . .

            My friend is out of earshot. Our ways divided
            Before we even knew we had missed each other.

            But he is gone where no hallooing voice
            Nor beckoning hand can ever call him back;
            And what is ours of him
            Must speak impartially for all the world;
            There is no personal word remains for me,
            And I pretend to find no meaning here.
            Though I might guess that other Singer's wisdom
            Who saw in Death a dark immaculate flower,
            And tenderness in every falling autumn,
            This abstract music will not bring again
            My friend to his warm room:
            Inscrutable the darkness covers him.
                    JOHN HEATH-STUBBS from *In Memory of Sidney Keyes*

235   Most men eddy about
            Here and there – eat and drink,
            Chatter and love and hate,
            Gather and squander, are raised
            Aloft, are hurled in the dust,
            Striving blindly, achieving
            Nothing; and then they die –
            Perish; – and no one asks
            Who or what they have been.
                    MATTHEW ARNOLD *Rugby Chapel*

One crowded hour of glorious life
Is worth an age without a name.   Thomas Osbert Mordaunt

236   All mankind is of one Author, and is one volume; when one man dies, one chapter is not torn out of the book, but translated into a better language; and every chapter must be so translated; God employs several translators; some pieces are translated by age, some by sickness, some by war, some by justice; but God's hand is in every translation; and his hand shall bind up all our scattered leaves again, for that Library where every book shall lie open to one another. As therefore the bell that rings to a sermon calls not upon the preacher only, but upon the congregation to come; so this bell calls us all . . . No man is an island, entire of itself; every man is a piece of the continent, a part of the main; if a clod be washed away by the sea, Europe is the less, as well as if a promontory were, as well as if a manor of thy friends or of thine own were; any man's death diminishes me, because I am involved in Mankind; and therefore never send to know for whom the bell tolls; it tolls for thee.

JOHN DONNE

237   What is our life? A play of passion,
Our mirth the music of division.
Our mothers' wombs the tiring-houses be,
Where we are dressed for this short comedy.
Heaven the judicious sharp spectator is,
That sits and marks still who doth act amiss.
Our graves that hide us from the searching sun
Are like drawn curtains when the play is done.
Thus march we, playing, to our latest rest.
Only we die in earnest, that's no jest.

SIR WALTER RALEIGH *All the World's a Stage*

Life isn't a dress rehearsal. The party's for real.   Charles Handy

238   This world a vale of soul-making –
         To what intent the finished wares?

         Is the ore enforced and fired through
         Harsh mills, only to fall aside?

         Who is this soulmaster? What say
         Do souls have in their made futures?

         We mourn the untried young, unmade
         In small coffins. What of grown graves?

         At times in cemeteries, you hear
         Their voices, sad and even-toned,

         Almost see the made souls, in their
         Curious glory. If you are old.

                              D. J. ENRIGHT *In Cemeteries*

239   I'll believe then that you are dead
         Only when the hills and flickering rivers,
         The wind roaring from North and South-West,
         When the cutting winter frost and the dews
         That lay on the grass today and yesterday –
         When all these are swallowed and fade away.

                    B. W. VILAKAZI from *Then I'll Believe*

*One must take all one's life to learn how to live, and . . . one must take
all one's life to learn how to die.*   Seneca

240   The force that through the green fuse drives the flower
       Drives my green age; that blasts the roots of trees
       Is my destroyer.
       And I am dumb to tell the crooked rose
       My youth is bent by the same wintry fever.

                                        DYLAN THOMAS

241   To see a World in a Grain of Sand
       And a Heaven in a Wild Flower,
       Hold Infinity in the palm of your hand
       And Eternity in an hour.

                    WILLIAM BLAKE from *Auguries of Innocence*

242   In the dark womb where I began
       My mother's life made me a man.
       Through all the months of human birth
       Her beauty fed my common earth.
       I cannot see, nor breathe, nor stir,
       But through the death of some of her.

                              JOHN MASEFIELD *C.L.M.*

243   Mad about the boy,
       It's pretty funny but I'm mad about the boy.
       He has a gay appeal
       That makes me feel
       There may be something sad about the boy.

                                        NOËL COWARD

The day of our birth is one day's advance towards our death.
                                        Thomas Fuller

244   It is not now as it hath been of yore; –
             Turn wheresoe'er I may,
                 By night or day,
         The things which I have seen I now can see no more.
                 WILLIAM WORDSWORTH from *Intimations of Immortality*

245   Lay your sleeping head, my love,
             Human on my faithless arm;
             Time and fevers burn away
             Individual beauty from
             Thoughtful children, and the grave
             Proves the child ephemeral:
             But in my arms till break of day
             Let the living creature lie,
             Mortal, guilty, but to me
             The entirely beautiful.
                                 W. H. AUDEN from *Lullaby*

246   Our birth is but a sleep and a forgetting:
         The Soul that rises with us, our life's Star
             Hath had elsewhere its setting,
                 And cometh from afar:
             Not in entire forgetfulness,
             And not in utter nakedness,
         But trailing clouds of glory do we come
             From God, who is our home:
         Heaven lies about us in our infancy!
                 WILLIAM WORDSWORTH from *Intimations of Immortality*

All thoughts, all passions, all delights, Whatever stirs this mortal
frame, All are ministers of Love, And feed his sacred flame.
                                 Samuel Taylor Coleridge

247   What though the radiance which was once so bright
        Be now for ever taken from my sight,
            Though nothing can bring back the hour
        Of splendour in the grass, of glory in the flower;
                We will grieve not, rather find
                Strength in what remains behind.
            WILLIAM WORDSWORTH from *Intimations of Immortality*

248   Stop all the clocks, cut off the telephone,
        Prevent the dog from barking with a juicy bone,
        Silence the pianos and with muffled drum
        Bring out the coffin, let the mourners come.

        Let aeroplanes circle moaning overhead
        Scribbling on the sky the message He Is Dead,
        Put crêpe bows round the white necks of the public doves,
        Let the traffic policemen wear black cotton gloves.

        He was my North, my South, my East and West,
        My working week and my Sunday rest,
        My noon, my midnight, my talk, my song;
        I thought that love would last for ever: I was wrong.

        The stars are not wanted now; put out every one;
        Pack up the moon and dismantle the sun;
        Pour away the ocean and sweep up the wood;
        For nothing now can ever come to any good.
                                        W. H. AUDEN *Funeral Blues*

Forgive, O Lord, my little jokes on Thee
And I'll forgive Thy great big one on me.   Robert Frost

249   Huge images of death lurk in my brain
           and track me where I go;
           here in this city, here in Summer's plain,
           I am smothered under shadow.

           Not being with friends nor even this tall day
           where the light sings
           brings peace, release from these; I cannot play
           nor find my joys in things.

           They are my thoughts of war and war's disease;
           I move with men
           and watch an equal dark behind each face
           striking them iron.

           Over my love and breaking on my joy
           this fear descends:
           I see guns shatter and slow fog destroy
           my friends, my lovely friends.

                                   RICHARD GOODMAN *Poem, 1933*

To those whom death again did wed,
This grave's their second marriage bed;
For though the hand of fate could force
'Twixt soul and body a divorce,
It could not sunder man and wife
Because they both liv'd but one life.
Peace, the lovers are asleep.
They, sweet turtles, folded lie
In the last knot that love could tie.   Richard Crashaw
                              from An Epitaph upon husband and wife;
                                 which died and were buried together

FAITH, HOPE, LOVE

250 Love doesn't end with dying
Or leave with the last breath.
For someone you've loved deeply,
Love doesn't end with death.

JOHN ADDEY For W.B.O.

251 One night I had a dream.
I dreamed I was walking along the beach with the Lord,
and across the sky flashed scenes from my life.
For each scene, I noticed two sets of footprints in the sand;
One belonged to me, the other to the Lord.
When the last scene of my life flashed before me,
I looked back at the footprints in the sand.
I noticed that many times along the path of life,
there was only one set of footprints.
I noticed that it happened at the very lowest and saddest times
in my life.
This really bothered me and I questioned the Lord about it:
"Lord, You said that once I decided to follow You,
You would walk with me all the way.
But I have noticed that during the most troublesome times in
my life, there is only one set of footprints. I don't understand
why in times when I needed You most, You would leave me."
The Lord replied:
"My precious, precious child, I love you and would never,
never leave you during your times of trial and suffering.
When you see only one set of footprints –
It was then that I carried you."

ANON

We must love one another or die.   W. H. Auden

252   Death is part of the future for everyone. It is the last post of
this life and the reveille of the next. Everywhere men fear
death – it is the end of our present life, it is parting from
loved ones, it is setting out into the unknown. We overcome
death by accepting it as the will of a loving God; by finding
him in it. Death, like birth, is only a transformation, another
birth. When I die I shall change my state, that is all. And in
faith in God, it is as easy and natural as going to sleep here
and waking up there.

BISHOP APPLETON from *Journey for a Soul*

253   The first Christians lived face to face with death but their
faith in the salvation that lay beyond their final death enabled
them to die daily to their immediate sufferings and to live in
the power of resurrection life. For many of us today, the
refusal to look death in the face robs us of the reality of that
resurrection experience. Tidying up the affairs of a person
who has died puts new perspective on all that person lived
for. What will be saved out of it all? The money – of no value
to him now. The property – standing empty. The clothes – to
be cast away. But the faith and the hope and the love by
which he lived – these surely are vindicated, these are of
eternal value, these are saved as his life reaches its ultimate
meaning beyond the grave, in the salvation that belongs to
our God.

PAULINE WEBB

Since faith is not knowledge, doubt is no sin.   Lord Hailsham

254   It matters not when I am dead
        Where this dull clay shall lie,
        Nor what the dogmas, creeds and rites
        Decree to us who die.
        I only know that I shall tread
        The paths my dead have trod,
        And where the hearts I love have gone,
        There shall I find my God.

KENDALL BANNING *It Matters Not*

255   Most near, most dear, most loved and most far,
        Under the window where I often found her
        Sitting as huge as Asia, seismic with laughter,
        Gin and chicken helpless in her Irish hand,
        Irresistible as Rabelais, but most tender for
        The lame dogs and hurt birds that surround her, –
        She is a procession no one can follow after
        But be like a little dog following a brass band.

        But she will not glance up at the bomber, or condescend
        To drop her gin and scuttle to a cellar,
        But leans on the mahogany table like a mountain
        Whom only faith can move, and so I send
        O all my faith and all my love to tell her
        That she will move from mourning into morning.

GEORGE BARKER *To My Mother*

If God sends us on stony paths he provides strong shoes.

Corrie ten Boom

256   Perhaps now I shall one day rise, and be worthy of him who
in his life both in peace and in war and in his death has shown
me 'the way more plain'. At any rate, if ever I do face danger
and suffering with some measure of his heroism, it will be
because I have learnt through him that love is supreme, that
love is stronger than death and the fear of death.

VERA BRITTAIN from *Testament of Youth*

257   O, my luve's like a red, red rose,
That's newly sprung in June:
O, my luve's like the melodie
That's sweetly played in tune.

As fair art thou, my bonnie lass,
So deep in luve am I;
And I will luve thee still, my dear,
Till a' the seas gang dry.

Till a' the seas gang dry, my dear,
And the rocks melt wi' the sun;
I will luve thee still, my dear,
While the sands o' life shall run.

And fare thee weel, my only luve!
And fare thee weel a while!
And I will come again, my luve,
Tho' it were ten thousand mile.

ROBERT BURNS

*Faith is much stronger in spite of something than because of
something.*   Arthur Koestler

258   No coward soul is mine,
       No trembler in the world's storm-troubled sphere:
       I see Heaven's glories shine,
       And faith shines equal, arming me from fear.

       O God within my breast,
       Almighty, every-present Deity !
       Life – that in me has rest,
       As I – undying Life – have power in thee!

       With wide-embracing love
       Thy spirit animates eternal years,
       Pervades and broods above,
       Changes, sustains, dissolves, creates, and rears.

       Though earth and man were gone,
       And suns and universes ceased to be,
       And thou were left alone,
       Every existence would exist in thee.

       There is not room for Death,
       Nor atom that his might could render void:
       Thou – thou art Being and Breath,
       And what thou art may never be destroyed.

                                        EMILY BRONTË
       (The last lines my sister Emily ever wrote – Charlotte Brontë)

*Sorrow, regret, anger, even thankfulness are passing emotions, and in
the end the only one that is everlasting is love.*

                                        June O'Carroll Robertson

259   All his beauty, wit and grace
        Lie forever in one place.
        He who sang and sprang and moved
        Now, in death, is only loved.

                                    ALICE THOMAS ELLIS *To Joshua*

260   The greatest griefs shall find themselves inside the smallest
           cage.
        It's only then that we can hope to take their rage,

        The monsters we must live with. For it will not do
        To hiss humanity because one human threw
        Us out of heart and home. Or part

        At odds with life because one baby failed to live.
        Indeed, as little as its subject, is the wreath we give –

        The big words fail to fit. Like giant boxes
        Round small bodies. Taking up improper room,
        Where so much withering is, and so much bloom.

                      D. J. ENRIGHT *On the Death of a Child*

261   Give me my Scallop shell of quiet,
        My staff of Faith to walk upon,
        My Scrip of Joy, Immortal diet,
        My bottle of salvation:
        My Gown of Glory, hopes true gage,
        And thus I'll take my pilgrimage.

        SIR WALTER RALEIGH from *The Passionate Man's Pilgrimage*
                (Supposed to be Written by One at the Point of Death)

Grief is not forever – but love is.   Anon

262   To Thee, my God, to thee I call !
            Whatever weak or woe betide,
        By thy command I rise or fall,
            In thy protection I confide.

        If, when this dust to dust's restored,
            My soul shall float on airy wing,
        How shall thy glorious name adored
            Inspire her feeble voice to sing !

        But, if this fleeting spirit share
            With clay the grave's eternal bed,
        While life yet throbs I raise my prayer,
            Though doom'd no more to quit the dead.

        To Thee I breathe my humble strain,
            Grateful for all thy mercies past,
        And hope, my God, to thee again
            This erring life may fly at last.

                    LORD BYRON from *The Prayer of Nature*

263   Only connect! That was the whole of her sermon. Only
        connect the prose and the passion, and both will be exalted,
        and human love will be seen at its height. Live in fragments
        no longer.

                    E. M. FORSTER from *Howard's End*

He that loveth flieth, runneth and rejoiceth. He is free.
                            Thomas à Kempis

264   Wilt thou forgive that sin where I begun,
             Which is my sin, though it were done before?
         Wilt thou forgive those sins through which I run,
             And do them still, though still I do deplore?
                 When thou hast done, thou hast not done,
                     For I have more.

         Wilt thou forgive that sin by which I won
             Others to sin? and made my sin their door?
         Wilt thou forgive that sin which I did shun
             A year or two, but wallowed in a score?
                 When thou hast done, thou has not done,
                     For I have more.

         I have a sin of fear, that when I have spun
             My last thread, I shall perish on the shore;
         Swear by thyself that at my death, thy Sun
             Shall shine as it shines now, and heretofore;
                 And, having done that, thou hast done,
                     I have no more.

                                        JOHN DONNE *A Hymn*

265   I said to the man who stood at the Gate of the Year, 'Give me
         a light that I may tread safely into the unknown'. And he
         replied, 'Go out into the darkness and put your hand into the
         hand of God. That shall be to you better than light and safer
         than a known way!'

                                 MINNIE LOUISE HASKINS *God Knows*

*Lord, I know you won't send any trouble today that you and I together
cannot handle.*   African prayer

266   Love is most nearly itself
         When here and now cease to matter.
         Old men ought to be explorers
         Here and there does not matter
         We must be still and still moving
         Into another intensity
         For a further union, a deeper communion
         Through the dark cold and the empty desolation,
         The wave cry, the wind cry, the vast waters
         Of the petrel and the porpoise. In my end is my beginning.

                              T. S. ELIOT from *East Coker*

267   Lord I am not entirely selfish
         Lord I am not entirely helpish
         O Lord to me be slightly lavish
         O Lord be in a minor way lovish

         Lord I am not completely bad-mannered
         Lord I am not a crusader, mad-bannered
         O Lord to me be quite well disposed
         O Lord to me be calm and composed

         Lord I am not a dog downed and to-heeled
         Lord I am not thick about what has been revealed
         O Lord you have it in your power to hurt me
         O Lord in your odd way please do not desert me

                                        GAVIN EWART *Prayer*

Faith is putting one's foot down in the mist and finding it on a rock.

                                                        Anon

268   The Soul a substance and a spirit is,
            Which God Himself doth in the body make,
            Which makes the Man: for every man from this
            The nature of a Man and name doth take.

            And though this spirit be to the body knit,
            As an apt mean her powers to exercise,
            Which are life, motion, sense, and will, and wit;
            Yet she survives, although the body dies.

SIR JOHN DAVIES *What the Soul Is*

269   So I beg you to incline with all eagerness to this lowly
            movement of love which is in your heart, and to follow it; it
            will be your guide in this life, and bring you to the bliss of
            heaven in the next. It is the essence of all good living, and
            without it no good work may be begun or ended. It is nothing
            other than a goodwill in harmony with God, and a kind of
            pleasure and gladness which you experience in your will at all
            that he does.

ANON from *The Cloud of Unknowing*
trans. Clifton Wolters

Learn you to live by faith, as I did live before,
Learn you to give in faith, as I did at my door.
Learn you to keep by faith, as God be still thy store,
Learn you to lend by faith, as I did to the poor;
Learn you to live, to give, to keep, to lend, to spend,
That God in Christ, at day of death, may prove thy friend.

John Porter, Norfolk yeoman, 1600

270   Chestnut candles are lit again
For the dead that died in spring:
Dead lovers walk the orchard ways,
And the dead cuckoos sing.

Is it they who live and we who are dead ?
Hardly the springtime knows
For which to-day the cuckoo calls,
And the white blossom blows.

Listen and hear the happy wind
Whisper and lightly pass:
Your love is sweet as hawthorn is,
Your hope green as the grass.

The hawthorn's faint and quickly gone,
The grass in autumn dies;
Put by your life, and see the spring
With everlasting eyes.

                    WILLIAM KERR *In Memoriam D.O.M.*

271   You gave me all that a mother could give;
You gave me your love and a reason to live.
You've been my best friend for so many years;
We've shared happy times and also our tears.
There's no-one that means as much as you do
After all you've done for me, and all we've been through.
So we'll never be parted – it just cannot be;
For you know I love you, and I know you love me.

                    LESLEY GRAY *For My Mum*

I do not fear to tread the road I cannot see,
Because the hand of One-who-loves is leading me   Nagata

272   My Lord God, I have no idea where I am going.
        I do not see the road ahead of me.
        I cannot know for certain where it will end.
        Nor do I really know myself,
        and the fact that I think I am following your will
        does not mean that I am actually doing so.

        But I believe that the desire to please you does in fact please
            you,
        and I hope that I have that desire in all that I am doing.
        I hope that I never do anything apart from that desire.
        And I know that if I do this
        you will lead me by the right road
        though I may know nothing about it.

        Therefore I will trust you always.
        Though I may seem to be lost and in the shadow of death
        I will not fear, for you are ever with me
        and you will never leave me to face my peril alone.

                                                    THOMAS MERTON

273   It seems such waste, such stupid senseless waste. His great
        thoughts, his fine body that loved life, all the friendship, the
        aspiration, the love . . . all thrown away, gone, wasted for
        ever.

        Who says that it is wasted? it is his body that has served its
        turn and is cast away. The great thoughts, the friendship, the
        aspiration, the love; can we say that these die? Nay, rather,
        these shall not die. These shall live in the Courts of the Lord,
        for ever.

                                                        E. NESBIT

274 Lay in the dead man's hand the Cross – the Cross upon his
   breast
Because beneath the shadow of the Cross he went to rest:
And let the Cross go on before – the Crucified was first
To go before the people and their chains of death to burst;
And be the widow's heart made glad with charitable dole,
And pray with calm, yet earnest faith for the departed soul.
And be the *De Profundis* said for one of Christ's own fold,
And – for a prisoner is set free – the bells be rung not tolled.
When face to face we stand with death, thus Holy Church
   records,
He is our slave, and we, through Her, his masters and his
   lords.
Deck the High Altar for the Mass! Let tapers guard the
   hearse!
For Christ, the Light that lighteneth all, to blessing turns our
   curse . . .

JOHN MASON NEALE
from *Oh, give us back the days of old*

Now I lay me down to sleep;
I pray the Lord my soul to keep.
If I should die before I wake,
I pray the Lord my soul to take.

New England Primer, 1781

A good life fears not life nor death.   Thomas Fuller

275   Does the road wind up-hill all the way ?
            Yes, to the very end.
        Will the day's journey take the whole long day ?
            From morn to night, my friend.

        But is there for the night a resting-place ?
            A roof for when the slow dark hours begin.
        May not the darkness hide it from my face ?
            You cannot miss that inn.

        Shall I meet other wayfarers at night ?
            Those who have gone before.
        Then must I knock, or call when just in sight ?
            They will not keep you standing at that door.

        Shall I find comfort, travel-sore and weak ?
            Of labour you shall find the sum.
        Will there be beds for me and all who seek ?
            Yes, beds for all who come.

                                CHRISTINA ROSSETTI *Up-Hill*

276   Though they go mad they shall be sane,
        Though they sink through the sea they shall rise again;
        Though lovers be lost love shall not;
        And death shall have no dominion.

                                    DYLAN THOMAS
                            from *Death shall have no Dominion*

*Now let the weeping cease; Let no one mourn again. These things are
in the hand of God.*   Sophocles

277   Man aspires
To good,
To love
Sighs;

Beaten, corrupted, dying
In his own blood lying
Yet heaves up an eye above
Cries, Love, love.
It is his virtue needs explaining,
Not his failing.

Away, melancholy,
Away with it, let it go.

STEVIE SMITH

278   I feel, and I wish you to feel for and with me, after the Rock
of eternal life and salvation; for as we are established thereon,
we shall be in the everlasting unity, which cannot be shaken
by all the changes of time, nor interrupted in a never-ending
eternity. We cannot approve or disapprove by parts the work
of Omnipotence rightly. We must approve the whole and say,
Thy will be done in all things . . . The desire of my heart is
the great blessing of time and the consolation of eternity . . .
let self be of no reputation; trust in the Lord, and he will carry
thee through all.

JOB SCOTT *Dying words, 1793*

Death surprises us in the midst of our hopes.   Thomas Fuller

279   Before the winter closes round the land – stripping the trees –
            along the windy lane; drift back in thought, across the waning
            year – Come let us dream – and live it all again.

            Daffodil time – and violets in the hedge; lilac in May – and
            bluebells in the rain; apple time, harvest and the hunter's
            moon – October mists . . . these memories remain.

            God made us so – that in the winter's gloom – through the
            dark hours, forgotten flowers may bloom; fear not, brave
            heart – for what the days may bring – dream on and hope –
            for yet another Spring.

                                                    PATIENCE STRONG
                                                    Another Spring

280   Loving with human love, one may pass from love to hatred;
            but divine love cannot change. Nothing, not even death, can
            shatter it. It is the very nature of the soul . . . Love is life. All,
            all that I understand, I understand only because I love. All is,
            all exists only because I love. All is bound up in love alone.
            Love is God, and dying means for me a particle of love, to go
            back to the universal and eternal source of love.

                                                    LEO TOLSTOY
                                                    from *War and Peace*

A man awaits his end
Dreading and hoping all.   W. B. Yeats

281   Strong Son of God, immortal Love,
           Whom we, that have not seen thy face,
           By faith, and faith alone, embrace,
       Believing where we cannot prove;

       Thine or these orbs of light and shade;
           Thou madest Life in man and brute;
           Thou madest Death; and lo, thy foot
       Is on the skull which thou has made.

       Thou wilt not leave us in the dust:
           Thou madest man, he knows not why;
           He thinks he was not made to die;
       And thou has made him: thou art just.

       Thou seemest human and divine,
           The highest, holiest manhood, thou:
           Our wills are ours, we know not how;
       Our wills are ours, to make them thine.

       Our little systems have their day;
           They have their day and cease to be:
           They are but broken lights of thee,
       And though, O Lord, art more than they.

       We have but faith: we cannot know;
           For knowledge is of things we see;
           And yet we trust it comes from thee,
       A beam in darkness: let it grow.

Unable are the Loved to die
For Love is Immortality.

                                    Emily Dickinson

Let knowledge grow from more to more,
     But more of reverence in us dwell;
     That mind and soul, according well,
May make one music as before,

But vaster. We are fools and slight;
     We mock thee when we do not fear:
     But help thy foolish ones to bear;
Help thy vain worlds to bear thy light.

Forgive what seem'd my sin in me;
     What seem'd my worth since I began;
     For merit lives from man to man,
And not from man, O Lord, to thee.

Forgive my grief for one removed,
     Thy creature, whom I found so fair.
     I trust he lives in thee, and there
I find him worthier to be loved.

Forgive these wild and wandering cries,
     Confusions of a wasted youth;
     Forgive them where they fail in truth,
And in thy wisdom make me wise.

                                   ALFRED, LORD TENNYSON
                                   from *In Memoriam*

*Faith is to believe what you do not yet see; the reward for this faith is
to see what you believe.*   St Augustine

282 Sunset and evening star,
    And one clear call for me !
And may there be no moaning of the bar,
    When I put out to sea,

But such a tide as moving seems asleep,
    Too full for sound and foam,
When that which drew from out the boundless deep
    Turns again home.

Twilight and evening bell,
    And after that the dark !
And may there be no sadness of farewell,
    When I embark;

For though from out our bourne of Time and Place
    The flood may bear me far,
I hope to see my Pilot face to face
    When I have crost the bar.
      ALFRED, LORD TENNYSON *Crossing the Bar*

283 There is no expeditious road
To pack and label men for God,
And save them by the barrel-load.
Some may perchance, with strange surprise,
Have blundered into Paradise.
      FRANCIS THOMPSON

The terrors of truth and dart of death
To faith alike are vain.   Herman Melville

284   Will you see the infancy of this sublime and celestial
greatness? Those pure and virgin apprehensions I had from
the womb, and that divine light wherewith I was born are the
best unto this day, wherein I can see the Universe. By the Gift
of God they attended me into the world, and by His special
favour I remember them till now. Verily they seem the
greatest gifts His wisdom could bestow, for without them all
other gifts had been dead and vain. They are unattainable by
book, and therefore I will teach them by experience. Pray for
them earnestly: for they will make you angelical, and wholly
celestial. Certainly Adam in Paradise had not more sweet and
curious apprehensions of the world, than I when I was a child.

All appeared new, and strange at first, inexpressibly rare and
delightful and beautiful. I was a little stranger, which at my
entrance into the world was saluted and surrounded with
innumerable joys. My knowledge was Divine. I knew by
intuition those things which since my Apostasy, I collected
again by the highest reason. My very ignorance was
advantageous. I seemed as one brought into the Estate of
Innocence. All things were spotless and pure and glorious:
yea, and infinitely mine, and joyful and precious. I knew not
that there were any sins, or complaints or laws. I dreamed not
of poverties, contentions or vices. All tears and quarrels were
hidden from mine eyes. Everything was at rest, free and
immortal. I knew nothing of sickness or death or rents or

*Death then, being the way and condition of life, we cannot love to live
if we cannot bear to die.*
                                        William Penn

exaction, either for tribute or bread. In the absence of these I was entertained like an Angel with the works of God in their splendour and glory, I saw all in the peace of Eden; Heaven and Earth did sing my Creator's praises, and could not make more melody to Adam, than to me. All Time was Eternity, and a perpetual Sabbath. Is it not strange, that an infant should be heir of the whole World, and see those mysteries which the books of the learned never unfold?

The corn was orient and immortal wheat, which never should be reaped, nor was ever sown. I thought it had stood from everlasting to everlasting. The dust and stones of the street were as precious as gold: the gates were at first the end of the world. The green trees when I saw them first through one of the gates transported and ravished me, their sweetness and beauty made my heart to leap, and almost mad with ecstasy, they were such strange and wonderful things. The Men! O what venerable and reverend creatures did the aged seem! Immortal Cherubims! And young men glittering and sparkling Angels, and maids strange seraphic pieces of life and beauty! Boys and girls tumbling in the street, and playing, were moving jewels. I knew not that they were born or should die; But all things abided eternally as they were in their proper places. Eternity was manifest in the Light of the Day, and something infinite behind everything appeared: which talked

Love is all we have, the only way that each can help the other.
                              Euripides, trans. William Arrowsmith

with my expectation and moved my desire. The city seemed
to stand in Eden, or to be built in Heaven. The streets were
mine, the temple was mine, the people were mine, their
clothes and gold and silver were mine, as much as their
sparkling eyes, fair skins and ruddy faces. The skies were
mine, and so were the sun and moon and stars, and all the
World was mine; and I the only spectator and enjoyer of it. I
knew no churlish properties nor bounds, nor divisions: but all
properties and divisions were mine: all treasures and
possessors of them. So that with much ado I was corrupted,
and made to learn the dirty devices of this world. Which now
I unlearn, and become, as it were, a little child again that I
may enter into the Kingdom of God.

THOMAS TRAHERNE
from *Centuries of Meditations*

285   Take him and cut him out in little stars,
       And he will make the face of heaven so fine
       That all the world will be in love with night
       And pay no worship to the garish sun.

WILLIAM SHAKESPEARE
from *Romeo and Juliet*

Faith – is the Pierless Bridge
Supporting what We see
Unto the Scene that We do not.   Emily Dickinson

286   To think well is to serve God in the interior court: To have a
mind composed of Divine Thoughts, and set in frame, to be
like Him within. To conceive aright and to enjoy the world, is
to conceive the Holy Ghost, and to see His Love: which is the
Mind of the Father. And this more pleaseth Him than many
Worlds, could we create as fair and great as this. For when
you are once acquainted with the world, you will find the
goodness and wisdom of God so manifest therein, that it was
impossible another, or better should be made. Which being
made to be enjoyed, nothing can please or serve him more,
than the Soul that enjoys it. For that Soul doth accomplish the
end of His desire in Creating it.

THOMAS TRAHERNE from *Centuries of Meditations*

287   I had thought that your death
Was a waste and a destruction
A pain of grief hardly to be endured.
I am only beginning to learn
That your life was a gift and a growing
And a loving left with me,
That desperation of death
Destroyed the existence of love,
But the fact of death
Cannot destroy what has been given.
I am learning to look at your life again
Instead of your death and your departing.

MARJORIE PIZER *The Existence of Love*

Hope is a strange invention –
A Patent of the Heart –
In unremitting action
Yet never wearing out.   Emily Dickinson

288   My soul, there is a country
        Far beyond the stars,
    Where stands a wingèd sentry
        All skilful in the wars:
    There, above noise and danger,
        Sweet Peace sits crown'd with smiles,
    And One born in a manger
        Commands the beauteous files.
    He is thy gracious Friend,
        And – O my soul, awake! –
    Did in pure love descend
        To die here for thy sake.
    If thou canst get but thither,
        There grows the flower of Peace,
    The Rose that cannot wither,
        Thy fortress, and thy ease.
    Leave then thy foolish ranges;
        For none can thee secure
    But one who never changes –
        Thy God, thy life, thy cure.

                         HENRY VAUGHAN *Peace*

289   True love is a durable fire
    In the mind ever burning,
    Never sick, never old, never dead,
    From itself never turning.

                         SIR WALTER RALEIGH

Eternal Love doth keep
In his complacent arms
The earth, the air, the deep.   William Cullen Bryant

290   Then, as the hour of his departure was fast approaching, he
       made all the Brethren that were in the place be called unto
       him and, consoling them for his death with words of comfort,
       exhorted them with fatherly tenderness unto the love of God.
       He spake long of observing patience, and poverty, and
       fidelity unto the Holy Roman Church, placing the Holy
       Gospel before all other ordinances. Then as all the Brethren
       sat around him, he stretched his hands over them, crossing his
       arms in the likeness of the Cross, for that he did ever love that
       sign, and he blessed all the Brethren present and absent alike,
       in the might and in the Name of the Crucified. He added,
       moreover, "Be strong, all ye my sons, in the fear of the Lord,
       and abide therein for ever. And since temptations will come
       and trials draw nigh, blessed are they who shall continue in
       the work that they have begun. I for my part make haste to go
       unto God, unto whose grace I commend you all."

                           ST BONAVENTURE *The Death of St Francis of Assisi*

291   When lilacs last in the dooryard bloom'd,
       And the great star early droop'd in the western sky in the
           night,
       I mourn'd, and yet shall mourn with ever-returning spring.

       Ever-returning spring, trinity sure to me you bring,
       Lilac blooming perennial and drooping star in the west,
       And thought of him I love.

                                                    WALT WHITMAN

Look for me in the nurseries of heaven.   Francis Thompson

CONSOLATION

292   For the flowers are great blessings,

For the Lord made a Nosegay in the meadow with his disciples and preached upon the lily.

For the angels of God took it out of his hand and carried it to the Height . . .

For there is no Height in which there are not flowers.

For flowers have great virtues for all the senses.

For the flower glorifies God and the root parries the adversary.

For the flowers have their angels even the words of God's Creation.

For the warp and woof of flowers are worked by perpetual moving spirits.

For flowers are good both for the living and the dead.

For there is a language of flowers.

For there is a sound reasoning upon all flowers.

For elegant phrases are nothing but flowers.

For flowers are peculiarly the poetry of Christ.

CHRISTOPHER SMART
from *Rejoice in the Lamb*

St Francis ordered a plot to be set aside for the cultivation of flowers when the convent garden was made, in order that all who saw them might remember the Eternal Sweetness.   Tomàs of Celano

293   In every age
         We relive history
         As if we ourselves were still in slavery
         And felt the breath
         Of the divine Spirit helping and saving us
         And leading us by the hand
         Into the land promised to our forefathers.

         And with hearts filled with gratitude and delight
         We celebrate and praise
         Him who has set us and our fathers free from slavery
         And who has saved us from our oppressors.
         It is he who changes sorrow into joy,
         Mourning into rejoicing
         And darkness into light.

                                                    ANON

294   You did not ask a lot from life,
         You just wanted someone to share
         All the treasures that this life can give,
         To know no restrictions, quite simply to live.

         People just didn't realise all your true worth;
         So now on this day, as you return to the earth,
         I'll be remembering you and the good times we had;
         And I'll look to the future and try not to be sad.

                                    LESLEY GRAY *To May*

*Rest eternal grant unto them O Lord; and let light perpetual shine
upon them.*   Roman Missal

295   A team of swans was flying down the valley,
        the hunter fired, one fell with broken wing
        and as she fell she knew that she was dying
        and calling to her friends, aspired to sing.

        They, from the frozen winds, replied:
        never shall we forget you, loved playmate,
        never in the meadow or on the fjord
        forget you, never . . . their departing wingbeats sighed.

                                    JIM BAILEY *War-Flying, 1940*

296   There would always be regrets. It was not something to be got
        over, but to be adapted to. Gradually, I saw my loss not as a
        special blow, but as a part of life, and I determined that if
        others could surmount such blows, I must and would, too.
        The pattern of life seemed grander and richer, and self-
        justifying, for its beauties and variety.

                                                BET CHERRINGTON

297   If it must be
        You speak no more with us,
        Nor smile no more with us,
        Nor walk no more with us
        Then let us take a patience and a calm
        For even now the green leaf explodes,
        Sun lightens stone, and all the river burns.

                                                         ANON

Where, unwilling, dies the rose
Buds the new, another year

                        Dorothy Parker

298
Regret not me;
Beneath the sunny tree
I lie uncaring, slumbering peacefully.

Swift as the light
I flew my faery flight;
Ecstatically I moved, and feared no night.

I did not know
That heydays fade and go.
But deemed that what was would be always so.

I skipped at morn
Between the yellowing corn,
Thinking it good and glorious to be born.

I ran at eves
Among the piled-up sheaves,
Dreaming, 'I grieve not, therefore nothing grieves.'

Now soon will come
The apple, pear and plum,
And birds will sing, and autumn insects hum.

Again you will fare
To cider-makings rare,
And junketings; but I shall not be there.

Grieve not; though the journey of life be bitter, and the end unseen,
there is no road which does not lead to an end.   Hafiz

> Yet gaily sing
> Until the pewter ring
> Those songs we sang when we went gipsying.
>
> And lightly dance
> Some triple-timed romance
> In coupled figures, and forget mischance;
>
> And mourn not me
> Beneath the yellowing tree;
> For I shall mind not, slumbering peacefully.
>
> THOMAS HARDY *Regret Not Me*

299   Remember me when I am gone away,
Gone far away into the silent land;
When you can no more hold me by the hand,
Nor I half turn to go yet turning stay.
Remember me when no more day by day
You tell me of our future that you planned:
Only remember me; you understand
It will be late to counsel then or pray.
Yet if you should forget me for a while
And afterwards remember, do not grieve:
For if the darkness and corruption leave
A vestige of the thoughts that once I had,
Better by far you should forget and smile
Than that you should remember and be sad.

CHRISTINA ROSSETTI *Remember*

*Then she is well, and nothing can be ill . . . And her immortal part
with angels lives*   William Shakespeare

300   When I am dead, my dearest,
            Sing no sad songs for me;
            Plant thou no roses at my head,
            Nor shady cypress tree:
            Be the green grass above me
            With showers and dewdrops wet;
            And if thou wilt, remember,
            And if thou wilt, forget.

            I shall not see the shadows,
            I shall not feel the rain;
            I shall not hear the nightingale
            Sing on, as if in pain;
            And dreaming through the twilight
            That doth not rise or set,
            Haply I may remember;
            And haply may forget.

                                        CHRISTINA ROSSETTI *Song*

301   but tragedy also
            teaches us that we are not the lords of this world
            tragedy also
            makes us know our place in this world

                        . . . .

            tragedy also
                elevates us to grander
                    levels
            tragedy also
                shows us the top of the mountains for the last time.

                                        TABAN LO LIYONG

*Art is long, and Time is fleeting, And our hearts, though stout and
brave, Still, like muffled drums, are beating Funeral marches to the
grave.*   Henry Wadsworth Longfellow

302   Doomed to know not Winter; only Spring – a being
            Trod the flowery April blithely for a while;
            Took his fill of music, joy of thought and seeing,
            Came and stayed and went; nor ever ceased to smile.

            Came and stayed and went; and now, when all is finished,
            You alone have crossed the melancholy stream.
            Yours the pang; but his, oh his, the undiminished
            Undecaying gladness, undeparted dream.

                                                    R. L. STEVENSON

303   Spring is past and over these many days,
            Spring and summer. The leaves of September droop,
            Yellowing and all but dead on the patient trees.
            Nor is there any hope in me. I walk
            Slowly homewards. Night is empty and dark
            Behind my eyes as it is dark without
            And empty round about me and over me.
            Spring is past and over these many days,
            But, looking up, suddenly I see
            Leaves in the upthrown light of a street lamp shining,
            Clear and luminous, young and so transparent,
            They seem but the coloured foam of air, green fire,
            No more than the scarce-embodied thoughts of leaves.
            And it is spring within that circle of light.
            Oh, magical brightness! The old leaves are made new.
            In the mind, too, some coloured accident
            Of beauty revives and makes all young again,
            A chance light shines and suddenly it is spring.

                                        ALDOUS HUXLEY *September*

Throughout all eternity, I forgive you, you forgive me.

                                                    William Blake

304   From too much love of living,
        From hope and fear set free,
        We thank with brief thanksgiving
        Whatever gods may be
        That no life lives for ever;
        That dead men rise up never;
        That even the weariest river
        Winds somewhere safe to sea.

        Then star nor sun shall waken,
        Nor any change of light:
        Nor sound of waters shaken,
        Nor any sound or sight:
        Nor wintry leaves nor vernal,
        Nor days nor things diurnal;
        Only the sleep eternal
        In an eternal night.

                                        A. C. SWINBURNE

305   Farewell dear babe, my heart's too much content,
        Farewell sweet babe, the pleasure of mine eye,
        Farewell fair flower that for a space was lent,
        Then ta'en away unto Eternity.
        Blest babe, why should I once bewail thy fate,
        Or sigh thy days so soon were terminate,
        Sith thou art settled in an Everlasting state?

                                        ANNE BRADSTREET
                In Memory of my dear grandchild Elizabeth Bradstreet,
                who deceased August, 1665, being a year and a half old

All things work together for good to them that love God.   St Paul

306   Yet we shall one day gain, life past,
           Clear prospect o'er our being's whole;
           Shall see ourselves, and learn at last
           Our true affinities of soul . . .

           And we, whose ways were unlike here,
           May then more neighbouring courses ply;
           May to each other be brought near,
           And greet across infinity.

                              MATTHEW ARNOLD from *A Farewell*

307   Goodnight; ensured release,
           Imperishable peace,
           Have these for yours,
           While sea abides, and land,
           And earth's foundations stand,
           And heaven endures.

           When earth's foundations flee,
           Nor sky nor land nor sea
           At all is found,
           Content you, let them burn:
           It is not your concern;
           Sleep on, sleep sound.

                              A. E. HOUSMAN *Parta Quies*

I hear a voice you cannot hear, that says I must not stay
I see a hand you cannot see, that beckons me away.
                              quoted by William Blake

308   Fear no more the heat o' the sun
        Nor the furious winter's rages;
Thou thy worldly task has done,
        Home art gone, and ta'en thy wages:
Golden lads and girls all must,
As chimney-sweepers, come to dust.

Fear no more the frown o' the great,
        Thou art past the tyrant's stroke;
Care no more to clothe and eat;
        To thee the reed is as the oak:
The sceptre, learning, physic, must
All follow this, and come to dust.

Fear no more the lightning-flash,
        Nor th'all-dreaded thunder-stone;
Fear not slander, censure rash;
        Thou hast finish'd joy and moan:
All lovers young, all lovers must,
Consign to thee, and come to dust.

No exorciser harm thee!
Nor no witchcraft charm thee!
Ghost unlaid forbear thee!
Nothing ill come near thee!
Quiet consummation have;
And renownèd be thy grave!

              WILLIAM SHAKESPEARE from *Cymbeline*

The only living life is in the past and future . . . the present is an interlude . . . strange interlude in which we call on past and future to bear witness we are living. Strange interlude ! Yes, our lives are merely strange dark interludes in the electrical display of God the Father!   Eugene O'Neill

309   The death of friends, or death
             Of every brilliant eye
             That made a catch in the breath –
             Seem but the clouds of the sky
             When the horizon fades;
             Or a bird's sleepy cry
             Among the deepening shades.

                                    W. B. YEATS from *The Tower*

310   Had I the heavens' embroidered cloths,
             Enwrought with golden and silver light,
             The blue and the dim and the dark cloths
             Of night and light and the half-light,
             I would spread the cloths under your feet:
             But I, being poor, have only my dreams;
             I have spread my dreams under your feet;
             Tread softly because you tread on my dreams.

                              W. B. YEATS *He Wishes for the Cloths of Heaven*

311   Though I am old with wandering
             Through hollow lands and hilly lands,
             I will find out where she has gone,
             And kiss her lips and take her hands;
             And walk among long dappled grass,
             And pluck till time and times are done
             The silver apples of the moon,
             The golden apples of the sun.

                          W. B. YEATS from *The Song of the Wandering Aengus*

*Old men must die, or the world would grow mouldy, would only breed
the past again.*
                                           Alfred, Lord Tennyson

312 About the Feast of the Nativity of our Lord Jesus Christ, as she lay very sick, she said, "The Word is made Flesh," and after a long silence, as though she were returning from some other place, she said, "Oh, every creature faileth, and the whole of the angelic understanding sufficeth not to comprehend this." Then she added, "My soul is washed and cleansed in the blood of Jesus Christ."

After this she said: "Christ Jesus, the Son of God, hath now presented me unto the Father, and these words have been spoken unto me –

" 'Oh bride and fair one, oh thou who art beloved of Me with perfect love, of a truth I would not that thou shouldst come unto Me with these exceeding great sufferings, but I would thou shouldst come with the utmost rejoicing and with joy unspeakable, even as it is seemly that the King should lead home the bride, whom He hath loved so long, and clothed with the royal robe.'

"And he showed me the robe, even as the bridegroom showeth it unto the bride whom he hath loved a long time. It was neither of purple nor of scarlet, but it was a certain marvellous light which clothed the soul. And then He showed unto me the Bridegroom, the Eternal Word, so that now I do understand what thing the Word is and what it doth mean – that is to say, this Word which for my sake was made Flesh. And the Word entered into me and touched me throughout and embraced me, saying, 'Come, My love, My bride, beloved of Me with true delight – come, for all the saints do await thee with exceeding great joy.' And he said again unto me, 'I will not commit thee in charge unto the blessed angels or other saints that they should lead thee unto Me, but I will come personally and fetch thee and will raise thee unto Myself, for thou hast made thyself meet for Me and pleasing unto My Majesty.' "

Now when she was nigh unto the time of her passing away, she did often repeat, "Father, into Thy Hands I do commend my soul and my spirit," Once, after repeating these words, she said unto us who were present:

"Now hath an answer unto those words been given unto me, and it is this: 'It is impossible that in death thou shouldst lose that which hath been impressed upon thine heart in life.'" Then did we say unto her, "Wilt thou, then, depart and leave us?" And she made answer: "A long time have I hidden it from you, but now will I conceal it no longer. I say unto you that I must needs depart."

And upon that same day ceased all those sufferings with which for many days previously she had been grievously tormented in all her limbs and afflicted in many ways. And she did then lie in such repose of the body and cheerfulness of spirit that she appeared as though she already tasted somewhat of the joy which had been promised unto her.

Then did we ask of her whether that aforesaid joy had yet been granted unto her, and she replied that the above-mentioned joy had commenced.

ANON *The Death of Blessed Angela of Foligno*

Though gifts of Nature yet thy gifts of Grace
The all Devouringe Grave cannot deface
Witness thy Godly Life thy Blessed End
Thy Conquest and thy Conflicts with Ye Fiende
When to thy present Friendes thy dying breath
Did sound thy Joyful Triumph over death
Thy Sacred Ashes in the earth shall rest
Till union make both Soule and Bodie blest.

Epitaph to Susanae Kinge, d. 1615, aged 23

313   Say not the struggle nought availeth,
       The labour and the wounds are vain,
The enemy faints not, nor faileth,
       And as things have been, things remain.

If hopes were dupes, fears may be liars;
       It may be, in yon smoke concealed,
Your comrades chase e'en now the fliers,
       And, but for you, possess the field.

For while the tired waves, vainly breaking,
       Seem here no painful inch to gain,
Far back through creeks and inlets making
       Comes, silent, flooding in, the main,

And not by eastern windows only,
       When daylight comes, comes in the light,
In front the sun climbs slow, how slowly,
       But westward, look, the land is bright.

                            ARTHUR HUGH CLOUGH

314   We take as due a longer term
       Than those frail few who fly
       This earth untimely;

       But may't be true, she shall affirm:
       "In death I do not die"
       And that sublimely.

                               ANDREW BEST
                   To Angelica, who died young

315   There's a blue patch way out yonder where the clouds are
thinning out. Keep on looking and you'll find that it will grow.
. . . There's a bright streak on the skyline you can see without
a doubt if you keep your eyes upon the distant glow.

Life is full of boons and blessings. Every day they come anew.
You will find them if you seek them everywhere. God is
somewhere in the darkness and is smiling down on you. In the
sunshine and the shadow He is there.

                                        PATIENCE STRONG

316   I have desired to go
                  Where springs not fail,
          To fields where flies no sharp and sided hail
                  And a few liles blow.

          And I have asked to be
                  Where no storms come,
          Where the green swell is in the havens dumb,
                  And out of the swing of the sea.

                        GERARD MANLEY HOPKINS *Heaven-Haven*

*I heard a voice from Heaven saying unto me, Write: from henceforth
blessed are the dead which die in the Lord; even so, saith the spirit,
for they rest from their labours.*

                        The Revelation of St John the Divine

317   When I have fears, as Keats had fears,
       Of the moment I'll cease to be
       I console myself with vanished years
       Remembered laughter, remembered tears,
       And the peace of the changing sea.

       When I feel sad, as Keats felt sad,
       That my life is so nearly done
       It gives me comfort to dwell upon
       Remembered friends who are dead and gone
       And the jokes we had and the fun.

       How happy they are I cannot know
       But happy am I who loved them so.

                                    NOËL COWARD

318   I can't remember how it came – this deep untroubled peace –
       I only know that one sweet day the heart found its release,
       from all the bondage of the past, its anguish and its fears –
       from all the hurts of yesterday and all its bitter tears I
       only know that fear has flown and every doubt has fled – and
       Faith goes with me light upon the pathway that I tread – For
       Death itself has been unmasked, and proved to be a friend –
       and I have found that God is good – as down Life's way we
       wend, we find that trials and troubles come to put us to the
       test – and in the end, we realize that all is for the best.

                                    PATIENCE STRONG *Meditation*

Hang there like fruit, my soul
Till the tree die!   William Shakespeare

319   The rooms and days we wandered through
        Shrink in my mind to one – there you
        Lie quite absorbed by peace – the calm
        Which life could not provide is balm
        In death. Unseen by me, you look
        Past bed and stairs and half-read book
        Eternally upon your home,
        The end of pain, the left alone.
        I have no friend, or intercessor,
        No psychopomp or true confessor
        But only you who know my heart
        In every cramped and devious part –
        Then take my hand and lead me out,
        The sky is overcast by doubt,
        The time has come, I listen for
        Your words of comfort at the door,
        O guide me through the shoals of fear –
        'Fürchte dich nicht, ich bin bei dir.'[1]

                                PETER PORTER from *An Exequy*

320   If I should die and leave you here awhile,
        Be not like others, sore undone, who keep
        Long vigils by the silent dust, and weep.
        For my sake turn again to life and smile,
        Nerving thy heart and trembling hands to do
        Something to comfort weaker hearts than thine.
        Complete those dear unfinished tasks of mine
        And I perchance may therein comfort you.

                                Attrib. A. PRICE HUGHES

[1] *Fear not, for I am with you.*

321   Sing the song of death, oh sing it!
       For without the song of death, the song of life
       becomes pointless and silly.

       Sing then the song of death, and the longest journey
       and what the soul carries with him, and what he leaves behind
       and how he finds the darkness that enfolds him into utter
           peace
       at last, at last, beyond innumerable seas.

                        D. H. LAWRENCE from *Song of Death*

322   For you,
       Let the dreams that are gone sleep fast my love,
       Let the tears and fears of yesterday's storm,
       For the darkness you saw is past my love,
       So smile and a new day is born.
       The seasons of life will go on my love,
       And the sails of your ship may be torn,
       But the secrets beneath your feet my love,
       Are the flowers that are yet to be born.
       Let the tears that you shed fall sweet my love,
       For the pain goes and rainbows come without warning.
       All the seasons will surely return my love
       And new life will be born in the dawning.

                                            ANON

When we lose one we love, our bitterest tears are called forth by the
memory of hours when we loved not enough.

                        Maurice Maeterlinck

323   You touched my life
             And turned my heart around.
             It seems when I found you
             It was me I really found.
             You opened my eyes
             And now my soul can see
             Our moments may be over,
             Of just you here with me.

             Love lives on beyond Goodbye
             The truth of us will never die.
             Our spirits will shine
             Long after we've gone,
             And so our love lives on.

             There was so much
             I didn't understand
             When you brought me here
             Far from where we all began.
             The changes you made
             To my life will never end.
             I'll look across the distance
             And know I have a friend.

             Love lives on beyond Goodbye
             The truth of us will never die.
             Our spirits will shine
             Long after we've gone,
             And so our love lives on.

             And so our love lives on.

                                                    ANON

This world is given us an as inn in which to stay, but not to dwell.

                                                    Cicero

324   When I must leave you for a while,
                Please do not grieve and shed wild tears
            And hug your sorrow to you through the years
            But start out bravely with a gallant smile;
                    And for my sake and in my name
                    Live on and do all things the same.
                Feed not your loneliness on empty days,
                    But fill each waking hour in useful ways.
            Reach out your hand in comfort and hold me dear,
            And I in turn will comfort you and hold you near,
                    And never, never be afraid to die,
                    For I am waiting for you in the sky!

                                                        ANON

325   Under the wide and starry sky,
        Dig the grave and let me lie.
        Glad did I live and gladly die,
        And I laid me down with a will.

        This be the verse you grave for me:
        Here he lies where he longed to be;
        Home is the sailor, home from sea,
        And the hunter home from the hill.

                                    R. L. STEVENSON *Requiem*

*We do on stage things that are supposed to happen off. Which is a
kind of integrity, if you look on every exit as being an entrance
somewhere else.*   Tom Stoppard

326   What ceremony can we fit
         You into now? If you had come
         Out of a warm and noisy room
         To this, there'd be an opposite
         For us to know you by. We could
         Imagine you in lively mood

         And then look at the other side,
         The mood drawn out of you, the breath
         Defeated by the power of death.
         But we have never seen you stride
         Ambitiously the world we know.
         You could not come and yet you go.

         But there is nothing now to mar
         Your clear refusal of our world.
         Not in our memories can we mould
         You or distort your character.
         Then all our consolation is
         That grief can be as pure as this.

                          ELIZABETH JENNINGS *For a Child Born Dead*

327   There is a comfort in the strength of love;
         'Twill make a thing endurable, which else
         Would overset the brain, or break the heart.

                          WILLIAM WORDSWORTH

*Earth's crammed with heaven, and every common bush afire with
God. But only he who sees takes off his shoes.*

                          Robert Browning

RECONCILIATION

328   When to the sessions of sweet silent thought
        I summon up remembrance of things past,
I sigh the lack of many a thing I sought,
        And with old woes new wail my dear time's waste:
Then can I drown an eye, unused to flow,
        For precious friends hid in death's dateless night,
And weep afresh love's long since cancelled woe,
        And moan the expense of many a vanished sight:
Then can I grieve at grievances foregone,
        And heavily from woe to woe tell o'er,
The sad account of fore-bemoanèd moan,
        Which I new pay as if not paid before.
           But if the while I think on thee, dear friend,
           All losses are restored and sorrows end.

                WILLIAM SHAKESPEARE *Sonnet XXX*

329   I'll be as patient as a gentle stream
And make a pastime of each weary step,
Till the last step have brought me to my love;
And there I'll rest, as after much turmoil
A blessed soul doth in Elysium.

        WILLIAM SHAKESPEARE from *Two Gentlemen of Verona*

We are such stuff As dreams are made on, and our little life
Is rounded with a sleep.   William Shakespeare

330   When you come to the end of a perfect day,
            And you sit alone with your thoughts,
            While the chimes ring out with a carol gay
            For the joy that the day has brought,
            Do you think what the end of a perfect day
            Can mean to a tired heart,
            When the sun goes down with a flaming ray,
            And the dear friends have to part ?

            Well, this is the end of a perfect day,
            Near the end of a journey, too;
            But it leaves a thought that is big and strong,
            With a wish that is kind and true.
            For mem'ry has painted this perfect day
            With colours that never fade,
            And we find, at the end of a perfect day,
            The soul of a friend we've made.

                                    CARRIE JACOBS BOND *Song*

331   I have got my leave. Bid me farewell my brothers. I bow to
            you all and take my departure.

                 Here I give back the keys of my door – and I give up all
            claims to my house. I only ask for last kind words from you.

                 We were neighbours for long, but I received more than I
            could give. Now the day has dawned and the lamp that lit my
            dark corner is out. A summons has come and I am ready for
            my journey.

                                    RABINDRANATH TAGORE

It is as natural to die as to be born.   Francis Bacon

332   [Death] can cast us down for more than the necessary period of mourning. It can blight our days, so that we exist forever in that chill, unexpected land. It can whisper to us that life is ultimately meaningless. If what awaits us at the end is our own obliteration, and the same grief we now feel is transferred like a disease to those who love us, what is the point of going on, of ambition, of rearing children who too will one day fail and fall ? It can hang like an albatross about our necks; or enclose our hearts in ice; or change us so deeply that even our closest friends turn away. At its worst, death has taken one life; and is offered another.

And yet it can enrich us. We can live for those who have gone. We can pack into our lives that extra time the dead have given us. For they *have* given us time: the expanded moment that comes when we realize that, for us, the blood still moves; the world is still there to be explored and made over; that, for now, this minute, this hour, this day, we are free of pain and hunger; that, though we still mourn in the deepest part of our being, death has liberated us, has made us see the transitory nature of everything; and life, being transitory, is thus infinitely more precious; commanding more attention than ever we gave it when we went on our way, still unthinking children, before death opened our minds, sharpened our eyes; and set us free . . . .

CHRISTOPHER LEACH
from *Letter to a Younger Son*

I was irrevocably betrothed to laughter, the sound of which has always seemed to me the most civilized music in the world.

Sir Peter Ustinov

333   Oh the losses into the All, Marina, the stars that are falling!
        We can't make it larger, wherever we fling ourselves,
            to whatever
        star we may go! In the Whole, all things are already
            numbered.
        So when anyone falls, the perfect sum is not lessened.
        Whoever lets go in his fall, dives into the source and
            is healed.

                                        RAINER MARIA RILKE
                        from *Elegy – to Marina Tsvetayeva-Efron*
                                        trans. Stephen Mitchell

334   It is not growing like a tree
        In bulk, doth make man better be;
        Or standing long an oak, three hundred year,
        To fall a log at last, dry, bald, and sere:
        A lily of a day
        Is fairer far in May,
        Although it fall and die that night,
        It was the plant and flower of light.
        In small proportions we just beauty see,
        And in short measures life may perfect be.

                                        BEN JONSON
                    from *To the Immortal Memory and Friendship of that
                    Noble Pair, Sir Lucius Cary and Sir Henry Morison*

*Cleave ever to the sunnier side of doubt,
And cling to Faith beyond the forms of Faith.*   Alfred, Lord Tennyson

335   Love is and was my Lord and King,
        And in his presence I attend
        To hear the tidings of my friend,
    Which every hour his couriers bring.

    Love is and was my King and Lord,
        And will be, though as yet I keep
        Within his court on earth, and sleep
    Encompassed by his faithful guard,

    And hear at times a sentinel
        Who moves about from place to place,
        And whispers to the worlds of space,
    In the deep night, that all is well.

            ALFRED, LORD TENNYSON from *In Memoriam*

336   For a son, the death of a father brings a profound ambivalence: fathers never quite let go; and, to the extent that they hold on to a little bit of power there, a little bit of influence here, to the right to silence, even – so to the same extent the son's true coming of age is diminished. In dying, the father may make his son two gifts: one, his second coming of age and, two, enabling his son to look upon his own approaching death with a new steadfastness. Although dispensed by death, these gifts are among life's blessings.

            ANON from *a private source*

If we do meet again, why, we shall smile;
If not, why then, this parting was well made.   William Shakespeare

337   Thus shall ye think of all this fleeting world: a star at dawn,
a bubble in a stream; a flash of lightning in a summer cloud,
a flickering lamp, a phantom, and a dream.

> BUDDHA from *The Lotus Sutra*

338   Weep you no more, sad fountains;
     What need you flow so fast?
Look how the snowy mountains
     Heaven's sun doth gently waste.
       But my sun's heavenly eyes
        View not your weeping,
        That now lies sleeping
      Softly, now softly lies
       Sleeping.

Sleep is a reconciling,
     A rest that peace begets.
Doth not the sun rise smiling
     When fair at even he sets?
      Rest you then, rest, sad eyes,
       Melt not in weeping,
       While she lies sleeping
      Softly, now softly lies
       Sleeping.

> ANON *Tears*

Touch with forgiving
Hand in darkness – as you did
When you were living.   Laurence Whistler

339   So, we'll go no more a-roving
           So late into the night,
       Though the heart be still as loving,
           And the moon be still as bright.

       For the sword outwears its sheath,
           And the soul wears out the breast,
       And the heart must pause to breathe,
           And love itself have rest.

       Though the night was made for loving,
           And the day returns too soon,
       Yet we'll go no more a-roving
           By the light of the moon.

                                        LORD BYRON

340   They are not long, the weeping and the laughter,
           Love and desire and hate:
       I think they have no portion in us after
           We pass the gate.

       They are not long, the days of wine and roses:
           Out of a misty dream
       Our path emerges for a while, then closes
           Within a dream.

                        ERNEST DOWSON *Vitae summa brevis . . .*

*He has outsoared the shadow of our night; Envy and calumny and
hate and pain, And that unrest which men miscall delight, Can touch
him not and torture not again.*   Percy Bysshe Shelley

341   He called for my will, and I resigned it at His
              call;
        But he returned me His own,
        In token of His love.

        He called for the world, and I laid it at His feet,
        With the crowns thereof;
        I withheld them not at the beckoning of His hand.

        But mark the benefit of exchange:
        For he gave me, instead of earth, a kingdom of eternal peace.
        And, in lieu of the crowns of vanity,
        A crown of glory.

              THOMAS STORY from *Song of praise to the saints in Zion*

342   Let all my songs gather together their diverse strains into a
        single current and flow to a sea of silence in one salutation to
        thee.

              Like a flock of homesick cranes flying night and day back
        to their mountain nests let all my life take its voyage to its
        eternal home in one salutation to thee.

                                        RABINDRANATH TAGORE

343   The humble, meek, merciful, just, pious and devout souls are
        everywhere of one religion, and when death has taken off the
        mask, they will know one another, though the divers liveries
        they wear here make them strangers.

                                        WILLIAM PENN

Living we lie asunder;
Dead we shall share one grave.   Helen Waddell

344　Even the outward order and economy of divine Providence affords instruction which often beautifully applies to our inward experiences. It is not all calm and sunshine. We have cold as well as heat, darkness as well as light, and cutting frosts as well as most refreshing dews, and a variety of other changes. All this is in infinite wisdom and goodness, and displays to the discerning eye the providential power and glory of the great Superintendent.

JOB SCOTT from *his journal, c. 1770*

345　Take of me what is not my own,
my love, my beauty, and my poem,
the pain is mine, and mine alone.

See how against the weight in the bone
the hawk hangs perfect in mid-air –
the blood pays dear to raise it there,
the moment, not the bird, divine.

And see the peaceful trees extend
their myriad leaves in leisured dance –
they bear the weight of sky and cloud
upon the fountain of the veins.

In rose with petals light as air
I bind for you the tides and fire –
the death that lives within the flower
oh gladly, love, for you I bear.

KATHLEEN RAINE *Envoi*

There is a land of the living and a land of the dead, and the bridge is love, the only survival, the only meaning.

Thornton Wilder

346   Death is natural. Nothing natural can be detrimental. Death is
rest. Rest is strength in disguise for a further adventure.

SRI CHINMOY

347   Birth and death play. They play together. Their game is the
game of harmony. And it is always played on the infinite
breast of Life.

SRI CHINMOY

348   There is a spirit which I feel that delights to do no evil, nor to
revenge any wrong, but delights to endure all things, in hope
to enjoy its own in the end. Its hope is to outlive all wrath and
contention, and to weary out all exaltation and cruelty, or
whatever is of a nature contrary to itself. It sees to the end of
all temptations. As it bears no evil in itself, so it conceives
none in thoughts to any other. If it be betrayed, it bears it, for
its ground and spring is the mercies and forgiveness of God.
Its crown is meekness, its life is everlasting love unfeigned.

JAMES NAYLER *Dying words, 1660*

And now sweet lovely Lord farewell!
go! sweetly rest in peace:
In that same peace I hope to dwell
with thee when life shal cease
Our mingled corps on earthen trunk
one stone shal them fast keep,
Till the last Judgement-sounding Trump
raise us from our last sleep.

Joseph Fletcher, 1577-1637
from Elegy upon his wife

349   . . . too thin to feel yet I must bear it.
– This scream, this pain, they are not mine,
Water and air is all I am,
A tree has shaken the staircase down –
Then what has rustled and entered in ?

I knew the other ones had come.
I knew my heart was theirs to claim.
I felt the millions in my room.
There is no being alone again.

JULIAN ORDE from *The Changing Wind*

350   I greet my cousins of the worlds beyond
Who bask in the freshness of their suns
Walking along the bans of wide rivers
They are with me in the dream
Through a vision that is my freedom
They greet me in the horizon of their home
Inviting me to a welcome feast.
I touch their flesh and it is soft like mine
I laugh, and they laugh with me
All the joys and pains are a single grain in the cosmos
And so are all the peoples and children of the earth.

MAZISI KUNENE *Dream of Planets*

When he dies, his marks will not be written on his gravestone. If he has loved a book, been kind to someone, enjoyed a certain colour in the sea – that is the the thing that will show whether he has lived.

Sylvia Plath

351   I think my body was my soul,
And when we are made thus
Who shall control
Our hands, our eyes, the wandering passion of our feet,
Who shall teach us
To thrust the world out of our hearts; to say (till
perhaps in death
When the race is run,
And it is forced from us with our last breath)
'Thy Will Be Done.'

CHARLOTTE MEW

352   Sometimes I have wanted
to throw you off
like a heavy coat.

Sometimes I have said
you would not let me
breathe or move.

But now that I am free
to choose light clothes
or none at all

I feel the cold
and all the time I think
how warm it used to be.

VICKI FEAVER *Coat*

Well, the fuel is gone that maintained that fire.   William Shakespeare

353   This is strange to say, but I've never been so happy in my life, because I've never had so little resistance, or self-doubt. I don't really know who I am but it doesn't matter, because nothing I think of myself as being seems to hold it for long anyway. Somehow I am always something else, and I don't know what that is. But it certainly is the most fulfilling exploration I have ever undertaken, because I am not going into it with a lot of knowing. I am going into it not knowing. My knowing has always blocked my understanding, filled me up, confused me. But now I am vulnerable to the truth, because I have nothing to lose. I had to lose it all to see that little of it was worth having in the first place. Somehow there is more to me than I ever imagined.

STEPHEN LEVINE
*a composite of what the author hears
many say as they approach death*
from *Who Dies?*

354   Dear Master, all the flowers are Thine,
And false the whisper, 'ours' and 'mine';
We lift our hearts to Thee and say,
'Lord, it was Thine to take away.'

And yet, though we would have it so,
Lord, it is very good to know
That Thou art feeling all our pain,
And we shall have our flowers again.

So help us now to be content
To take the sorrow Thou has sent.
Dear Lord, how fair Thy house must be
With all the flowers we've lent to Thee

AMY CARMICHAEL

It is better to grieve than not to grieve.   Mary Shelley

355   Our dying has a quality of healing when all about us are
touched by the recognition of the preciousness of each
moment. Our dying is a healing when all that has been unsaid
is touched with forgiveness and love, when all imagined
unpaid obligations of the past are resolved in mercy and
loving kindness.

STEPHEN LEVINE
from *Healing into Life and Death*

356   I have as much to do with the dead
     And the dying, as with the living
Nowadays; and failing them is
     Past forgiving.

As soon be absolved for that, as if
     A tree, or a sea, should be shriven;
And yet the truth is, fail we must
     And be forgiven.

DONALD DAVIE from *G.M.B.*

357   I am glad I was here. Now I am clear, I am fully clear . . . All
is well; the Seed of God reigns over all and over death itself.
And though I am weak in body, yet the spirit of God is over
all, and the Seed reigns over all disorderly spirits.

GEORGE FOX *Dying words, 1691*

Let mourning stop when one's grief is fully expressed.   Confucius

358   Fear death? – to feel the fog in my throat,
           The mist in my face,
When the snows begin, and the blasts denote
           I am nearing the place,
The power of the night, the press of the storm,
           The post of the foe;
Where he stands, the Arch Fear in visible form,
           Yet the strong man must go:
For the journey is done and the summit attained,
           And the barriers fall,
Though a battle's to fight ere the guerdon be gained,
           The reward of it all.
I was ever a fighter, so – one fight more,
           The best and the last!
I would hate that death bandaged my eyes, and forebore,
           And made me creep past.
No! let me taste the whole of it, fare like my peers
           The heroes of old,
Bear the brunt, in a minute pay glad life's arrears
           Of pain, darkness, and cold.
For sudden the worst turns the best to the brave,
           The black minute's at end,
And the elements' rage, the fiend-voices that rave,
           Shall dwindle, shall blend,
Shall change, shall become first a peace, then a joy,
           Then a light, then thy breast,
O thou soul of my soul! I shall clasp thee again,
           And with God be the rest.

                          ROBERT BROWNING *Prospice*

How sweet to have a common faith!
To hold a common scorn of death!   Alfred, Lord Tennyson

359 We are one people, one community and the death of one is the concern of all. In the face of death man can achieve grandeur, but if he turns his back on death he remains a child, clinging to a land of make-believe. For death is not the ending of the pattern of life's unwinding, but a necessary interruption. Through the painful work of grieving we rediscover the past and weave it afresh into a new reality.

Our aim cannot be to cancel out the past, to try to forget, but to ensure that the strength and meaning which gave beauty to the old pattern is remembered and reinterpreted in the pattern now emerging. Every man must die but the world is permanently changed by each man's existence . . . . There is no easy way through the long valley but we have faith in the ability of each one to find his own way, given time and the encouragement of the rest of us.

COLIN MURRAY PARKES

360 As the tender twilight covers in its fold of dust-veil marks of hurt and wastage from the dusty day's prostrations, even so let my great sorrow for thy loss, Beloved, spread one perfect golden-tinted silence of its sadness o'er my life.

Let all its jagged fractures and distortions, all unmeaning scattered scraps and wrecks and random ruins, merge in the vastness of some evening stilled with thy remembrance, filled with endless harmony of pain and peace united.

RABINDRANATH TAGORE

Not as we wanted it,
But as God granted it.   Sir Arthur Quiller-Couch

361   Though we never know
Where life will take us,
I know it's just a ride
On the wheel.
And we never know
When death will shake us
And we wonder how
It will feel.

So Goodbye my friend.
I know I'll never see you again.
But the time together
Through all the years,
Will take away these tears.
It's OK now – Goodbye my friend.

I see a lot of things
That make me crazy,
And I guess I held on to you.
You could have run away
And left – well maybe,
But it wasn't time
And we both knew.

So Goodbye my friend.
I know I'll never see you again.
But the love you gave me
Through all the years
Will take away these tears.
I'm OK now – Goodbye my friend.

ANON

Better by far you should forget and smile
Than that you should remember and be sad.   Christina Rossetti

362   Time passing, and the memories of love
         Coming back to me, carissima, no more mockingly
         Than ever before; time passing, unslackening,
         Unhastening, steadily; and no more
         Bitterly, beloved, the memories of love
         Coming into the shore.

         How will it end? Time passing, and our passages of love
         As ever, beloved, blind
         As ever before; time binding, unbinding
         About us; and yet to remember
         Never less chastening, nor the flame of love
         Less like an ember.

         What will become of us? Time
         Passing, beloved, and we in a sealed
         Assurance unassailed
         By memory. How can it end,
         This siege of a shore that no misgivings have steeled,
         No doubts defend ?

                          DONALD DAVIE *Time Passing, Beloved*

363   I have seen death too often to believe in death.
         It is not an ending, but a withdrawal.
         As one who finishes a long journey
         Stills the motor, turns off the lights,
         Steps from his car,
         And walks up the path to the home that awaits him.

                                            ANON

*Life is a great surprise. I do not see why death should not be an even
greater one.*   Vladimir Nabokov

364   One would like to be able to write something for them
            not for the sake of the writing but because
            a man should be named in dying as well as living,
            in drowning as well as on death-bed, and because
            the brain being brain must try to establish laws.

            Yet these events are not amenable
            to any discipline that we can impose
            and are not in the end even imaginable.
            What happened was simply this, bad luck for those
            who have lain here twelve years in a changing pose.

            These things happen and there's no explaining,
            and to call them 'chosen' might abuse a word.
            It is better also not to assume a mourning,
            moaning stance. These may have well concurred
            in whatever suddenly struck them through the absurd

            or maybe meaningful. One simply doesn't
            know enough, or understand what came
            out of the altering weather in a fashioned
            descriptive phrase that was common to each name,
            or may have surrounded each like a dear frame.

            Best not to make much of it and leave these seamen
            in the equally altering acre they now have
            inherited from strangers though yet human.
            They fell from sea to earth from grave to grave
            and, griefless now, taught others how to grieve.

                                                    IAIN CRICHTON SMITH
                                        For the Unknown Seamen of the
                                        1939-45 War Buried in Iona Churchyard

Let time shape, and there's an end.   William Shakespeare

365   I dreamed of Miriam for the last time. I was walking down Shepperton High Steet on my way to the shops when I saw her by the traffic lights at the crossroads. She was as young and beautiful as I ever remembered her, and I was filled with a deep sense of love for her, and relief that we would meet again. I was glad that the nightmare of the past months was over and that we would be reunited with the children in our little house. I called to her as she strode confidently across the road, her skirt swinging at her knees. She looked back, recognising me with a cheery smile, and walked on. I called to her again, but she strode past the shops, and I saw her disappear among the cars and pedestrians.

     Waking from the dream, I listened to my children sleeping in their rooms. I lay in the darkness and knew that Miriam had set me free.

J. G. BALLARD from The Kindness of Women

366   From quiet homes and first beginning,
Out to the undiscovered ends,
There's nothing worth the wear of winning,
But laughter and the love of friends.

HILAIRE BELLOC Dedicatory Ode

367   Teach us Delight in simple things,
And Mirth that has no bitter springs;
Forgiveness free of evil done,
And Love to all men 'neath the sun.

RUDYARD KIPLING Children's Song

There is no fear in love; but perfect love casteth out fear.   St John

368   Ah, close the chapter on this hour!
     The grass so green, the air so sweet,
     All springtime burning in a flower,
     All summer blossoming at our feet.

     If what's to come be past our mending,
     All that has been has led to this;
     Then give the tale a happy ending
     And close the chapter with a kiss.

     What if estrangements follow greetings?
     What if our lovely loves grow cold?
     Since journeys end in lovers' meetings
     Keep silence now; this tale is told.

                          WINIFRED HOLTBY *Happy Ending*

369   Lady, when your lovely head
     Droops to sink among the Dead,
     And the quiet places keep
     You that so divinely sleep;
     Then the dead shall blessed be
     With a new solemnity,
     For such Beauty, so descending,
     Pledges them that Death is ending,
     Sleep your fill – but when you wake
     Dawn shall over Lethe break.

                         HILAIRE BELLOC *On a Sleeping Friend*

I'm not afraid of death. It's the stake one puts up in order to play the game of life.   Jean Giraudoux

370   Not I, not I, but the wind that blows through me!
         A fine wind is blowing the new direction of Time.
         If only I let it bear me, carry me, if only it carry me!
         If only I am sensitive, subtle, oh, delicate, a winged gift!
         If only, most lovely of all, I yield myself and am borrowed
         By the fine, fine wind that takes its course through the chaos
              of the world
         Like a fine, an exquisite chisel, a wedge-blade inserted;
         If only I am keen and hard like the sheer tip of a wedge
         Driven by invisible blows,
         The rock will split, we shall come at the wonder, we shall find
              the Hesperides.

         Oh, for the wonder that bubbles into my soul;
         I would be a good fountain, a good well-head,
         Would blur no whisper, spoil no expression.

         What is the knocking?
         What is the knocking at the door in the night?
         It is somebody wants to do us harm.

         No, no, it is the three strange angels.
         Admit them, admit them.
              D. H. LAWRENCE *Song of a Man who has Come Through*

              The Grace of God and a Loving Wife
              A Contented Mind and a quiet Life
              A good Report and a Friend in store
              What should a Man desire more?

                                        Norfolk, 1571

The art of living well and the art of dying well are one.

                                             Epicurus

371   Raking long furrows with his little boat's prow,
       Gathering small harvests with his scything net,
       All his time he farmed acres of the sea.

       By nature as by circumstance solitary,
       He knew no hollowness in his shallow dug-out
       Considering the pathways of the fish, and of the clouds and
           stars,
       Learning the geometry of waters and the verse of weathers.

       To catalogue his virtues and relegate his failures
       Can avail him nothing, nor much avail us.

       What we can do for him ultimate now
       is rest him calm in the narrowest of craft,
       Point him desolately towards the horizon.
                    A. L. HENDRIKS *Requiem for a Caribbean Fisherman*

372   And slowly answered Arthur from the barge:
       'The old order changeth, yielding place to new,
       And God fulfils Himself in many ways,
       Lest one good custom should corrupt the world.
       Comfort thyself: what comfort is in me?
       I have lived my life, and that which I have done
       May He within Himself make pure! but thou,
       If thou shouldst never see my face again,
       Pray for my soul. More things are wrought by prayer
       That this world dreams of. Wherefore, let thy voice
       Rise like a fountain for me night and day.'
                    ALFRED, LORD TENNYSON from *Morte d'Arthur*

The ground that gave them first has them again:
Their pleasures here are past, so is their pain.   William Shakespeare

CELEBRATION AND THANKS

373   Strange is the vigour in a brave man's soul. The strength of his spirit and irresistible power, the greatness of his heart and the height of his condition, his mighty confidence and contempt of dangers, his true security and repose in himself, his liberty to dare and do what he pleaseth, his alacrity in the midst of fears, his invincible nature, are advantages which make him master of fortune. His courage fits him for all attempts, makes him serviceable to God and man.

THOMAS TRAHERNE

374   Only in your dying, Lady, could I offer you a poem.

Never in life could I capture that free live spirit of girl.

From the gutter of my defeated dreams
you pulled me to heights almost your own.

Only in your dying, Lady, could I offer you a poem.

I do not grieve for you
in our little square plot of indiscriminate clay
for now you shall truly dance.

O great heart
O best of all my songs
the dust be merciful on your holy bones.

CHRISTY BROWN *For My Mother*

Strew on her roses, roses
And never a spray of yew.   Matthew Arnold

375   And what shall we remember him by?
           Not by the high throne of office
               he sat on,
           Not his golden mention in the scrolls
               of the nation's great,
           Neither power, which he never knew,
               to summon or dismiss,
           Nor his quarried likeness set
               in the centre of the Square.

       What then shall we remember him by?
           Children sleep-drunk around the dying fire,
           Old folk weary with their life,
           Workmen home from days of dusty toil, and
           Lovers cloistered in the stillness
               of moonlit shadows –
           All who listened to his voice,
               Spell-bound.

       We shall remember him
           By the truths he dared to speak,
           The songs of hope he gave us
               To sing.

                          JOE DE GRAFT *In Memory of a Poet*

376   There falls across this one December day
       The light remembered from those days of June
       That you reflected in the summer's play
       Of perfect strokes across the afternoon.
               JOHN ARLOTT *For Sir Jack Hobbs on his 70th birthday*

Fare thee well! and if forever,
Still forever, fare thee well.   Lord Byron

377   They said on his first day on earth,
        Better far if he'd died at birth.
        How could they know.
        How could they tell the joy he'd bring,
        He taught our hearts the way to sing,
        We loved him so.

        We learned together through the years
        To show the joy, but hide the tears,
        They must not see.
        They'd never learn the hurt they caused
        Through thoughtless stares that on him paused
        So carelessly.

        And as he grew, we never grieved
        To see how little he achieved,
        No praise he'd lose.
        His progress made in life's tough school
        We measured with a shorter rule
        Than scholars use.

        I can't believe he owed his day
        To some genetic disarray
        Wrongly conceived.
        He came into this world, and there
        He lived to teach us how to care.
        This he achieved.

                                ANON *To a Mongol Child*

378   When timely death my life and fortunes ends,
        Let not my hearse be vext with mourning friends;
        But let all lovers, rich in triumph, come
        And with sweet pastimes grace my happy tomb.
        THOMAS CAMPION from *Vivamus, Mea Lesbia, atque Amenum*

But being so much too good for earth,
Heaven vowed to keep him.
                                        Ben Jonson

379 She walks in beauty, like the night
        Of cloudless climes and starry skies;
    And all that's best of dark and bright
        Meet in her aspect and her eyes:
    Thus mellowed to that tender light
        Which heaven to gaudy day denies.

    One shade the more, one ray the less,
        Had half impaired the nameless grace
    Which waves in every raven tress,
        Or softly lightens o'er her face;
    Where thoughts serenely sweet express
        How pure, how dear their dwelling-place.

    And on that cheek, and o'er that brow,
        So soft, so calm, yet eloquent,
    The smiles that win, the tints that glow,
        But tell of days in goodness spent,
    A mind at peace with all below,
        A heart whose love is innocent.

                                        LORD BYRON

380 I believe man will not merely endure, he will prevail. He is
    immortal, not because he, alone among creatures, has an
    inexhaustible voice but because he has a soul, a spirit capable
    of compassion and sacrifice and endurance.

                                        WILLIAM FAULKNER
                                    from *Nobel Prize speech, 1950*

Death takes away the commonplace of life.   Alexander Smith

381   There's a breathless hush in the Close to-night –
                Ten to make and the match to win –
            A bumping pitch and a blinding light,
                An hour to play and the last man in.
            And it's not for the sake of a ribboned coat,
                Or the selfish hope of a season's fame,
            But his Captain's hand on his shoulder smote –
                Play up! Play up! and play the game!

            To set the Cause above renown,
                To love the game beyond the prize,
            To honour, while you strike him down,
                The foe that comes with fearless eyes
            To count the life of battle good,
                And dear the land that gave you birth,
            And dearer yet the brotherhood
                That binds the brave of all the earth.

                                    SIR HENRY NEWBOLT
                        from *This Island Race, Clifton Chapel*

382   Oh, Adam was a gardener, and God who made him sees
            That half a proper gardener's work is done upon his knees,
            So, when your work is finished, you can wash your hands and
                pray
            For the Glory of the Garden, that it may not pass away!
            And the Glory of the Garden it shall never pass away!

                                    RUDYARD KIPLING

'Tisn't life that matters! 'Tis the courage you bring to it.

                                    Sir Hugh Walpole

383   We are the music makers,
          And we are the dreamers of dreams,
      Wandering by lone sea-breakers,
          And sitting by desolate streams; –
      World-losers and world-forsakers,
          On whom the pale moon gleams:
      Yet we are the movers and shakers
          Of the world for ever, it seems.

A. H. O'SHAUGHNESSY from *Ode*

384   When Earth's last picture is painted and the tubes are
          twisted and dried,
      When the oldest colours have faded, and the youngest
          critic has died,
      We shall rest, and, faith, we shall need it – lie down
          for an hour or two,
      Till the Master of All Good Workmen shall put us to
          work anew . . . .

      And only The Master shall praise us, and only The
          Master shall blame;
      And no one shall work for money, and no one shall work
          for fame,
      But each for the joy of the working, and each, in his
          separate star,
      Shall draw the Thing as he sees It for the God of
          Things as They are!

RUDYARD KIPLING

*You cannot know a man's life before the man has died, then only can
you call it good or bad.*   Sophocles

385   I don't believe in death
       Who mocks in silent stealth
       He robs us only of a breath,
       Not of a life-time's wealth.

       I don't believe the tomb
       Imprisons us in earth;
       It's but another loving womb
       Preparing our new birth.

       I do believe in Life
       Empowered from above;
       Till, freed from stress and worldly strife,
       We soar through realms above.

       I do believe that then,
       In joy that never ends,
       We'll meet all those we've loved, again,
       And celebrate our friends.

                                    PAULINE WEBB

386   His strongest characteristic was his gaiety. His smile, his
       laugh, the light of happiness in his eyes – these are the things
       which those who knew him will recall when they think of
       him. He allowed nothing to be sombre. Having expressed
       himself with vigour, even with passion, when anything
       touched the depths of his feelings, he was quick to banish the
       serious look, to laugh away the serious situation, to smother
       the bitter disappointment.

                            THE EARL OF LYTTON from *Antony*

Your son, my lord, has paid a soldier's debt . . . Why then, God's
soldier be he!
                                    William Shakespeare

387 Death cannot deprive me of that living spark which feeds on all given it, and which is now triumphant in sorrow. I love, and shall enjoy happiness again.

MARY SHELLEY from *Diary, 11 November 1822*

388 Fly, envious Time, till thou run out thy race;
Call on the lazy leaden-stepping hours,
Whose speed is but the heavy plummet's pace;
And glut thyself with what thy womb devours,
Which is no more than what is false and vain,
And merely mortal dross;
So little is our loss,
So little is thy gain.
For when as each thing bad thou hast entombed,
And last of all thy greedy self consumed,
Then long eternity shall greet our bliss
With an individual kiss;
And joy shall overtake us as a flood,
When every thing that is sincerely good
And perfectly divine,
With truth, and peace, and love shall ever shine
About the supreme throne
Of him, to whose happy-making sight alone
When once our heavenly-guided soul shall climb,
Then all this earthy grossness quit,
Attired with stars, we shall for ever sit,
    Triumphing over Death, and Chance, and thee,
        O Time.

JOHN MILTON *On Time*

From joy all beings are born
By joy they are all sustained,
And into joy they again return.   Taittiriya Upanishad

389   Cricket began here yesterday, the air heavy, suitable
For medium-paced bowlers. Deck-chairs, though, mostly
    were vacant,
Faces white over startling green. Later, trains will decant
People with baskets, litter and opinions, the seaside's staple
Ingredients. To-day Langridge pushes the ball for unfussed
Singles; ladies clap from check rugs, talk to retired colonels.
On tomato-red verandas the scoring rate is discussed.

Sussex v. Lancashire, the air birded and green after rain,
Dew on syringa and cherry. Seaward the water
Is satin, pale emerald, fretted with lace at the edges,
The whole sky rinsed easy like nerves after pain.
May here is childhood, lost somewhere between and never
Recovered, but again moved nearer, as a lever
Turned on the pier flickers the Past into pictures
A time of immediacy, optimism, without strictures.

Postcards and bathing-machines and old prints.
Something comes back, the inkling, the momentary hint
Of what we had wanted to be, though differently now,
For the conditions are different and what we had wanted
We wanted as we were then, without conscience, unhaunted,
And given the chance must refuse to want it again,
Only, occasionally, we escape, we return where we were:
Watching cricket at Brighton, Cornford bowling through sea-
    scented air.

ALAN ROSS *Cricket at Brighton*

His utmost wishes were to please
A friend or foe, and live at ease:
May he now join the choirs above
In lasting harmony and love.

J. Clarke 1798-1861

390   Come, my Way, my Truth, my Life;
Such a Way as gives us breath,
Such a Truth as ends all strife,
Such a Life as killeth death.

Come, my Light, my Feast, my Strength;
Such a Light as shows a Feast,
Such a Feast as mends in Strength,
Such a Strength as makes his guest.

Come, my Joy, my Love, my Heart;
Such a Joy as none can move,
Such a Love as none can part,
Such a Heart as joys in Love.

GEORGE HERBERT *The Call*

391   So did she move; so did she sing
Like the Harmonious spheres that bring
    Unto their Rounds their music's aid;
Which she performèd such a way.
As all th'inamour'd world will say
    The Graces danced, and Apollo played.

RICHARD LOVELACE
from *Gratiana dancing and singing*

In the third revelation when I saw that God does everything I saw no sin, and I saw that everything was all right. But it was when God showed me sin that he said, "Everything is going to be all right."

Julian of Norwich

392   For those who had the power
       of the forest fires that burn
Leaving their source in ashes
       to flush the sky with fire:
Those whom a famous urn
       could not contain, whose passion
Brimmed over the deep grave
       and dazzled epitaphs:
For all that have won us wings
       to clear the tops of grief,
My friend who within me laughs
       bids you dance and sing.

               C. DAY-LEWIS from *A Time to Dance*

393   Let me live harmlessly, and near the brink
       Of Trent or Avon have a dwelling-place,
Where I may see my quill, or cork, down sink,
       With eager bite of pike, or bleak, or dace;
And on the world and my Creator think:
       Whilst some men strive ill-gotten goods t'embrace
And others spend their time in base excess
       Of wine, or worse, in war, or wantonness.

Let them that will, these pastimes still pursue,
       And on such pleasing fancies feed their fill;
So I the fields and meadows green may view,
       And daily by fresh rivers walk at will,
Among the daisies and the violets blue,
       Red hyacinth and yellow daffodil.

                     J. DAVORS

Life is a novel written by God.   George Horner

394   Few on the whole have had such a happy life, and it could not
       have been as happy without his jolly miseries, which were as
       entrancing as all the rest of him. Perhaps his laugh was his
       richest part. However grim the mood, it was sure to be caught
       out by his laugh. I have never heard a more glorious laugh in
       man or boy; it overfilled him: I think he laughed last in his
       last moment, or one prefers to believe that his laugh
       accompanies him still.

                          J. M. BARRIE from *Foreword to Antony*

395   Because of you we will be glad, and pray,
       Remembering you we may be brave and strong:
       And hail the advent of each dangerous day,
       And meet the last adventure with a song.
       And, as you proudly gave your jewelled gift,
       We'll give our lesser offering with a smile,
       Nor falter on the path where, all too swift,
       You led the way and leapt the golden stile.

       Whether new paths, new heights to climb you find,
       Or gallop through the unfooted asphodel,
       We know you know we shall not lag behind,
       Nor halt to waste a moment on a fear:
       And you will speed us onward with a cheer,
       And wave beyond the stars that all is well.

                          MAURICE BARING

Speak the truth, laughing.   Horace

396   In old age wandering on a trail of beauty lively may
            I walk.
        In old age wandering on a trail of beauty living
            again may I walk.
        It is finished in beauty.

                                          AMERICAN INDIAN

397   Not, how did he die, but how did he live?
        Not, what did he gain, but what did he give?
        These are the units to measure the worth
        Of a man as a man, regardless of birth.
        Not what was his church, nor what was his creed?
        But had he befriended those really in need?
        Was he ever ready, with word of good cheer,
        To bring back a smile, to banish a tear?
        Not what did the sketch in the newspaper say,
        But how many were sorry when he passed away?

                                                   ANON

398   The splendours of the firmament of time
            May be eclipsed, but are extinguished not;
            Like stars to their appointed height they climb,
            And death is a low mist which cannot blot
            The brightness it may veil.

                                        WINIFRED HOLTBY

Dying is as natural as living.   Thomas Fuller

399 Come not to mourn for me with solemn tread
Clad in dull weeds of sad and sable hue,
Nor weep because my tale of life's told through,
Casting light dust on my untroubled head.
Nor linger near me while the sexton fills
My grave with earth – but go gay-garlanded,
And in your halls a shining banquet spread
And gild your chambers o'er with daffodils.

Fill your tall goblets with white wine and red,
And sing brave songs of gallant love and true,
Wearing soft robes of emerald and blue,
And dance, as I your dances oft have led,
And laugh, as I have often laughed with you –
And be most merry – after I am dead.

WINIFRED HOLTBY *No Mourning, By Request*

400 Unto each man his handiwork, unto each his crown,
    The just Fate gives;
Whoso takes the world's life on him and his own lays down,
    He, dying so, lives.

Whoso bears the whole heaviness of the wronged world's
        weight
    And puts it by,
It is well with him suffering, though he face man's fate;
    How should he die?

A. C. SWINBURNE

*I can't think of a more wonderful thanksgiving for the life I have had
than that everyone should be jolly at my funeral.*

Lord Louis Mountbatten

401   There was a glorious sight in the sky, one of the grand
spectacles of the Universe. There was not a cloud in the deep
wonderful blue of the heavens. Along the Eastern horizon
there was a clear deep intense glow neither scarlet nor
crimson but a mixture of both. This red glow was very
narrow, almost like a riband and it suddenly shaded off into
the deep blue. Opposite in the west the full moon shining in
all its brilliance was setting upon the hill beyond the church
steeple. Thus the glow in the east bathed the church in a
warm rich tinted light, while the moon from the west was
casting strong shadows. The moon dropped quickly down
behind the hill bright to the last, till only her rim could be
seen sparkling among the tops of the orchards on the hill. The
sun rose quickly and his rays struck red upon the white walls.

R. F. KILVERT *Diary, 16 April 1870*

402   The benevolence of the good and the courage of the
undefeated remain, like the creative achievements of the
richly gifted, a part of the heritage of humanity for ever.

VERA BRITTAIN from *Testament of Friendship*

He studied nature in her varying look,
And all around was but a glorious book
Of mute intelligence, to it he clung
With all the enthusiasm of the young
Inspir'd boy-bard, and knit his very soul
To God, to nature, to the wondrous whole.

WILLIAM FLETCHER *from* Monody on the
Death of Robert Bloomfield

Farewell and love yourself, for in so doing you will love me also.
Lorenzo de' Medici

403   Thanks to the human heart by which we live,
Thanks to its tenderness, its joys, and fears,
To me the meanest flower that blows can give
Thoughts that do often lie too deep for tears.

         WILLIAM WORDSWORTH from *Intimations of Immortality*

404   It is not for the love of a husband that a husband is dear;
but for the love of the Soul in the husband that a husband is
dear.

       It is not for the love of a wife that a wife is dear; but for
the love of the Soul in the wife that a wife is dear . . . .

       It is not for the love of all that all is dear; but for the love
of the Soul in all that all is dear.

         BRIHAD-ARANYAKA UPANISHAD

405   My heart's in the Highlands, my heart is not here;
My heart's in the Highlands a-chasing the deer;
Chasing the wild deer, and following the roe –
My heart's in the Highlands wherever I go.
Farewell to the Highlands, farewell to the North.
The birth-place of valour, the country of worth;
Wherever I wander, wherever I rove,
The hills of the Highlands for ever I love.

Farewell to the mountains high cover'd with snow;
Farewell to the straths and green valleys below;
Farewell to the forests and wild hanging woods;
Farewell to the torrents and loud-pouring floods.
My heart's in the Highlands, my heart is not here,
My heart's in the Highlands a-chasing the deer;
Chasing the wild deer, and following the roe –
My heart's in the Highlands, wherever I go.

         ROBERT BURNS

406 How straight it flew, how long it flew,
    It clear'd the rutty track
And soaring, disappeared from view
    Beyond the bunker's back –
A glorious, sailing, bounding drive
That made me glad I was alive.

And down the fairway, far along
    It glowed a lonely white;
I played an iron sure and strong
    And clipp'd it out of sight,
And spite of grassy banks between
I knew I'd find it on the green.

And so I did. It lay content
    Two paces from the pin;
A steady putt and then it went
    Oh, most securely in.
The very turf rejoiced to see
That quite unprecedented three.

Ah, seaweed smells from sandy caves
    And thyme and mist in whiffs,
In-coming tide, Atlantic waves
    Slapping the sunny cliffs,
Lark song and sea sounds in the air
And splendour, splendour everywhere.

JOHN BETJEMAN
Seaside Golf

Ah! the clock is always slow; it is later than you think.
Robert W. Service

407   O how shall I warble myself for the dead one there
              I loved?
          And how shall I deck my song for the large sweet
              soul that has gone?
          And what shall my perfume be for the grave of him
              I love?
          Sea-winds blown from east and west,
          Blown from the Eastern sea and blown from the
              Western sea, till there on the prairies meeting,
          These and with these and the breath of my chant,
          I'll perfume the grave of him I love.

          O what shall I hang on the chamber walls?
          And what shall the pictures be that I hang on the walls,
          To adorn the burial-house of him I love?

          Pictures of growing spring and farms and homes,
          With the Fourth-month eve at sundown, and the grey
              smoke lucid and bright,
          With floods of the yellow gold of the gorgeous,
              indolent sinking sun, burning, expanding the air,
          With the fresh sweet herbage under foot, and the pale
              green leaves of the trees prolific,
          In the distance the flowing glaze, the breast of the
              river, with a wind-dapple here and there,
          With ranging hills on the banks, with many a line
              against the sky, and shadows,
          And the city at hand with dwellings so dense, and
              stacks of chimneys,
          And all the scenes of life and the workshops, and the
              workmen homeward returning.

                                              WALT WHITMAN
                             from *When Lilacs last in the dooryard bloom'd*

408   In the time of your life, live so that in the wondrous time you
       shall not add to the misery and sorrow of the world but shall
       smile to the infinite delight and mystery of it.

WILLIAM SAROYAN

409   Thanks to life for giving so much
       It gave me eyes to see light and darkness in the sky
       The stars above and to find the man I love in the crowd.

       Thanks to life for giving so much
       It gave me sounds and letters, words for thoughts
       And to my mother, friend, brother,
       And light to show the way of the soul in love.

       Thanks to life for giving strength to my tired feet
       To walk cities and rivers, beaches, deserts and
           mountains and plains
       And to walk to your house, your street, your garden.

       Thanks to life for giving me the heart that beats
       When I admire the fruits of the mind
       When I see the bad far from the good
       When I look into the depths of your clear eyes.

       Thanks to life for giving me laughter and tears
       That teach me the difference between joy and sadness
       The two parts that make up my song
       And your song, which is also mine,
       And the song of everyone which is also my song.

MERCEDES SOSA *Song,* Gracias a la Vida

410   From your wisdom I nourished my youth
        And my tomorrows grew like a long line of reeds
        The beat of your feet echoed round the young plant
        And my vision rose like a mountain.
        I was like the morning star shying away from the sun
        They said: 'How beautiful is this boy!'
        And my eyes bloomed with your words of praise
        I was fed in your calabashes of wisdom.
        And you, by your love, spoke to me:
        'Those who are before us are those who shall follow
        Their heritage is like an unending rain
        In each cycle we create what is unfinished
        We are the beginning and the end of our season.'

                        MAZISI KUNENE *To My Elder Kinsman*

411   The names of those who in their lives fought for life
        Who wore at their hearts the fire's centre.
        Born of the sun they travelled a short while towards the sun,
        And left the vivid air signed with their honour.

                        STEPHEN SPENDER from *I think continually*
                                of those who were truly great

412   Sleep; and if Life was bitter to thee, pardon;
            If sweet, give thanks; thou hast no more to live;
            And to give thanks is good, and to forgive.

                                A. C. SWINBURNE
                                from *Ave atque Vale*

413   I have made tales in verse, but this man made
Waggons of elm to last a hundred years;
The blacksmith forged the rims and iron gears,
His was the magic that the wood obeyed.

Each deft device that country wisdom bade,
Or farmers' practice needed, he preserved.
He wrought the subtle contours, straight and curved,
Only by eye, and instinct of the trade.

No weakness, no offence in any part,
It stood the strain in mired fields and roads
In all a century's struggle for its bread;
Bearing, perhaps, eight thousand heavy loads.
Beautiful always as a work of art,
Homing the bride, and harvest, and men dead.

JOHN MASEFIELD *The Waggon-Maker*

414   He was indeed an heavenly-minded man, zealous for the name of the Lord, and preferred the honour of God before all things. He was valiant for the truth, bold in asserting it, patient in suffering for it, unwearied in labouring in it, steady in his testimony to it, immovable as a rock.

THOMAS ELLWOOD *concerning George Fox, 1694*

415   Sleep after toil,
Port after stormy seas,
Ease after war,
Death after Life
Doth greatly please.

GEOFFREY CHAUCER

416   my father moved through dooms of love
through sames of am through haves of give
singing each morning out of each night
my father moved through depths of height

this motionless forgetful where
turned at his glance to shining here;
that if (so timid air is firm)
under his eyes would stir and squirm

newly as from unburied which
floats the first who, his april touch
drove sleeping selves to swarm their fates
woke dreamers to their ghostly roots

and should some why completely weep
my father's fingers brought her sleep:
vainly no smallest voice might cry
for he could feel the mountains grow.

Lifting the valleys of the sea
my father moved through griefs of joy;
praising a forehead called the moon
singing desire into begin

joy was his song and joy so pure
a heart of star by him could steer
and pure so now and now so yes
the wrists of twilight would rejoice

keen as midsummer's keen beyond
conceiving mind of sun will stand,
so strictly (over utmost him
so hugely) stood my father's dream

his flesh was flesh his blood was blood:
no hungry man but wished him food;
no cripple wouldn't creep one mile
uphill to only see him smile.

Scorning the pomp of must and shall
my father moved through dooms of feel;
his anger was as right as rain
his pity was as green as grain

septembering arms of year extend
less humbly wealth to foe and friend
than he to foolish and to wise
offered immeasurable is

proudly and (by octobering flame
beckoned) as earth will downward climb,
so naked for immortal work
his shoulders marched against the dark

his sorrow was as true as bread:
no liar looked him in the head;
if every friend became his foe
he'd laugh and build a world with snow.
. . .

E. E. CUMMINGS

I loved the man, and do honour his memory (on this side Idolatry) as
much as any. He was (indeed) honest, and of an open and free nature:
had an excellent Phantasie; *brave notions, and gentle expressions:*
wherein he flowed with that facility, that sometime it was necessary he
should be stopped: . . . His wit was in his own power; would the rule
of it had been so too . . . There was ever more in him to be praised
than to be pardoned.   Ben Jonson (on Shakespeare)

417   Mother died yesterday. I sat by the bed and held her hand
      until she died. I have no complaints and no regrets. It was as I
      always hoped it would be. She was ninety-one years old and I
      was with her close, close, close until her last breath. Over and
      above this sensible, wise philosophy I know it to be the
      saddest moment of my life [after] years of love and
      tenderness and crossness and devotion and unswerving
      loyalty. Without her I could only have achieved a quarter of
      what I have acheived, not only in terms of success and career,
      but in terms of personal happiness. We have quarrelled, often
      violently, over the years, but she has never stood between me
      and my life, never tried to hold me too tightly, always let me
      go free. Goodbye, my darling.

                              NOËL COWARD *Diaries, 1 July 1954*

418   I believe you died in God's will, and that you are eternal, but
      of your place and condition I know nothing, and I do not
      speculate about it . . .

      If I am ever in any kind of sense of the word to *know* you
      again, there will be no jealousies and angers and arrogances
      and impatiences, but only joy. And sorrow and pain shall be
      no more, neither sighing, but life everlasting.

      And if such things are never to be, then I give thanks this
      day for what is and has been. And I can doubly give thanks,
      for during the writing of these words, I have come out of the
      valley of darkness.

      Did you intercede for me?

                              ALAN PATON from *Kontakion for You Departed*

*There must be a beginning of any great matter, but the continuing
unto the end until it be thoroughly finished yields the true glory.*

                              Sir Francis Drake

419   As you love me, let there be
            No mourning when I go –
            No tearful eyes, no hopeless sighs,
            No woe, nor even sadness.
            Indeed, I would not have you sad,
            For I myself shall be full glad
            With the high triumphant gladness
            Of a soul made free
            Of God's sweet liberty.
            No windows darkened, for my own
            Will be flung wide, as ne'er before,
            To catch the radiant in-pour
            Of Love that shall in full atone
            For all the ills that I have done.
            No voices hushed; my own, full-flushed
            With an immortal hope, will rise
            In ecstasies of new-born bliss
            And joyful melodies.
            Rather, of your sweet courtesy
            Rejoice with me
            At my soul's loosing from captivity.
            Wish me 'Bon Voyage' as you do a friend
            Whose joyous visit finds its happy end
            And bid me both 'Adieu' and 'Au revoir'
            Since, though I come no more
            I shall be waiting there to greet you
            At His door.
            And, as the feet of the bearers tread
            The ways I trod,
            Think not of me as dead, but rather –
            Happy, thrice happy, he whose course is sped
            He has gone home – to God,
            His Father.

                                      attrib. JOHN OXENHAM

420   There's a far bell ringing
        At the setting of the sun,
    And a phantom voice is singing
        Of the great days done.
    There's a far bell ringing,
    And a phantom voice is singing
    Of renown for ever clinging
        To the great days done.

SIR HENRY NEWBOLT

421   Abou Ben Adhem (may his tribe increase!)
    Awoke one night from a deep dream of peace,
    And saw, within the moonlight in his room,
    Making it rich, and like a lily in bloom,
    An angel writing in a book of gold: –
    Exceeding peace had made Ben Adhem bold,
    And to the presence in the room he said,
        'What writest thou?' – The vision raised its head,
    And with a look made of all sweet accord,
    Answered, 'The names of those who love the Lord.'
    'And is mine one?' said Abou. 'Nay, not so,'
    Replied the angel. Abou spoke more low,
    But cheerly still; and said, 'I pray thee, then,
    Write me as one that loves his fellow men.'
        The angel wrote, and vanished. The next night
    It came again with a great wakening light,
    And showed the names whom love of God had blest,
    And lo! Ben Adhem's name led all the rest.

JAMES LEIGH HUNT

For though the day be never so long,
At last the bells ringeth to evensong.   Stephen Hawes

422   Do not stand at my grave and weep
I am not there. I do not sleep.
I am a thousand winds that blow.
I am the diamond glints on snow.
I am the sunlight on ripened grain,
I am the gentle autumn rain.
When you awaken in the morning's hush
I am the swift uplifting rush
Of quiet birds in circled flight
I am the soft stars that shine at night.
Do not stand at my grave and cry,
I am not there; I did not die.

ANON *left by Stephen Cummins,*
a soldier killed in Northern Ireland

423   My experience of people reacting to death is quite simply that
they want to have inhibitions and doubts removed: they want
to know more. Sentiments such as 'Rest in Peace' give little
satisfaction: they amount to a sort of 'Holy Blank' which
brings with it neither help nor comfort. They want to know
what happens at and after death, to know – and then perhaps
forget – what the Christian churches do not teach: that the
after life is *tremendous* and that it is entirely possible to be in
close touch with those who die.

ROSALIND RICHARDS from *a letter to the authors*

*He did not lose his place in the minds of men because he was out of
their sight*   John Henry Newman

424 Not marble, nor the gilded monuments
    Of princes, shall outlive this powerful rhyme;
But you shall shine more bright in these contents
    Than unswept stone, besmeared with sluttish time.
When wasteful war shall statues overturn,
    And broils root out the work of masonry,
Nor Mars his sword nor war's quick fire shall burn
    The living record of your memory.
'Gainst death and all oblivious enmity
    Shall you pace forth; your praise shall still find room
Even in the eyes of all posterity
    That wear this world out to the ending doom.
      So, till the judgement that yourself arise,
      You live in this, and dwell in lovers' eyes.
                WILLIAM SHAKESPEARE *Sonnet LV*

425 Death is nothing at all . . . I have only slipped away into the next room. I am I and you are you. Whatever we were to each other that we are still. Call me by my old familiar name, speak to me in the easy way which you always used. Put no difference in your tone; wear no forced air of solemnity or sorrow. Laugh as we always laughed at the little jokes we enjoyed together. Play, smile, think of me, pray for me. Let my name be ever the household word that it always was. Let it be spoken without effort, without the ghost of a shadow on it. Life means all that it ever meant. It is the same as it ever was; there is absolutely unbroken continuity. Why should I be out of mind because I am out of sight? I am waiting for you for an interval, somewhere very near, just around the corner. All is well.

                HENRY SCOTT HOLLAND

There is an Absence Real as a Presence   John Montague

426   I fall asleep in the full and certain hope
That my slumber shall not be broken;
And that though I be all-forgetting,
Yet shall I not be all-forgotten,
But continue that life in the thoughts and deeds
Of those I loved.

SAMUEL BUTLER

427   What concerns us most about individual death, perhaps more even than our own, is the loss of loved people out of our lives. This loss and grief is greatest when the one who dies is young, perhaps a child. The future seems cheated, and even if we believe that there is a meaningful future somewhere and somehow for the person after death, there is still the feeling that this death was untimely, perhaps before experiences could be enjoyed, functions fulfilled or wrongs put right and wounds healed. Even if we are satisfied in these things, there is still our loss so heavy and grievous to those who remain. I have never felt that the physical death of a human being was the total losing out of this world of what that person had been. To me, personality persists in Relationship, and relationship which has become part of me also, will persist wherever the other partner is – here or there, alive or dead. In this sense, therefore, my loved ones still have a 'presence' here with me.

CAROL JEFFREY

Persuade our hearts that when our dear ones die neither we nor they are parted from you   Dick Williams

428   As virtuous men pass mildly away,
                And whisper to their souls to go,
        Whilst some of their sad friends do say
                'The breath goes now,' and some say, 'No':

        So let us melt, and make no noise,
                No tear-floods, nor sigh-tempests move,
        'Twere profanation of our joys
                To tell the laity our love.

        Moving of the earth brings harms and fears,
                Men reckon what it did and meant;
        But trepidation of the spheres,
                Though greater far, is innocent.

        Dull sublunary lovers' love
                (Whose soul is sense) cannot admit
        Absence, because it doth remove
                Those things which elemented it.

        But we by a love, so much refin'd,
                That ourselves know not what it is,
        Inter-assurèd of the mind,
                Care less, eyes, lips, and hands to miss.

        Our two souls therefore, which are one,
                Though I must go, endure not yet
        A breach, but an expansion,
                Like gold to airy thinness beat.

To live in hearts we leave Is not to die   Thomas Campbell

If they be two, they are two so
    As stiff twin compasses are two,
Thy soul the fixed foot, makes no show
    To move, but doth, if th'other do.

And though it in the centre sit,
    Yet when the other far doth roam
It leans, and hearkens after it,
    And grows erect, as that comes home.

Such wilt thou be to me, who must
    Like th'other foot, obliquely run;
Thy firmness makes my circle just,
    And makes me end, where I begun.
                JOHN DONNE *A Valediction: forbidding mourning*

429   Let the new faces play what tricks they will
            In the old rooms; night can outbalance day,
            Our shadows rove the garden gravel still,
            The living seem more shadowy than they.
                            W. B. YEATS from *The New Faces*

430   They shall grow not old, as we that are left grow old:
                Age shall not weary them, nor the years condemn.
            At the going down of the sun and in the morning
                We will remember them.

                                        LAURENCE BINYON

Yet meet we shall, and part, and meet again
Where dead men meet, on lips of living men   Samuel Butler

431   What would the dead want from us
Watching from their cave?
Would they have us forever howling?
Would they have us rave
Or disfigure ourselves, or be strangled
Like some ancient emperor's slave?

None of my dead friends were emperors
With such exorbitant tastes
And none of them were so vengeful
As to have all their friends waste
Waste quite away in sorrow
Disfigured and defaced.

I think the dead would want us
To weep for what *they* have lost.
I think that our luck in continuing
Is what would affect them most.
But time would find them generous
And less self-engrossed.

And time would find them generous
As they used to be
And what else would they want from us
But an honoured place in our memory,
A favourite room, a hallowed chair,
Privilege and celebrity?

And so the dead might cease to grieve
And we might make amends
And there might be a pact between
Dead friends and living friends.
What our dead friends would want from us
Would be such living friends.

JAMES FENTON *For Andrew Wood*

432   When we are weary and in need of strength,
           When we are lost and sick at heart,
           We remember him.

           When we have a joy we crave to share
           When we have decisions that are difficult to make
           When we have achievements that are based on his
           We remember him.

           At the blowing of the wind and in the chill of winter
           At the opening of the buds and in the rebirth of spring,
           We remember him.

           At the blueness of the skies and in the warmth of summer
           At the rustling of the leaves and in the beauty of autumn,
           We remember him.

           At the rising of the sun and at its setting,
           We remember him.

           As long as we live, he too will live
           For he is now a part of us,
           As we remember him.

                              adapted from THE YIZKOR SERVICE

433   The flowers left thick at nightfall in the wood
           This Eastertide call into mind the men,
           Now far from home, who, with their sweethearts, should
           Have gathered them and will do never again.

                              EDWARD THOMAS from *In Memoriam*

*He who has gone, so we but cherish his memory, abides with us, more
potent, nay, more present, than the living man.*

                                        Antoine de Saint-Exupéry

434   And what the dead had no speech for, when living,
They can tell you, being dead: the communication
Of the dead is tongued with fire beyond the language
    of the living.

T. S. ELIOT from *Little Gidding*

435   Do not say that I'll depart tomorrow
because even today I still arrive.

Look at me: I arrive in every second
to be a bud on a spring branch,
to be a tiny bird, whose wings are still fragile,
    learning to sing in my new nest,
to be a caterpillar in the heart of a flower,
to be a jewel hiding itself in a stone.

I still arrive, in order to laugh and to cry,
    in order to fear and to hope,
the rhythm of my heart is the birth and death
    of all that are alive.

THICH NHAT HANH from *Please Call Me by My True Names*

436   A cigarette that bears a lipstick's traces,
An airline ticket to romantic places;
And still my heart has wings
These foolish things
Remind me of you.

HOLT MARVELL *Song*

The song is ended (but the melody lingers on).   Irving Berlin

437   'I don't need a "thing" to remember Jane by,' said one of her
friends. 'Jane taught me how to make bread. Whenever I
make bread, I think of her.'

Before she died, we had talked of how people live on in
what they do, in their actions, in the memories of those they
have influenced. That was how Jane hoped she would live on.
And she will.

> ROSEMARY & VICTOR ZORZA, *writing of their*
> *daughter Jane, who died aged 25 from cancer*

438   Peace, peace! he is not dead, he doth not sleep –
He hath awakened from the dream of life –
'Tis we, who lost in stormy visions, keep
With phantoms an unprofitable strife . . .

He lives, he wakes – 'tis Death is dead, not he;
Mourn not for Adonais. – Thou young Dawn,
Turn all thy dew to splendour, for from thee
The spirit thou lamentest is not gone . . .

He is made one with Nature: there is heard
His voice in all her music, from the moan
Of thunder, to the song of night's sweet bird;
He is a presence to be felt and known
In darkness and in light, from herb and stone,
Spreading itself where'er that Power may move
Which has withdrawn his being to its own;
Which wields the world with never-wearied love,
Sustains it from beneath, and kindles it above.

> PERCY BYSSHE SHELLEY from *Adonais*

The dead don't die. They look on and help.   D. H. Lawrence

439

I'd a dream to-night
As I fell asleep,
Oh! the touching sight
Makes me still to weep:
Of my little lad,
Gone to leave me sad,
Aye, the child I had,
But was not to keep.

As in heaven high,
I my child did seek,
There, in train, came by
Children fair and meek,
Each in lily white,
With a lamp alight;
Each was clear to sight,
But they did not speak.

Then, a little sad,
Came my child in turn,
But the lamp he had,
Oh! it did not burn;
He, to clear my doubt,
Said, half turned about,
'Your tears put it out;
Mother, never mourn.'

WILLIAM BARNES
The Mother's Dream

The hour which gives us life begins to take it away.   Seneca

440   When the Present has latched its postern behind my
                  tremulous stay,
              And the May month flaps its glad green leaves like wings,
          Delicate-filmed as new-spun silk, will the neighbours
                  say,
              "He was a man who used to notice such things"?

          If it be in the dusk when, like an eyelid's soundless
                  blink,
              The dewfall-hawk comes crossing the shades to alight
          Upon the wind-warped upland thorn, a gazer may think,
              "To him this must have been a familiar sight."

          If I pass during some nocturnal blackness, mothy and
                  warm,
              When the hedgehog travels furtively over the lawn,
          One may say, "He strove that such innocent creatures
                  should come to no harm,
              But he could do little for them; and now he is gone."

          If, when hearing that I have been stilled at last,
                  they stand at the door,
              Watching the full-starred heavens that winter sees,
              Will this thought rise on those who will meet my face
                  no more,
              "He was one who had an eye for such mysteries"?

          And will any say when my bell of quittance is heard in
                  the gloom,
              And a crossing breeze cuts a pause in its out-rollings,
          Till they rise again, as they were a new bell's boom,
              "He hears it not now, but used to notice such things"?

                                                  THOMAS HARDY
                                                  Afterwards

441   Death is not an end, but a beginning. It is but an incident in
the 'life of the ages', which is God's gift to us *now*. It is the
escape of the spirit from its old limitations and its freeing for
a larger and more glorious career. We stand around the grave,
and as we take our last, lingering look, too often our thoughts
are *there*; and we return to the desolate home feeling that all
that made life lovely has been left behind on the bleak hillside
... Yet the spirit now is *free*, and the unseen angel at our side
points upwards from the grave and whispers, 'He is not here,
but is risen'. The dear one returns with us to our home, ready
and able, as never before, to comfort, encourage, and beckon
us onward.

WILLIAM LITTLEBOY

442   Music, when soft voices die,
Vibrates in the memory;
Odours, when sweet violets sicken,
Live within the sense they quicken.

Rose leaves, when the rose is dead,
Are heaped for the beloved's bed;
And so thy thoughts, when thou art gone,
Love itself shall slumber on.

PERCY BYSSHE SHELLEY

*I have my dead, and I have let them go,
and was amazed to see them so contented,
so soon at home in being dead, so cheerful ....*

Rainer Maria Rilke

443   Come into the candlelight. I'm not afraid
        to look the dead in the face. When they return,
        they have a right, as much as other Things do,
        to pause and refresh themselves within our vision.
            Come; and we will be silent for a while.
        Look at this rose on the corner of my desk:
        isn't the light around it just as timid
        as the light on you? It too should not be here,
        it should have bloomed or faded in the garden,
        outside, never involved with me. But now
        it lives on in its small porcelain vase:
        what meaning does it find in my awareness?

RAINER MARIA RILKE from *Requiem for a Friend*
trans. Stephen Mitchell

444   It is often said that something may survive of a person after
        his death, if that person was an artist and put a little of
        himself into his work. It is perhaps in the same way that a sort
        of cutting taken from one person and grafted on to the heart
        of another continues to carry on its existence even when the
        person from whom it had been detached has perished.

MARCEL PROUST from *Remembrance of Things Past*
trans. C. K. Scott Moncreiff

445   Tree at my window, window tree,
        My sash is lowered when night comes on;
        But let there never be curtain drawn
        Between you and me.

ROBERT FROST

Heard melodies are sweet, but those unheard are sweeter.

John Keats

446   I will not say that I have all the answers,
Or that your life from trouble will be free.
I cannot promise blue skies will be over you,
Or that the darkness you will never see.

But I am here and I will stand beside you.
I would not leave you now to march alone.
I know we'll win – because we fight together.
We'll build a bridge of love to take us safely home.

Walk tall, my friend, you cannot be defeated.
Be proud, my friend, you're beautiful to me.
Stand firm, my friend, for you will be victorious.
Let's build a bridge across this raging sea.

We'll take the bricks they throw called fear and prejudice.
We'll use their blindness as our guiding rope.
And with your hand in mine we'll strive together;
We'll work to build a bridge of love from fear to hope.

VIVIENNE PRESCOTT
(to the tune of Londonderry Air)

447   When the news [of my son's death] reached my friend John
Wilhelm Rowntree, he experienced a profound sense of
Divine Presence enfolding him and me, and his comfort and
love were an immense help to me in my trial. I know now, as
I look back across the years, that nothing has carried me up
into the life of God, or done more to open out the infinite
meaning of love, than the fact that love can span this break of
separation, can pass beyond the visible and hold right on
across the chasm. The mystic union has not broken and
knows no end.

RUFUS M. JONES

448   Her full grey eyes look far beyond
                  The little room and me
            To village church and village pond
                  And ample rectory.

            She sees her children each in place
                  Eyes downcast as they wait,
            She hears her Harry murmur Grace,
                  Then heaps the porridge plate.

            Aroused at seven, to bed by ten,
                  They fully lived each day,
            Dead sons, so motor-bike-mad then,
                  And daughters far away.

            Now when the bells for Eucharist
                  Sound in the Market Square,
            With sunshine struggling through the mist
                  And Sunday in the air,

            The veil between her and her dead
                  Dissolves and shows them clear,
            The Consecration Prayer is said
                  And all of them are near.

                           JOHN BETJEMAN from *House of Rest*

449   Were a star quenched on high
            For ages would its light,
            Still travelling downwards from the sky
            Shine on our mortal night.
            So, when a good man dies,
            For years beyond our ken
            The light he leaves behind him
            Shines upon the paths of men.   ANON

I'll see you again,
Whenever Spring breaks through again.   Noël Coward

450   You must remain very much alone,
– quietness of the fragile movement,
anxiety of perception –
that the presences may come.

Do not be afraid,
the dead never die;
even the most humble and forgotten
exist, and when you are very much alone
they come near you
invested with the mystic silence
of the ineradicable,
the incomparable presence of man.

ZOË KARÈLLI *Presences*
trans. Kimon Friar

451   No room for mourning: he's gone out
Into the noisy glen, or stands between the stones
Of the gaunt ridge, or you'll hear his shout
Rolling among the screes, he being a boy again.
He'll never fail nor die
And if they laid his bones
In the wet vaults or iron sarcophagi
Of fame, he'd rise at the first summer rain
And stride across the hills to seek
His rest among the broken lands and clouds.
He was a stormy day, a granite peak
Spearing the sky; and look, about its base
Words flower like crocuses in the hanging woods,
Blank though the dalehead and the bony face.

SIDNEY KEYES *William Wordsworth*

The tongues of dying men
Enforce attention like deep harmony.   William Shakespeare

452   *Is the kitchen tap still dripping?*
You should always chain the door at nights.
Soon the roof will need repairing.
What's happening these days at the office?
Too much coffee agitates the nerves.
Now don't forget to spray the roses.
Do see the doctor about those twinges.

But tell me where you are! How is it there?
Are you in pain or bliss? And what is bliss?
Are you lonely? Do we live for ever?
How do you pass the time, if time there is?
Does God exist? Is God loving?
Why must his ways be so mysterious?
Is there a purpose in our living?

Why won't you speak of things that matter?
You used to be so wise, so serious.
Now all our talk is roofs and roses
Like neighbours chatting at the corner.

Here wisdom is as common as the air,
Great matters are the ground I tread.
Tell me, what weather are you having?
Are the planes still noisy overhead?
Ask my old mates how work is going –

Don't be angry, dear. This hasn't changed:
Those things we lack are what we covet.
I am the guest, the one to be indulged.

D. J. ENRIGHT *Guest*

I shall have more to say when I am dead.

Edwin Arlington Robinson

453   Last Saturday,
          wearing old clothes,
          I cleared out the garage:
          finding, at the very back
          behind a stack of deckchairs,
          the dismantled cot.
          And as I had no further use for it
          I gave it away.

          But ever since
          I have been troubled
          by a trace of memory:
          the scent of other women's flowers,
          a nurse sponging my arms,
          tears wept for want
          of anything else
          over a borrowed copy
          of *True Life Romances*.

          And more clearly,
          eating a whole bar of chocolate
          in relief at getting home
          with no expense,
          no after-effects.

          Or so I thought.
          But damp blooms
          on a newly painted wall,
          weeds have pushed through concrete
          in the yard, and you –
          fifth child who was never born –
          are not so easily
          disposed of after all.

                           VICKI FEAVER *Last Saturday*

He is made one with nature; there is heard
His voice in all her music . . .
                               Percy Bysshe Shelley

454   They told me, Heraclitus, they told me you were dead,
            They brought me bitter news to hear and bitter tears
                to shed.
            I wept as I remembered how often you and I
            Had tired the sun with talking and sent him down
                the sky.

            And now that thou art lying, my dear old Carian guest,
            A handful of grey ashes, long, long ago at rest,
            Still are thy pleasant voices, thy nightingales,
                awake;
            For Death, he taketh all away, but them he cannot
                take.

                                                    W. J. CORY

455   They that love beyond the world cannot be separated by it.
            Death cannot kill what never dies. Nor can spirits ever be
            divided that love and live in the same divine principle: the
            root and record of their friendship.
                Death is but crossing the world as friends do the seas; they
            live in one another still. For they must needs be present that
            love and live in that which is omnipresent. In this divine glass
            they see face to face; and their converse is free as well as
            pure. This is the comfort of friends, that though they may be
            said to die, yet their friendship and society are, in the best
            sense, ever present, because immortal.

                                WILLIAM PENN from *More Fruits of Solitude*

*Saul and Jonathan were lovely and pleasant in their lives; and in their
death they were not divided.*   2 Samuel

456   Listen more often to things than to beings
        Hear the fire's voice
        Hear the voice of water.
    Hear, in the wind, the sobbing of the trees.
    It is the breath of the ancestors.

    The dead are not gone forever
    They are in the paling shadows,
    They are in the darkening shadows.

        The dead are not beneath the ground,
        They are in the rustling tree,
        In the murmuring wood,
        The flowing water,
        The still water,
        In the lonely place, in the crowd;
        The dead are never dead.

    Listen more often to things than to beings.
        Hear the fire's voice.
        Hear the voice of water.
        In the wind hear the sobbing of the trees.
        It is the breath of the ancestors.
        They are not gone
        They are not beneath the ground
        They are not dead.

Death is nothing else but a process of nature; and if anyone is afraid of a process of nature, he is a child.   Marcus Aurelius

The dead are not gone forever.
>   They are in a woman's breast,
>   A child's cry, a glowing ember.
>   The dead are not beneath the earth,
>   They are in the flickering fire,
>   In the weeping plant, the groaning rock,
>   The wooded place, the home.
>   The dead are never dead.

Listen more often to things than to beings
>   Hear the fire's voice
>   Hear the voice of water.
>   Hear, in the wind, the sobbing of the trees.
>   It is the breath of the ancestors.

>   BIRAGO DIOP *Souffles (Breath of the Ancestors)*
>   *trans. Samuel Allen*

457   I know that our deceased friends are more really with us than
when they were apparent to our mortal part. Thirteen years
ago I lost a brother, and with his spirit I converse daily and
hourly in the spirit, and see him in my remembrance, in the
regions of my imagination. I hear his advice, and even now
write from his dictate. Forgive me for expressing to you my
enthusiasm, which I wish all to partake of, since it is to me a
source of immortal joy, even in this world. By it I am the
companion of angels. May you continue to be so more and
more; and to be more and more persuaded that every mortal
loss is an immortal gain. The ruins of Time build mansions in
Eternity.

WILLIAM BLAKE from *a letter to William Hayley, 6 May 1800*

Death is nothing but a gateway to Divinity and Eternity.
>   Gobind Singh Mansukhani

458   With you a part of me hath passed away;
For in the peopled forest of my mind
A tree made leafless by this wintry wind
Shall never don again its green array.
Chapel and fireside, country road and bay,
Have something of their friendliness resigned;
Another, if I would, I could not find,
And I am grown much older in a day.

But yet I treasure in my memory
Your gift of charity, and young heart's ease,
And the dear honour of your amity;
For these once mine, my heart is rich with these.
And I scarce know which part may greater be –
What I keep of you, or you rob from me.

GEORGE SANTAYANA *For These Once Mine*

459   It has been given to me to see our progress to God as a road divided in the middle by a low wall, which we call death. Whatever our age or stage of development, or relationship with other human beings, there is no real change involved in crossing the low wall. We simply continue in parallel course with those who loved us in our development and relationship. I do not believe that God altered one whit your responsibility or service for your child.

I do believe that she will grow side by side with you, in spirit, as she would have done on earth; and that your prayer and love will serve her development as they would have done on earth. There is nothing static about the other life . . . The companionship which was given you, you still have. The growth to which you look forward will still be yours to watch over and care for.

ANON from *a letter to Bishop George Reindorp whose daughter died young*

460   People do not die for us immediately, but remain bathed in a sort of aura of life which bears no relation to true immortality but through which they continue to occupy our thoughts in the same way as when they were alive. It is as though they were travelling abroad.

> MARCEL PROUST from *Remembrance of Things Past*
> trans. *C. K. Scott Moncreiff*

461   I have a feeling – no, more than that, a presentiment – that when we eventually and in the fullness of time go to heaven we travel not singly but in groups. After death, we would wait for those who are nearest to us in affection, and then move off together. This could lead to surprising associations; for a mother will have persuaded herself that she was close to her husband, or to her daughter, yet she finds herself voyaging to heaven, not with them, but with her baker, and at that, the baker is not a part of her family but she has become part of his . . .

When Roman mercenaries fought each other during the Roman elections, they used first to greet their enemy with a 'Salve'. I do not doubt that when Christian and Muslim killed each other on the edges of Europe, there will have been many occasions when the slaughtered of both sides picked each other up and moved off happily together. During this last war who is to suppose that this was not sometimes the case?

> JIM BAILEY *Preface to The Sky Suspended*

I am the enemy you killed, my friend.   Wilfred Owen

462   The ecstasy of dying is something I can never, never express. It is suddenly like becoming light itself. It is so wonderful. It is heat and coolness. It is a warmth in the mind. It is clarity of vision and understanding. It is like a clap of Divine Thunder and Hey presto, there I am out of my tiresome old body, leaping about in the glorious ether . . . [Dying] is a Communion, a Sacrament of Living on a higher level . . . I am overcome with Joy.

Dictated by Fr Andrew Glazewski

463   The memorial service was a great releasing and setting free, as you knew. All you did with letters and thoughts to procure forgiveness and peace was of inestimable help. So many people are tied down by the rope-like resentments and unresolved bitternesses, and this keeps them incomplete.

Don't underestimate flowers: you never did. This is just to confirm what a true influence they have, and that is why people have them at funerals.

It is the *gloom* that is so difficult for the passing soul. I do not identify gloom with grief. Grief is a passion, and purges, and has to be faced and gone through with courage. But the warmth of love and the friends and the flowers and the candle-lit vigil are perhaps more help than you have any idea of. So I bless you for the blessing with which you helped me through. It has been so easy for me, and that is why I am so buoyant and active.

ANON from *Life in a New Dimension (private source)*

464   Never fear that we shall not find one another. *We* have freedom from time, so it is not hard to wait for you, and it is our mutual love that keeps us in close touch and that makes me already to know your greater states, and you to apprehend my own – expansion, I think is the word. So that it will be a great coming together, a great reunion, not at all a strangeness, when you, one by one, come across. There is such infinite care and love poured out for those who come over: there is no fierce judgement and condemnation, only loving help and the abounding joy of tackling all there is to do.

ANON from *Life in a New Dimension (private source)*

465   God is here, and the man or woman who seeks Him on earth will find Him in heaven, and the discovery can be repaid. The need then is to accustom oneself to God as he comes in the everyday environment, and react as is best for each one. You will have to imagine a sort of response like that of plants to the sun. It comes slowly but inevitably where there is the existing readiness, and the spirit can be saturated with God as the surroundings are.

Dictated to the Reverend Charles Fryer by his father

466   Say maiden wilt thou go with me
In this strange death of life to be
To live in death and be the same
Without this life or home or name
At once to be and not to be
That was and is not – yet to see
Things pass like shadows – and the sky
Above, below, around us lie

The land of shadows wilt thou trace
And look – nor know each others face
The present mixed with reasons gone
And past, and present all as one
Say maiden can thy life be led
To join the living with the dead
Then trace thy footsteps on with me
We're wed to one eternity

JOHN CLARE from *An Invite to Eternity*

467   I never think upon eternity without receiving great comfort. For I say to myself: how could my soul grasp the idea of everlastingness, if the two were not related in some way? But as soon as I feel how close the yearning of my heart folows upon the thought of eternity, my happiness becomes incomparably greater. For I am certain that, according to his nature, man can yearn only for that which can be attained. And so my yearning makes me certain that I shall reach eternity.

ST FRANCIS DE SALES

The face of death is towards the sun of life.   Alfred, Lord Tennyson

468   I looked upon the broadly-blushing sea:
              The mid-day sun from his unclouded throne
              Was with a glow of glory, smiling down
         Upon that emblem of immensity
         And soon came bounding onwards, fair and free,
              A stately bark, – so gallant was her trim,
              No ocean-bird upon the wave could swim
         In prouder daring, or less heedful glee.

         I gazed awhile. The gaudy ship was gone
              And all was vacant to my 'wildered eye.
         "And thus", I cried "doth man's life journey on
              A vessel bound unto eternity!
         A moment seen: whilst all things else remain
         Unchanged and constant as this watery plain."
                                WILLIAM BRANWHITE CLARKE *Life*

469   I am standing upon that foreshore. A ship at my side spreads
         her white sails to the morning breeze and starts for the blue
         ocean. She is an object of beauty and strength and I stand and
         watch her until at length she hangs like a speck of white cloud
         just where the sea and sky come down to mingle with each
         other. Then someone at my side says, "There! She's gone!"
         "Gone where?" "Gone from my sight, that's all". She is just
         as large in mast and spar and hull as ever she was when she
         left my side; just as able to bear her load of living freight to
         the place of her destination. Her diminished size is in me, not
         in her. And just at that moment when someone at my side
         says, "There! She's gone!" there are other eyes watching her
         coming and other voices ready to take up the glad shout,
         "Here she comes!" And that is dying.
                                VICTOR HUGO from *Toilers of the Sea*
                                (a passage often attributed to Bishop Brent)

The loneliness does linger. Life will indeed never be the same.
Nevertheless, it may yet be good.   Anon

470   O may I join the choir invisible
        Of those immortal dead who live again
        In minds made better by their presence: live
        In pulses stirred to generosity,
        In deeds of daring rectitude, in scorn
        For miserable aims that end with self,
        In thoughts sublime that pierce the night like stars,
        And with their mild persistence urge man's search
        To vaster issues . . .
                This is the life to come,
        Which martyred men have made more glorious
        For us who strive to follow. May I reach
        That purest heaven, be to other souls
        The cup of strength in some great agony,
        Enkindle generous ardour, feed pure love,
        Beget the smiles that have no cruelty –
        Be the sweet presence of a good diffused,
        And in diffusion ever more intense.
        So shall I join the choir invisible
        Whose music is the gladness of the world.

                                        GEORGE ELIOT

471   The first and the most important thing is to know that life is
        one and immortal. Only the forms, countless in number, are
        transient and brittle. The life everlasting is independent of
        any form but manifests itself in all forms. Life then does not
        die; but the forms are dissolved.

                                        SRI AUROBINDO

Then while we live, in love let's so persever
That, when we live no more, we may live ever.   Anne Bradstreet

472

Lord, who created man in wealth and store,
though foolishly he lost the same,
decaying more and more,
till he became
most poor,

with thee
Oh let me rise,
as larks, harmoniously,
and sing this day the victory:
then shall that fall further the flight in me.

My tender age in sorrow did begin,
and still with sickness and shame
thou didst so punish sin
that I became
most thin.

With thee
let me combine,
and feel this day thy victory:
for if I graft my wing on thine,
affliction shall advance the flight in me.

GEORGE HERBERT *Easter Wings*

473

Immortal in thy passion and thy pain,
For ever crowned art thou,
The dew of the Eternal on thy head,
Its light upon thy brow.

HELEN WADDELL from *the Chinese*

Sorrow and sighing shall flee away.   Isaiah

474 As I stand by the cross on the lone mountain's crest,
   Looking over the ultimate sea;
 In the gloom of the mountain a ship lies at rest,
   And one sails away from the lea:
 One spreads its white wings on a far-reaching track,
   With pennant and sheet flowing free;
 One hides in the shadow with sails laid aback, –
   The ship that is waiting for me !

 But lo ! in the distance the clouds break away,
   The Gate's glowing portals I see;
 And I hear from the outgoing ship in the bay
   The song of the sailors in glee.
 So I think of the luminous footprints that bore
   The comfort o'er dark Galilee,
 And wait for the signal to go to the shore,
   To the ship that is waiting for me.

         BRET HARTE *The Two Ships*

475 Even such is Man, who heaps up sorrow,
 Lives but this day, and dies tomorrow.
 The Lightning's past, the Post must go,
 The Song is short, the Journey's so,
 The Pear doth rot, the Plum doth fall,
 The Snow dissolves, and so must all.

 Even so this Death, Man's life bereaves,
 But being dead, Man death deceives,
 The Seed it springeth, Lazarus standeth,
 Tabitha walks, and Jonas landeth.
 The Night is past, the Stars remain:
 So Man that dies, shall live again.

      FRANCIS QUARLES from *Like as the Damask Rose*

476   In process of time, there came a post to the town again, and his business was with Mr Ready-to-halt.

So he inquired him out, and said, I am come to thee in the name of Him whom thou hast loved and followed, though upon crutches; and my message is, to tell thee, that he expects thee at his table, to sup with him, in his kingdom, the next day after Easter: wherefore prepare thyself for thy journey.

Then he also gave him a token that he was a true messenger, saying, I have 'broken the golden bowl, and loosed the silver cord'.

After this, Mr Ready-to-halt called for his fellow-pilgrims, and told them, saying, I am sent for, and God shall surely visit you also.

So he desired Mr Valiant to make his will; and because he had nothing to bequeath to them that should survive him, but his crutches and his good wishes, therefore thus he said: These crutches I bequeath to my son that shall tread in my steps, with an hundred warm wishes that he may prove better than I have been.

Then he thanked Mr Great-heart for his conduct and kindness, and so addressed himself to his journey.

When he came to the brink of the river, he said, Now I shall have no more need of these crutches, since yonder are chariots and horses for me to ride on.

The last words he was heard to say, were Welcome life! So he went his way.

JOHN BUNYAN from *The Pilgrim's Progress*

Forget not yet the tried intent
Of such a truth as I have meant;
My great travail so gladly spent
Forget not yet!

Sir Thomas Wyatt *from* Steadfastness

477   After this it was noised about, that Mr Valiant-for-truth was
taken with a summons by the same post as the other; and had
this for a token that the summons was true, that 'His pitcher
was broken at the fountain'.

When he understood it, he called of his friends, and told
them of it. Then said he, I am going to my Father's; and
though with great difficulty I have got higher, yet now I do
not repent me of all the trouble I have been at to arrive where
I am.

My sword I give to him that shall succeed me in my
pilgrimage, and my courage and skill to him that can get it.
My marks and scars I carry with me, to be a witness for me,
that I have fought his battles, who will now be my rewarder.

When the day that he must go hence was come, many
accompanied him to the river-side, into which as he went, he
said, Death, where is thy sting? and as he went down deeper,
Grave where is thy victory? So he passed over, and all the
trumpets sounded for him on the other side.

JOHN BUNYAN from *The Pilgrim's Progress*

478   Heaven is everlasting, for God is everlasting, and it is the
fulfilment of man's meaning as created in the divine image
and of God's infinite love for each and all. Thus heaven gives
perspective to man's present existence, and man's life in this
world is but a brief prelude to the goal for which he was
created.

ARTHUR MICHAEL RAMSEY from *Sacred and Secular*

Death is the supreme festival on the road to freedom.

Dietrich Bonhoeffer

479   I went to sleep; and now I am refreshed.
A strange refreshment: for I feel in me
An inexpressive lightness, and a sense
Of freedom, as I were at length myself,
And ne'er had been before. How still it is!
I hear no more the busy beat of time,
No, nor my fluttering breath, nor struggling pulse;
Nor does one moment differ from the next . . .

JOHN HENRY NEWMAN
from *the Dream of Gerontius*

480   Take me away, and in the lowest deep
     There let me be,
And there in hope the lone night-watches keep,
     Told out for me.
There will I sing my absent Lord and Love:
     Take me away,
That sooner I may rise, and go above,
And see Him in the truth of everlasting day.

JOHN HENRY NEWMAN
from *The Dream of Gerontius*

481   I stretch my arms to Jesus Christ,
To him I now betake me,
And fall asleep in perfect rest,
No man again can wake me.
For Jesus Christ, God's only Son,
Will open wide the Gates of heaven,
To life eternal take me.

NIKOLAUS HERMANN *Hymn*

The ruins of Time build mansions in eternity.   William Blake

482   They are all gone into the world of light!
                And I alone sit ling'ring here;
            Their very memory is fair and bright,
                And my sad thoughts doth clear.

            It glows and glitters in my cloudy breast
                Like stars upon some gloomy grove,
            Or those faint beams in which this hill is dress'd,
                After the sun's remove.

            I see them walking in an air of glory,
                Whose light doth trample on my days:
            My days, which are at best but dull and hoary,
                Mere glimmering and decays.

            O Father of Eternal life, and all
                Created glories under Thee!
            Resume Thy spirit from this world of thrall
                Into true liberty.

            Either disperse these mists, which blot and fill
                My perspective (still) as they pass,
            Or else remove me hence unto that hill,
                Where I shall need no glass.

                                        HENRY VAUGHAN

483   I would have such knowledge about God, in my reason and in
            my understanding, that nothing could disturb me nor bring me
            into any doubt.

                                        KING ALFRED THE GREAT

Oh immortality, you are wholly mine!   Heinrich von Kleist

484   Faire is the Heaven where happy soules have place
In full enjoyment of felicitie;
Whence they do still behold the glorious face
Of the Divine, Eternall Majestie;
Yet farre more faire be these bright Cherubims,
Which all with golden wings are overdight,
And those eternall burning Seraphims,
Which from their faces dart out fiery light;
Yet fairer than they both and much more bright
Be th'Angels and Archangels which attend
On God's owne person without rest or end
These then in faire each other farre excelling
As to the highest they approach more neare
Yet is that Highest farre beyond all telling
Fairer than all the rest which there appeare
Though all their beauties joynd together were;
How then can mortall tongue hope to expresse
The image of such endlesse perfectnesse.

                                        EDMUND SPENSER

485   I was not aware of the moment when I first crossed the threshold of this life. What was the power that made me open out into this vast mystery like a bud in the forest at midnight! When in the morning I looked upon the light I felt in a moment that I was no stranger in this world, that the inscrutable without name and form had taken me in its arms in the form of my own mother. Even so, in death the same unknown will appear as ever known to me.

                                        RABINDRANATH TAGORE

Upon Easter Day, mother, my rising shall be; O the sun and the moon shall uprise with me.   Anon *The Cherry Tree Carol*

486
Though inland far we be,
Our souls have sight of that immortal sea
Which brought us hither.

WILLIAM WORDSWORTH
from *Intimations of Immortality*

487   You say that you cannot see the kingdom of goodness and truth on earth. Neither have I seen it: nor is it possible for any one to see it who looks upon this life as the sum and end of all. On the earth, that is to say on this earth (Pierre pointed to the fields), there is no truth; all is falsehood and evil: but in the universe, in the whole universe, truth has its kingdom; and we who are now children of the earth are none the less children of the universe. Do not I feel in my soul that I am actually a member of this vast harmonious whole? Do not I feel that in this countless assemblage of beings, wherein the Divinity, the First Cause – or however you may term it – is manifested, I make one link, one step between the lower beings and the higher? If I see and clearly see the ladder leading from plant to man, then why must I suppose that it breaks off at me, and does not lead on further and beyond? I feel not only that I cannot utterly perish, since nothing in the universe is annihilated, but that I always shall be, and always was. I feel that besides me are spirits that live above me, and that in this universe there is truth.

LEO TOLSTOY from *War and Peace*

Haste, therefore, each degree, To welcome destiny: Heaven is our heritage, Earth but a player's stage.   Thomas Nashe

488   Now finalè to the shore,
            Now land and life finalè and farewell,
            Now Voyager depart, (much, much for thee is yet in store)
            Often enough hast thou adventur'd o'er the seas,
            Cautiously cruising, studying the charts,
            Duly again to port and hawser's tie returning;
            But now obey thy cherish'd secret wish,
            Embrace thy friends, leave all in order,
            To port and hawser's tie no more returning,
            Depart upon thy endless cruise old Sailor.

                                            WALT WHITMAN

489   Death, be not proud, though some have callèd thee
            Mighty and dreadful, for thou art not so;
            For those whom thou think'st thou dost overthrow
            Die not, poor death, nor yet canst thou kill me.
            From rest and sleep, which but thy pictures be,
            Much pleasure – then, from thee much more must flow;
            And soonest our best men with thee do go,
            Rest of their bones and soul's delivery.
            Thou 'rt slave to fate, chance, kings and desperate men,
            And dost with poison, war, and sickness dwell,
            And poppy or charms can make us sleep as well,
            And better than thy stroke. Why swell'st thou then?
            One short sleep past, we wake eternally,
            And death shall be no more. Death, thou shalt die.

                                            JOHN DONNE

'Tis Death is dead, not he.   Percy Bysshe Shelley

490   Sweet day, so cool, so calm, so bright!
            The bridal of the earth and sky;
            The dew shall weep thy fall to-night:
            For thou must die.

            Sweet rose, whose hue angry and brave
            Bids the rash gazer wipe his eye,
            Thy root is ever in its grave,
            And thou must die.

            Sweet spring, full of sweet days and roses,
            A box where sweets compacted lie;
            My music shows ye have your closes,
            And all must die.

            Only a sweet and virtuous soul,
            Like season'd timber, never gives;
            But though the whole world turn to coal,
            Then chiefly lives.

                            GEORGE HERBERT *Virtue*

491   You shall be glorified, you shall live in communion with Him,
            you shall ascend into the Throne of the highest Heavens; you
            shall be satisfied, you shall be made greater than the Heavens,
            you shall be like Him, when you enjoy the world as He doth;
            you shall converse with His wisdom, goodness, and power
            above all words, and therefore shall know Him. To know
            Whom is a sublime thing; for it is Life Eternal.

                THOMAS TRAHERNE from *Centuries of Meditations*

*Love is not changed by death And nothing is lost And all in the end is
harvest.*   Edith Sitwell

492   Part of myself is the God within every creature,
        Keeps that nature eternal, yet seems to separate . . .
        When the Lord puts on a body, or casts it from Him,
        He enters or departs, taking the mind and senses
        Away with Him, as the wind steals perfume
        Out of the flowers.

                                        THE BHAGAVAD-GITA

493   To know GOD is Life Eternal. There must therefore some
        exceeding Great Thing be always attained in the Knowledge
        of Him. To know God is to know Goodness. It is to see the
        beauty of infinite Love.

                        THOMAS TRAHERNE from *Centuries of Meditations*

494   Yet if so be you are indeed my friend,
        Then in the end,
        There is one road, a road I've never gone,
        And down that road you shall not pass alone.
        And there's one night you'll find me by your side.
        The night that they shall tell me you have died.

                            HELEN WADDELL from *the Chinese*

Light, more light, more light.   Goethe, *Dying words*

495   There is time of weeping and there is time of laughing. But as
you see, he setteth the weeping time before, for that is the
time of this wretched world and the laughing time shall come
after in heaven. There is also a time of sowing, and a time of
reaping too. Now must we in this world sow, that we may in
the other world reap: and in this short sowing time of this
weeping world, must we water our seed with the showers of
our tears, and then shall we have in heaven a merry laughing
harvest for ever.

SIR THOMAS MORE

496   And if, in the changing phases of man's life
I fall in sickness and in misery
my wrists seem broken and my heart seems dead
and strength is gone, and my life is only the
        leavings of a life:

and still, among it all, snatches of lovely obvlivion
        and snatches of renewal
odd, wintry flowers upon the withered stem, yet
        new, strange flowrs
such as my life has not brought forth before, new
        blossoms of me –

then I must know that still
I am in the hands of the unknown God,
he is breaking me down to his new oblivion
to send me forth on a new morning, a new man.

D. H. LAWRENCE *Shadows*

I have good hope that there is something after death.   Plato

497   Now is the time for stripping the spirit bare,
             Time for the burning of days ended and done,
             Idle solace of things that have gone before:
             Rootless hope and fruitless desire are there;
             Let them go to the fire with never a look behind.
             The world that was ours is a world that is ours
                 no more.

             They will come again, the leaf and the flower,
                 to arise
             From squalor of rottenness into the old splendour,
             And magical scents to a wondering memory bring;
             The same glory, to shine upon different eyes.
             Earth cares for her own ruins, naught for ours.
             Nothing is certain, only the certain spring.
                             LAURENCE BINYON from *The Burning of the Leaves*

498   They are gone for now,
                          But we shall rejoin them,
                          Be one with them again,
                     Happy with each other, for eternity,
                            In God's kingdom,
                              A place for all.
                           They shall not grow old,
                             Nor will they die.
                 Reunited we can live the life that never was,
                           Together, not apart,
                            A family once more.
                     DAN BOVINGTON from *Loss, on the death of pupils
                        in the Hadleigh High School minibus disaster*

Death does not kill love; in some ways it deepens it.   J. Neville Ward

499   He who bends himself to a joy
Doth the wingèd life destroy;
But he who catches the joy as it flies
Lives in Eternity's sunrise.

WILLIAM BLAKE

500   He who fears death either fears the loss of feeling or fears a
different kind of feeling. But if you are to be bereft of feeling,
you cannot feel any hurt; and if you are to acquire another
kind of feeling, you will be a different kind of living being,
and you shall not cease to live.

MARCUS AURELIUS

501   Never weather-beaten sail more willing bent to shore,
Never tirèd pilgrim's limbs affected slumber more,
Than my weary sprite now longs to fly out of my
      troubled breast.
    0! come quickly, sweetest Lord, and take my soul
      to rest.

Ever blooming are the joys of Heaven's high Paradise.
    Cold age deafs not there our ears, nor vapour dims
      our eyes;
    Glory there the sun outshines, whose beams the blessèd
      only see.
    0! come quickly, glorious Lord, and raise my sprite
      to thee.

THOMAS CAMPION

Open the windows wide, there is nothing to fear.
                         Jim Winskill, Dorset forester *Dying words*

502   Life and death are one, even as the river and the sea are one.
          In the depth of your hopes and desires lies your silent
          knowledge of the beyond;
                  And like seeds dreaming beneath the snow your heart
          dreams of spring.
                  Trust the dreams, for in them is hidden the gate to eternity
          . . .

          For what is it to die but to stand naked in the wind and to melt
               it into the sun?
          And what is it to cease breathing but to free the breath from
               its restless tides, that it may rise and expand and seek God
               unencumbered?
          Only when you drink from the river of silence shall you
               indeed sing.
          And when you have reached the mountain top, then you shall
               begin to climb.
          And when the earth shall claim your limbs, then shall you
               truly dance.

                                                          KAHLIL GIBRAN

503   The Spirit that is in all beings is immortal in them all: for the
          death of what cannot die, cease thou to sorrow.
                                                          THE BHAGAVAD GITA
                                                          trans. Juan Mascaró

*Death is not the extinguishing of the light, but the putting out of the
lamp, because Dawn has come.*   Rabindranath Tagore

504   What a day that will be, – When I go Home.

Perhaps the last words which I shall hear and grasp on earth will be those uttered by doctor or nurse or priest at my bedside, "I'm sorry but I am afraid he's going." Yes, indeed going, going Home.

When the majestic procession will come to greet me: the Cherubim and Seraphim, Angels and Archangels, Patriarchs and Prophets, The Apostles and Martyrs, All the Saints and my Queen, my Patrons and my own dear Guardian; there too my loved ones who have gone before me and for whom my heart has ached.

What a day that will be, what a day, when I shall go to Everlasting Light and Life; to the one who held me in love before time and creation began, and to Whom I return.

How my heart has leaped at the magic of a dawn, or the glory of a sunset; heard the repeated mantra of waves breaking on the beach; rejoiced at the birds' morning chorus; caught the sweet scent of roses; bathed in the gold of summer days or crunched winter's snow beneath my feet; relaxed at the sound of best-loved music; delighted at hearing my dear grandchildren's voices; known the happiness of loving and being loved, and the friendship and goodness of others.

So what a day that will be when all that love and joy and delight and happiness will be known and experienced at their Source in the One who is the True, the Beautiful and the Good. And I shall live forever. My last breath will be the first note of my eternal Canticle of Joy.

What a day that will be, what a day – when I go Home.

MAURICE O'CONNOR *Canticle of Joy*

505   All men come to the hills
Finally . . . .
Men come from the deeps of the plains of the sea –
Where a wind-in-the-sail is hope,
That long desire, and long weariness fulfils –
Come again to the hills.

And men with dusty, broken feet;
Proud men, lone men like me,
Seeking again the soul's deeps –
Or a shallow grave
Far from the tumult of the wave –
Where a bird's note motions the silence in . . .
The white kiss of silence that the spirit stills
Still as a cloud of windless sail horizon-hunt
above the blue glass of the sea-
Come again to the hills . . .
Come ever, finally.

ROGER MAIS

506   Joy, shipmate, joy!
(Pleas'd to my soul at death I cry,)
Our life is closed, our life begins,
The long, long anchorage we leave,
The ship is clear at last, she leaps!
She swiftly courses from the shore,
Joy, shipmate, joy.

WALT WHITMAN

Non nobis Domine, non nobis; sed nomini tuo da gloriam.
Not unto us, O Lord, not unto us; but unto thy name
   be the glory given.

Hymns

The following hymns can be found variously in Hymns Ancient & Modern New Standard (1983); Hymns Ancient & Modern Revised (1950); The Anglican Hymn Book (1965, 1978); The Church Hymnal for the Christian Year (1917, 1920); Hymns and Psalms (1983); and The New English Hymnal (1986). These are referred to in the following list respectively as A&MNS; A&MR; AHB; CH; H&P; NEH. These hymns are expressive of a wide range of mood and feeling. You will have your own favourites, but you may well wish to refresh your memory of some of these hymns by looking them up and deciding for yourself whether the mood expressed is appropriate. One word of warning: many hymn books advise that certain verses should be omitted. These are almost always verses which refer to death. For a funeral service, therefore, such verses should be included. The sub-heading 'Music' gives you the composer of the tune and the name of the tune. Many hymns have more than one tune. The tunes will be found in the index to the music editions of the hymn books referred to, one or more of which the church organist will have. You will soon find your favourite.

Abide with me; fast falls the eventide The darkness deepens; Lord, with me abide	A&MNS **13**; A&MR **27**; NEH **331** Words: H. F. Lyte, 1792-1847 Music: W. H. Monk, 1823-89 *Eventide* S. S. Wesley, 1810-76 *Orisons*
Alleluya ! sing to Jesus ! His the Sceptre, His the Throne	A&MNS **262**; A&MR **399**; NEH **271** Words: W. Chatterton Dix, 1837-98 Music: R. H. Prichard, 1811-87 *Hyfrydol* S. S. Wesley, 1810-76 *Alleluya*

All creatures of our God and King,
Lift up your voice and with us sing
	A&MNS **105**; A&MR **172**; NEH **263**
	Words: St Francis of Assisi, trans. Wm
	    Draper, 1855-1933
	Music: *Lasst uns Erfreuen* (Geistliche
	    Kirchengesang *or* Cölner
	    Gesangbuch, 1623)

All things bright and beautiful
All creatures great and small

A&MNS 116; A&MR **442**; NEH **264**
Words: Mrs C. F. Alexander, 1818-95
Music: W. H. Monk, 1823-89 *All things bright and beautiful*
Trad. Arr. Martin Shaw, 1875-1958 *Royal Oak*

All my hope on God is founded;
He doth still my trust renew.

A&MNS **336**; H&P **63**; NEH **333**
Words: Robert Bridges, 1844-1930
Music: H. Howells, 1892-1983 *Michael*

All ye who seek a comfort sure
    or for sure relief
In trouble and distress

A&MNS **64**; A&MR **104**; NEH **63**
Words: 18th century
Music: 1741 *St Bernard*

And did those feet in ancient time
Walk upon England's mountains green

A&MNS **254**; A&MR **578**; NEH **488**
Words: William Blake, 1757-1827
Music: C. H. H. Parry, 1848-1918 *Jerusalem*

Be still my soul, the Lord is on thy side;
Bear patiently the cross of grief or pain

AHB **520**
Words: Katherina A. D. von Schlegel, 1752
trans. Jane Borthwick 1855
Music: Orlando Gibbons, 1583-1625 *Song 1*
J. Sibelius, 1865-1957 *Finlandia*

Blest are the pure in heart,
For they shall see our God

A&MNS **238**; A&MR **335**; NEH **341**
Words: J. Keble, 1792-1866
Music: W. H. Havergal, 1793-1870 *Franconia*

Come, Holy Ghost, our souls inspire,
And lighten with celestial fire

A&MNS **93**; A&MR **157**; NEH **138**
Words: Bishop J. Cosin, 1594-1672, from the Latin
Music: *Veni Creator*, mode viii Mechlin version

Commit thou all thy griefs
And ways into His hands

AHB **525**; H&P **672**
Words: P. Gerhardt 1607-76 trans. J.
    Wesley 1739
Music: S. Wesley,1766-1837 *Doncaster*
    Franconia (König Choralbuch)
    O. Gibbons, 1583-1625 *Song 20*

Dear Lord and Father of mankind
Forgive our foolish ways !

A&MNS **115**; A&MR **184**; NEH **353**
Words: J. G. Whittier, 1807-92
Music: C. H. H. Parry, 1848-1918 *Repton*
    F. C. Maker 1844-1927 *Rest*

Eternal Father, strong to save
Whose arm doth bind the restless wave

A&MNS **292**; A&MR **184**; NEH **354**
Words: W. Whiting, 1825-78
Music: J. B. Dykes, 1823-76 *Melita*

Eternal Ruler of the ceaseless round
Of circling planets singing on their way

A&MNS **353**; NEH **355**
Words: J. W. Chadwick, 1840-1904
Music: Orlando Gibbons, 1583-1625
    Song 1

Fight the good fight with all thy might,
Christ is thy strength, and Christ thy right

A&MNS **220**; A&MR **304**; NEH **359**
Words: J.S.B. Monsell 1811-75
Music: J. Hatton, d.1793 *Duke Street*
    W. Boyd, 1847-1928 *Pentecost*

For all the saints who from their labours
    rest,
Who thee by faith before the world
    confest

A&MNS **305**; A&MR **527**; NEH **197**
Words: W. Walsham How, 1823-97
Music: R. Vaughan Williams, 1872-1958
    Sine nomine
J. Barnby, 1838-96 *For all the Saints*
C. V. Stanford, 1852-1924 *Engelberg*

'For ever with the Lord !'
Amen; so let it be;

A&MR **346**
Words: J. Montgomery, 1771-1854
Music: I. B. Woodbury, 1819-58 (arr.
    Sullivan) *Nearer Home*

For the beauty of the earth
For the beauty of the skies

A&MNS **104**; A&MR **171**; NEH **285**
Words: F. S. Pierpoint 1835-1917
Music: H. Smart, 1813-1879 *Heatherlands*
    C. Kocher, 1786-1872 *Dix*
    arr. G. Shaw, 1879-1943 *England's Lane*

God moves in a mysterious way
His wonders to perform

A&MNS **112**; A&MR **181**; NEH **365**
Words: W. Cowper, 1731-1800
Music: Playford's Psalms, 1671 *London New*

God, that madest earth and heaven,
Darkness and light

A&MNS **12**; A&MR **26**; NEH **245**
Words: Bishop Heber 1827
Music: Welsh traditional *Ar Hyd y Nos*

Guide me, O thou great Redeemer
   or Jehovah
Pilgrim through this barren land

A&MNS **214**; A&MR **296**; NEH **368**
Words: W. Williams, 1717-91
Music: John Hughes, 1873-1932 *Cwm Rhondda*

Hark, Hark my Soul,
Angelic songs are swelling

A&MR **354**
Words: F. W. Faber
Music: H. Smart, 1813-79 *Pilgrims*

Hark, my soul, it is the Lord
'Tis thy Saviour, hear his Word

A&MNS **244**; A&MR **344**; H&P **521**
Words: W. Cowper, 1731-1800
Music: J. B. Dykes 1823-1876 *St Bees*
    J. Wesley's *Foundery Collection* 1742

He who would valiant be
'Gainst all disaster *or*
Who would true valour see
Let him come hither

A&MNS **212**; A&MR **293**; NEH **372**
Words: John Bunyan, 1628-88, and others
Music: English traditional *Monks Gate*

Holy Father, cheer our way
With thy love's perpetual ray;

A&MR **22**; NEH **246**
Words: David Evans
Music: J. Stainer, 1840-1901 *Vesper*

How sweet the name of Jesus sounds
In a believer's ear !

A&MNS **122**; A&MR **192**; NEH **374**
Words: John Newton, 1725-1807
Music: A. Reinagle, 1799-1877 *St Peter*
C. Howard, 1856-1927 *Lloyd*

I vow to thee, my country – all earthly
    things above –
Entire and whole and perfect, the service
    of my love

A&MNS **295**; A&MR **579**
Words: Sir Cecil Spring-Rice, 1859-1918
Music: Gustav Holst, 1874-1934 *Thaxted*

Immortal, invisible, God only wise,
In light inaccessible hid from our eyes

A&MNS **199**; A&MR **372**; NEH **377**
Words: W. Chalmers Smith, 1824-1908
Music: Welsh Hymn Melody *St Denio*

Immortal Love, for ever full
For ever flowing free

A&MNS **133**; A&MR **208**; NEH **378**
Words: J. G. Whittier, 1807-92
Music: J. Clark, 1673-1707 *Bishopthorpe*

In heavenly love abiding
No change my heart shall fear

AHB **524**; CH **548**; H&P **678**
Words: Anna L. Waring, 1823-1910
Music: C. Urban, 1790-1845 *Rutherford*
D. Jenkins, 1848-1915 *Penlan*

Jerusalem the golden
With milk and honey blest

A&MNS **184**; A&MR **278**; NEH **381**
Words: Bernard of Cluny, 12th century
    trans. J. M. Neale, 1818-66
Music: A. Ewing, 1830-95 *Ewing*

Jesu, Lover of my soul,
Let me to thy bosom fly

A&MNS **123**; A&MR **193**; NEH **383**
Words: Charles Wesley, 1707-88
Music: Joseph Parry, 1841-1903
    Aberystwyth
J. B. Dykes, 1823-76 *Hollingside*

Jesus lives ! thy terrors now
Can, O Death, no more appal us

A&MNS **82**; A&MR **140**; NEH **112**
Words: C. F. Gellert, 1715-69
Music: H. J. Gauntlett, 1805-76
    St Albinus

Jesus, still lead on,
Till our rest be won

A&MR **206**; CH **479**
Words: Count N. L. Zinzendorf, 1700-60
Trans. J. Borthwick, 1846
Music: A. Drese, 1620-1701 (arr. S. S.
　　　　Wesley) *Rochelle*
　　　　G. Bullivant, 1883-1937 *Bow Church*

Jesus, where'er thy people meet,
There they behold thy mercy-seat

A&MR **245**; H&P **549**; NEH **390**
Words: W. Cowper, 1731-1800
Music: T. Turton, 1780-1864 *Ely*
　　　　R. Redhead, adap. 1820-1901
　　　　Redhead No. 4
　　　　G. Cooper 1820-1876 *St Sepulchre*
　　　　P. Armes 1836-1908 *Galilee*

Lead, kindly Light, amid the encircling
　　　gloom,
Lead thou me on

A&MNS **215**; A&MR **298**; NEH **392**
Words: J. H. Newman, 1801-90
Music: J. B. Dykes, 1823-76 *Lux Benigna*
　　　　W. H. Harris, 1883-1973 *Alberta*
　　　　C. H. Purday, 1799-1885 *Sandon*

Lead us, Heavenly Father, lead us
O'er the world's tempestuous sea

A&MNS **224**; A&MR **311**; NEH **393**
Words: J. Edmeston, 1791-1867
Music: F. Filitz, 1804-76 *Mannheim*

Let saints on earth in concert sing
With those whose work is done

A&MNS **182**; NEH **396**
Words: Charles Wesley, 1707-88
Music: Scottish Psalter *Dundee*

Light's abode, celestial Salem,
Vision dear whence peace doth spring

A&MNS **185**; A&MR **279**; NEH **401**
Words: St Thomas à Kempis, 1330-1471
Music: H. Smart, 1813-79 *Regent Square*

Lord of all hopefulness, Lord of all joy
Whose trust, ever child-like, no cares
　　　could destroy

A&MNS **294**; H&P **552**; NEH **239**
Words: Jan Struther, 1901-53
Music: Irish traditional *Slane*

Lord, thy Word abideth,
And our footsteps guideth

A&MNS **166**; A&MR **250**; NEH **407**
Words: Sir H. W. Baker, 1821-77
Music: arr. W. H. Monk *Ravenshaw*
　　　　(Leisentritt's Gesangbuch, 1527)

Love divine, all loves excelling,
Joy of heaven, to earth come down

A&MNS **131**; A&MR **205**; NEH **408**
Words: Charles Wesley, 1707-88
Music: J. Stainer, 1840-1901 *Love divine*
      W. Rowlands, 1860-1937 *Blaenwern*

Love's redeeming work is done;
Fought the fight, the battle won

A&MNS **83**; A&MR **141**; NEH **113**
Words: Charles Wesley, 1707-88
Music: *Savannah (Herrnhut* c.1740)

Loving shepherd of thy sheep
Keep thy lamb, in safety keep

A&MNS **134**; A&MR **444**
Words: Jane E. Leeson, 1807-82
Music: L. G. Hayne, 1836-83 *Buckland*

Mine eyes have seen the glory of the
    coming of the Lord
He is trampling out the vintage where the
    grapes of wrath are stored

H&P **242**
Words: Julia Ward Howe, 1819-1910
Music: *Battle Hymn of the Republic*

Most Glorious Lord of life, that on this
    day
Didst make thy triumph over death and
    sin

AHB **73**; NEH **255**
Words: Edmund Spenser, 1552-99
Music: H. Lawes, 1596-1602 *Farley
    Castle*

My song is love unknown
My Saviour's love to me

A&MNS **63**; A&MR **102**; NEH **86**
Words: Samuel Crossman, c.1624-84
Music: J. Ireland, 1879-1962 *Love
    Unknown*
    J. B. Calkin, 1827-1905 *St John*

My soul, there is a country
Far beyond the stars

A&MNS **191**; A&MR **286**; NEH **412**
Words: Henry Vaughan 1622-95
Music: Melchior Vulpius, 1560-1616
    Christus der ist Mein Leben

Nearer, my God, to thee
Nearer to thee!

A&MR **352**; H&P **451**
Words: Sarah F. Adams, 1805-48
Music: J. B. Dykes, 1823-76 *Horbury*
    L. Mason, 1792-1872 *Bethany*

Now thank we all our God
With heart and hands and voices

A&MNS **205**; H&P **566**; NEH **413**
Words: M. Rinkart, 1586-1649
    trans. C. Winkworth, 1827-78
Music: J. Cruger, 1598-1662 *Nun Danket*

O God, our help in ages past,
Our hope for years to come

A&MNS **99**; A&MR **165**; NEH **417**
Words: I. Watts, 1674-1748
Music: Dr Croft, 1678-1727 *St Anne*

O love that wilt not let me go
I rest my weary soul in thee

CH **233**; H&P **685**
Words: G. Matheson, 1842-1906
Music: A. L. Pearce, 1844-1912
    St Margaret

O Strength and Stay, upholding all
    creation,
Who ever dost thyself unmoved abide

A&MNS **7**; A&MR **17**; NEH **248**
Words: Ascribed to St Ambrose, 340-97
Music: J. B. Dykes, 1823-76 *Strength
    and Stay*
    J. Barnby, 1838-96 *O Perfect Love*

Pleasant are thy courts above
In the land of light and love

A&MR **240**; AHB **563**
Words: H. F. Lyte, 1793-1847
Music: W. B. Gilbert, 1829-1910
    Maidstone

Praise, my soul, the King of Heaven,
To his feet thy tribute bring.

A&MNS **192**; A&MR **365**; NEH **436**
Words: H. F. Lyte, 1793-1847
Music: J. Goss, 1800-80 *Praise my soul*

Rejoice for a brother deceased
Our loss is his infinite gain

Methodist Hymn Book (1904) **83**
Words: Charles Wesley, 1707-88
Music: J. Goss, 1800-80 *St Cyprian*

Rejoice, the Lord is King,
Your Lord and King adore

A&MNS **139**; A&MR **216**; NEH **443**
Words: Charles Wesley, 1707-88
Music: G. F. Handel, 1685-1759 *Gopsal*
    J. Darwall, 1731-89 *Darwall's 148th*

Rock of ages, cleft for me,
Let me hide myself in thee

A&MNS **135**; A&MR **210**; NEH **445**
Words: A. M. Toplady, 1740-78
Music: R. Redhead, 1820-1901 *Redhead
    No. 76*
    T. Hastings, 1784-1872 *Petra*

Round me falls the night;
Saviour, be my Light

A&MNS **18**; A&MR **35**; NEH **249**
Words: W. Romanis, 1824-99
Music: A Drese, 1620-1701
  Seelenbräutigam

Saviour, again to thy dear name we raise
With one accord our parting hymn of
    praise

A&MNS **15**; A&MR **31**; NEH **250**
Words: J. Ellerton, 1826-93
Music: E. J. Hopkins, 1818-1901 *Ellers*

Soul of my saviour, sanctify my breast
Body of Christ, be thou my saving guest

NEH **305**
Words: Latin, 14th century Trans. Anon
Music: William Maher, 1823-1877 *Anima
    Christi*

Sun of my soul, thou Saviour dear,
It is not night if thou be near

A&MNS **11**; A&MR **24**; NEH **251**
Words: J. Keble, 1792-1866
Music: H. P. Smith, 1825-1898 *Maryton*
    H. S. Oakeley, 1830-1903 *Abends*
    From a melody in Katholisches
    Gesangbuch, Vienna, 1774 *Hursley.*
    From an early 19th cent. ms harm.
    G. Shaw, 1879-1943, *Birling*

Teach me, my God and King,
In all things thee to see

A&MNS **240**; A&MR **337**; NEH **456**
Words: G Herbert, 1593-1633
Music: English traditional *Sandys*

Ten thousand times ten thousand
In sparkling raiment bright

A&MNS **189**; A&MR **284**
Words: H. Alford, 1810-71
Music: J. B. Dykes 1823-1876 *Alford*

The day thou gavest, Lord, is ended,
The darkness falls at thy behest

A&MNS **16**; A&MR **33**; NEH **252**
Words: J. Ellerton, 1826-93
Music: C. C. Scholefield, 1839-1905
    St Clement

The day is past and over
All thanks, O Lord, to thee

A&MR **21**
Words: St Anatolius, 8th century
Trans. J. M. Neale, 1862
Music: A. H. Brown, 1830-1926
    St Anatolius

The God of love my Shepherd is,
And He that doth me feed

A&MNS **110**; A&MR **178**; NEH **77**
Words: George Herbert, 1593-1633
Music: C. Collignon, 1725-1785
  University

The King of love my Shepherd is,
Whose goodness faileth never

A&MNS **126**; A&MR **197**; NEH **457**
Words: Sir H. W. Baker, 1821-77
Music: Ancient Irish Hymn Melody
  St Columba
  J. B. Dykes, 1823-76 *Dominus regit me*

The Lord's my Shepherd, I'll not want
He makes me down to lie
In pastures green

A&MNS **426**; H&P **70**; NEH **459**
Words: Scottish Psalter 1650
Music: J. Irvine, 1836-87 *Crimond*

The Lord my pasture shall prepare
And feed me with a Shepherd's care

A&MNS **111**; A&MR **179**; NEH **458**
Words: Joseph Addison, 1672-1719
Music: H. Carey, c.1690-1743 *Surrey*

The spacious firmament on high
With all the blue ethereal sky

A&MNS **103**; A&MR **170**; NEH **267**
Words: J. Addison, 1672-1719
Music: E. J. Hopkins, 1818-1901
  Creation
  J. Sheeles, 1688-1761 *London* (or *Addison's*)

The strife is o'er, the battle done;
Now is the Victor's triumph won

A&MNS **78**; A&MR **135**; NEH **119**
Words: Latin 17th cent. trans. F. Pott, 1832-1909
Music: G. P. da Palestrina, c.1525-1594
  Victory

There is a land of pure delight,
Where Saints immortal reign

A&MNS **190**; A&MR **285**; NEH **460**
Words: I. Watts, 1674-1748
Music: George M. Garrett, 1834-97
  Beulah

There's a Friend for little children
Above the bright blue sky

A&MR **452**
Words: A. Midlane, 1825-1909
Music: J. Stainer, 1840-1901 *In Memoriam*

Thine be the glory, risen, conquering Son
Endless is the victory thou o'er death hast
    won

A&MNS **428**; H&P **212**; NEH **120**
Words: Edmond Budry, 1854-1932
        trans. Richard Hoyle, 1875-1939
Music: G. F. Handel, 1685-1759
     Maccabaeus

Thine for ever ! God of love,
Hear us from thy throne above

A&MNS **234**; A&MR **330**; NEH **463**
Words: Mrs M. F. Maude, 1820-1913
Music: W. Maclagan, 1826-1910
     Newington

What a friend we have in Jesus
All our sins and griefs to bear

AHB **612**; H&P **559**
Words: J. Scriven, 1819-1886
Music: W. P. Rowlands, 1860-1937
     Blaenwern
     C. C. Converse, 1832-1918 *Converse*

Where is death's sting? We were not born
    to die,
Nor only for the life beyond the grave;

Songs of Praise (1926) **296**
Words: G. F. Bradby
Music: Orlando Gibbons, 1583-1625
     Song 1

Who would true valour see
Let him come hither

H&P **688** *and see* He who would valiant be
'Gainst all disaster

For the second impression of this book, with corrections, we have taken belated note of the fine collection Hymns and Psalms (1983), prepared by representatives of the British Methodist Conference and by members of the Baptist Union, Churches of Christ, Church of England, Congregational Federation, Methodist Church in Ireland, United Reformed church, and the Wesleyan Reform Union, and published by Methodist Publishing House, Peterborough. Hymns and Psalms contains approximately fifty of the hymns listed above, but due to the exigencies of time and to the typographical layout of the first impression of this book, it has only been possible to indicate Hymns and Psalms as a source in a few instances.

Music

The following are merely suggestions. You may know a piece of music that was a favourite of the deceased; you will certainly know one that is a favourite of yours. You can have your choice played at the funeral service (CD or cassette tape) by arrangement with the celebrant. Your local Public Library should have a copy of The Gramophone: Classical Catalogue (Master Edition), *which will help you to locate the recordings, for which the 'look-up' references are given in italics. Where we indicate a movement of a particular work (e.g. Beethoven Piano Concerto No.4, 1st movement) it is not that we are suggesting that the whole of the first movement should be played; rather, that the first movement should commence and can then be stopped or faded out at the moment that seems appropriate to you. For each piece of classical and church music (there is some overlap between these) and for each piece of popular music we recommend a currently available recording or simply indicate that there is a wide choice. Most have a contemplative or consoling mood; some are triumphant, even defiant. An asterisk* indicates that the words set to music may be found, in whole or in part, in the text of this book.*

Classical Music

ALBINONI, T.	*Adagio in G minor* (organ and strings) (many recordings)
BACH, J. S.	*Concerto in D Minor for two violins* 2nd movement (solo violins and orchestra) (many recordings)
	Have mercy, Lord *St Matthew Passion, No. 47, Erbarme dich,* (contralto and orchestra) Kathleen Ferrier (Decca)
	Jesu, joy of man's desiring *Cantata No. 147, No. 10, Jesu bleibet meine Freude* (choir or other arrangements) (many recordings)
	Jesu, Priceless Treasure *Motet No. 3, Jesu meine Freude* (choir) Trinity College Choir, Cambridge (Conifer Records)

Sheep may safely graze *Cantata No. 208, No. 9 Schafe konnen sicher weiden* (choir or other arrangements) Academy of St Martins (EMI Classics)

Toccata and Fugue in D Minor (organ) (many recordings)

BACH, J. S.
arr, GOUNOD, C.F.

Ave Maria (song) (many recordings)

BARBER, S.

Adagio for Strings (string orchestra) (many recordings)

BEETHOVEN, L. van

Piano Concerto No. 4, 1st movement (piano and orchestra) (many recordings)

Symphony No. 6 "Pastoral", last movement (orchestra) (many recordings)

Symphony No. 9 "Choral", last movement (choir and orchestra) (many recordings)

Violin Concerto in D major, second movement (violin and orchestra) (many recordings)

BRAHMS, J.

How lovely are thy dwellings fair* *Ein Deutsches Requiem, No. 4 Wie lieblich sind deine Wohnungen* (choir and orchestra) (many recordings)

Lord, let me know mine end* *Ein Deutsches Requiem, No. 3 Herr, lehre doch mich* (baritone, choir and orchestra) (many recordings)

Ye now have sorrow* *Ein Deutsches Requiem, No. 5 Ihr habt nun Traurigkeit* (soprano, choir and orchestra) (many recordings)

Symphony No. 3, last movement (orchestra) (many recordings)

BRITTEN, B.

Simple Symphony 3rd Movement, Sentimental sarabande (string orchestra) (many recordings)

CAMPION, T.

Never weather-beaten sail* *First Booke of Ayres No.12* (song) Michael Chance and C. Wilson (Chandos)

CARTER, S.

The Lord of the Dance (song) Bach Choir (Chandos)

CHOPIN, F.

Nocturne No.8 in D flat (piano) Dinu Lipatti (EMI Classics)

Prelude No.4 in E minor (piano) Shura Cherkassky (Decca)

"Funeral Sonata", *Sonata No. 2 in B flat minor*, third movement (piano) (many recordings)

COPLAND, A.　　　　　*Fanfare for the Common Man* (orchestra) Aaron
　　　　　　　　　　　Copland (Sony Classical)

DEBUSSY, C.　　　　　Clair de lune *Suite Bergamasque, No.3* (piano) (many
　　　　　　　　　　　recordings)
　　　　　　　　　　　The Girl with the flaxen hair *Préludes No.8 "La Fille
　　　　　　　　　　　aux cheveux de lin"* (orchestra) W. Smith,
　　　　　　　　　　　Philharmonia Orch. (Sony Classics)

DELIUS, F.　　　　　　The Walk to the Paradise Garden *"A Village Romeo and
　　　　　　　　　　　Juliet" No.19* (orchestra) Academy of St Martins
　　　　　　　　　　　(Decca)

DVOŘÁK, A.　　　　　The Lord is my Shepherd* (Psalm 23) *10 Biblical
　　　　　　　　　　　Songs, No.4* (song) (choir and orchestra) B. Rayner
　　　　　　　　　　　Cook, Royal Scottish National Orch. (Chandos)
　　　　　　　　　　　I will lift up mine eyes* (Psalm 121) *10 Biblical Songs,
　　　　　　　　　　　No.9* (song) (choir and orchestra) B. Rayner Cook,
　　　　　　　　　　　Royal Scottish National Orch. (Chandos)
　　　　　　　　　　　"Going Home" *Symphony No. 9 "From the New
　　　　　　　　　　　World"*, second movement (orchestra) (many
　　　　　　　　　　　recordings)

ELGAR, E.　　　　　　*Cello Concerto* (concerto for cello and orchestra) (many
　　　　　　　　　　　recordings)
　　　　　　　　　　　Nimrod *Variations on an Original Theme, "Enigma"
　　　　　　　　　　　No.9* (orchestra) (many recordings)
　　　　　　　　　　　Proficiscere *The Dream of Gerontius No.8* Proficiscere
　　　　　　　　　　　anima Christiana! Go forth upon thy journey
　　　　　　　　　　　Christian soul* (bass, choir and orchestra) Adrian
　　　　　　　　　　　Boult, New Philharmonia Orch. (EMI Classics)
　　　　　　　　　　　Serenade, second movement (string orchestra) Academy
　　　　　　　　　　　of St Martins. (Decca)
　　　　　　　　　　　Symphony No. 1, first movement (orchestra) Adrian
　　　　　　　　　　　Boult, London Philharmonic (EMI Classics)
　　　　　　　　　　　Symphony No. 2, slow movement (orchestra) Adrian
　　　　　　　　　　　Boult, London Philharmonic (EMI Classics)

FAURÉ, G.　　　　　　*Elégie* (cello and orchestra) Paul Tortelier (EMI
　　　　　　　　　　　Classics)
　　　　　　　　　　　In Paradisum *Requiem No.7* (choir and orchestra) (many
　　　　　　　　　　　recordings)
　　　　　　　　　　　Libera me *Requiem No.6* (baritone and orchestra) (many
　　　　　　　　　　　recordings)

Pie Jesu *Requiem No.4* (soprano and orchestra) (many recordings)

Sanctus *Requiem No.3* (choir and orchestra) (many recordings)

GIBBONS, O.   *The Silver Swan* (choir) Cambridge Singers (Collegium)

GÓRECKI, H.   *Symphony No.3*, 3rd movement (soprano and orchestra) Dawn Upshaw, London Sinfonietta (Elektra Nonesuch)

GOUNOD, C. F.   O Divine Redeemer *Repentir* (soprano and orchestra) Jessye Norman (Philips Classics)

Sanctus *Messe Solennelle de Sainte Cécile* (soprano and orchestra) Jessye Norman (Philips Classics)

GRIEG, E.   Air *Holberg Suite No.4* (string orchestra) (many recordings)

Last Spring *Two Elegiac Melodies, No. 2* (string orchestra) Eugene Ormandy, Philadelphia Orchestra (Sony Classics)

HANDEL, G. F.   Comfort ye *Messiah No.2* (tenor and orchestra) (many recordings)

I know that my Redeemer liveth *Messiah No.45* (soprano and orchestra (many recordings)

The Trumpet shall sound *Messiah No.51* (bass and orchestra) (many recordings)

Handel's Largo *Ombra mai fu Serse No.1b* (song) Kathleen Ferrier (Decca)

Handel's Water Music *Water Music No.1f "Air"* (orchestra) (many recordings)

Where'er you walk *Semele No.9f* (song) Anna-Sophie von Otter, Drottningholm Baroque Ensemble (Proprius)

HAYDN, J.   *Seven last words* The Seven Last Words of our Saviour on the Cross (string quartet) Lindsay Quartet (ASV)

Emperor quartet *String Quartet Op.76, No.3 in C*, 2nd movement Amadeus Quartet (Deutsche Grammophon)

HOLST, G.   Jupiter *The Planets No.4* (orchestra) (many recordings)

HUMPERDINCK, E.   *Hänsel und Gretel*, Prelude (orchestra) H. von Karajan, Berlin Philharmonic Orchestra (EMI Classics)

KARG-ELERT, S.   Nun Danket alle Gott *66 Choral-improvisationen No.59* (organ) S. Preston (Decca)

MacDOWELL, E.   To a Wild Rose *Woodland Sketches, No.1* (piano) Moura Lympany (EMI Laser)

MAHLER, G.   "Death in Venice" *Symphony No. 5, No.4 "Adagietto"* (orchestra) Leonard Bernstein and New York Philharmonic Orchestra (Sony Classical)

MASCAGNI, P.   *Ave Maria* (song) M. Hayward Segal, etc. (Symposium)
     Cavallieria Rusticana No.13 "Intermezzo" (orchestra) H. van Karajan and Berlin Philharmonic Orchestra (Deutsche Grammophon)

MENDELSSOHN, F.   Be thou faithful unto death St Paul *Paulus* (tenor and orchestra) Leipzig Gewandhaus (Philips)
     Cast thy burden *Elijah No.15* (tenor and orchestra) Richard Hickox, London Symphony Orchestra (Chandos)
     Hear my prayer (treble, choir and organ) (many recordings)
     He that shall endure to the end *Elijah No.32* (treble, choir and organ) (many recordings)
     Rest in the Lord *Elijah No.31* (contralto) Kathleen Ferrier, Boyd Neel Orchestra (Decca)
     Octet last movement (strings) Vienna Octet (Decca)
     O God have Mercy St Paul *Paulus* (bass and orchestra) Leipzig Gewandhaus (Philips)

MESSIAEN, O.   *L'Ascension* (organ) S. Cleobury (Collins Classics)

MONTEVERDI, C.   Ave Maris Stella *Vespro della Beata Virgine, No.12* (soloists, choir and orchestra) John Eliot Gardiner, Monteverdi Choir and Orchestra (Decca)

MOZART, W. A.   "Elvira Madigan" *Piano concerto No. 21 in C*, second movement (piano and orchestra) (many recordings)

PUCCINI, G.   One fine day *Un bel di vedremo Madam Butterfly No.10* (soprano and orchestra) (many recordings)
     Symphonic Prelude *Preludio sinfonico* (orchestra) Berlin Radio Symphony Orchestra (Decca)

PURCELL, H.	"Dido's Lament" *Dido and Aeneas, No.43* (soprano and orchestra) Janet Baker, English Chamber Orchestra (Decca)
RAVEL, M.	Pavane for a Dead Infanta *Pavane pour une Enfante défunte* (orchestra) (many recordings)
SCHOENBERG, A.	*Verklärte Nacht* (string sextet) Juillard quartet (Sony Classics)
SCHUBERT, F.	"To Music" *An die Musik* (song) Kathleen Ferrier (Decca)
	Ave Maria (song) Leontyne Price, Vienna Philharmonic Orchestra (Decca)
	"Death and the Maiden" *String Quartet No.14 in D Minor*, 2nd movement (strings) (many recordings)
	Sonata for Piano No. 21 in B flat, 2nd movement (piano) (many recordings)
	String Quintet in C, 1st movement and 2nd movement (strings) (many recordings)
	"The Lord is my Shepherd"* *Psalm 23* (choir) King's College Choir, Cambridge (Classics for Pleasure)
	Impromtus No.3 in G Flat, No.4 in A Flat (piano) (many recordings)
	Litanei (auf das Fest Allerseelen) (song) D. Fischer-Dieskau (Deutsche Grammophon)
SCHÜTZ, H.	*Musikalisches Exequien* (soloists, choir, continuo and instruments) John Eliot Gardiner, Monteverdi Choir and Orchestra (Archiv)
SIBELIUS, R.	The Swan of Tuonela *Legends No.2* (orchestra) (many recordings)
STRAUSS, R.	Four Last Songs *Vier Letzte Lieder* No.4 "Im Abendrot" (At Sunset) (soprano and orchestra) Jessye Norman (Philips)
	Metamorphosen (strings) J. Barbirolli, New Philharmonia (EMI Classics)
TAVENER, J.	*The Protecting Veil* opening (cello and orchestra) Steven Isserlis, London Symphony Orchestra (Virgin Classics)
VAUGHAN WILLIAMS, R.	*Fantasia on a theme of Thomas Tallis* (strings) (many recordings)

VAUGHAN WILLIAMS, R.   *The Lark Ascending* (violin and orchestra) (many recordings)

WAGNER, R.   Liebestod (Death in love) *Tristan und Isolde, No.19* (orchestra) (many recordings)

Siegfried's funeral march *Götterdammerung, No.37* (orchestra) (many recordings)

WIDOR, C.   Toccata *Symphony No. 5, Toccata* (organ) (many recordings)

Church Music

ANERIO, G.   *Missa pro Defunctis* Kyrie & Sanctus (choir) Westminster Cathedral Choir (Hyperion)

BAINTON, E. L.   And I saw a new Heaven* (anthem) King's College Choir, Cambridge (EMI Classics)

BAIRSTOW, E. C.   *Jesu, grant me this I pray* (anthem) York Minster Choir (Priory Records)

Save us, O Lord (anthem) York Minister Choir (Priory Records)

BYRD, W.   Agnus Dei "O Lamb of God" *Four-part Mass* (choir) King's College Choir, Cambridge (Decca)

Ave verum corpus "Hail True Body" (choir) King's College Choir, Cambridge (Decca)

Iustorum Animae "The Souls of the righteous"* *Gradualia Vol.1/i (Feast of All Saints) No. 4* (anthem) King's College Choir, Cambridge (Classics for Pleasure)

Nunc Dimittis "Lord, now lettest thou thy servant depart in peace" *Short Service, No.7* (choir) Worcester Cathedral Choir (Pickwick)

CROFT, W.   I am the Resurrection and the Life* *Funeral Sentences "Burial Service"* (choir) King's College Choir, Cambridge (Decca)

ELGAR, E.   *Ave verum corpus* "Hail True Body" (choir) Trinity College Choir, Cambridge (Conifer)

GIBBONS, O.   *Almighty and Everlasting God** (choir) King's College Choir (Decca)

Nunc Dimittis "Lord lettest thou thy servant depart in peace"* *First (short) Service* (choir) King's College Choir, Cambridge (Decca)

GOSS, J.

O Saviour of the World (choir) Clare College Choir, Cambridge (Gamut)

O taste and see how gracious the Lord is (choir) Clare College Choir, Cambridge (Gamut)

HARRIS, W. H.

*Bring us, O Lord God** (choir) Salisbury Cathedral Choir (Meridian)

*Faire is the Heaven** (choir) Salisbury Cathedral Choir (Meridian)

HOWELLS, H.

Take him, earth, for cherishing (In Memoriam JFK) (choir) St Paul's Cathedral Choir (Hyperion)

IRELAND, J.

Greater love hath no man than this (choir) St Paul's Cathedral Choir (Hyperion)

MORLEY, T.

Nunc Dimittis "Lord, now lettest thou thy servant depart in peace" *Short Service, No.2* (choir) Norwich Cathedral Choir (Priory)

MOZART, W. A.

Ave verum Corpus Hail true body (choir) (many recordings)

PALESTRINA, G. P. da

Agnus dei (O Lamb of God) *Missa Brevis* (choir) Westminster Cathedral Choir (Hyperion)

PARRY, C. H. H.

I know my soul hath power* *Songs of Farewell, No.5* (choir) Trinity College Choir, Cambridge (Conifer)

Lord, let me know mine end *Songs of Farewell, No.6* (choir) Trinity College Choir. Cambridge (Conifer)

My Soul, there is a country* *Songs of Farewell, No.1* (choir) Trinity College Choir, Cambridge (Conifer)

Never weather-beaten sail* *Songs of Farewell, No.3* (choir) Trinity College Choir, Cambridge (Conifer)

*Sunset and evening star "Crossing the Bar"** (choir) Wellington College Choir (Herald)

There is an old belief *Songs of Farewell, No.4* (choir) Trinity College Choir, Cambridge (Conifer)

PARSONS, R.

Ave Maria (choir) Oxford Christ Church Cathedral Choir (Gamut)

PHILLIPS, P.   Ave verum Corpus "Hail true body" *Christi in five parts, 1612* (choir) King's College Choir, Cambridge (Classics for Pleasure)

PURCELL, H.   *Music for the funeral of Queen Mary II* March and Canzona and Funeral Sentences (brass, drums and choir) Winchester Cathedral Choir (Argo)

                          Now that the sun hath veiled his light *"Evening Hymn"* (song) J. Bowman and King's Consort (Hyperion)

                          Thou knowest, Lord, the secrets of our hearts *Music for the funeral of Queen Mary II* (choir) Winchester Cathedral Choir (Argo)

RUTTER, J.   *God be in my head* (choir) Cambridge Singers (Collegium)

STAINER, J.   God so loved the world *The Crucifixion, No.5* (choir) St John's College Choir, Cambridge (Decca)

STANFORD, C. V.   Beati quorum via "Blessed are they that walk in the law of the Lord" *3 Motets, No.3* (choir) Trinity College Choir, Cambridge (Conifer)

                          Justorum animae "The souls of the righteous"* *3 Motets, No.1* (choir) Trinity College Choir, Cambridge (Conifer)

                          Nunc Dimittis "Lord, now lettest thou thy servant depart in peace"* *Services in B flat (Evening Service No.3b)* (choir, orchestra and organ) Winchester Cathedral Choir (Argo)

TALLIS, T.   *If ye love me, keep my commandments** (choir) Worcester Cathedral Choir (Abbey)

TOMKINS, T.   Nunc Dimittis "Lord, now lettest thou thy servant depart in peace"* *Third Service No.4* (choir) St George's Chapel Choir (Hyperion)

WALFORD DAVIES, H.   *God be in my head** (choir) Trinity College Choir, Cambridge (Conifer)

                          Solemn Melody (organ) C. Curley (RCA Victor)

WALMISLEY, T. A.   Nunc Dimittis "Lord, now lettest thou thy servant depart in peace"* *Evening Service in D Minor, No.2* (choir) St Paul's Cathedral Choir (Hyperion)

WALTON, W.	A Litany *Drop, drop slow tears* (choir and organ) Trinity College Choir, Cambridge (Conifer)
	Where does the uttered music go ? (choir) Trinity College Choir, Cambridge (Conifer)
WESLEY, S. S.	*Let us lift up our heart* (choir) Worcester Cathedral Choir (Hyperion)
	Man that is born of woman (choir) Worcester Cathedral Choir (Hyperion)
	Thou wilt keep him in perfect peace* (choir) Worcester Cathedral Choir (Hyperion)

Popular Music

Tori AMOS	Happy Phantom *Little Earthquakes* (East/West Warner)
Joan ARMATRADING	Only One *Walk Under Ladders* (A & M)
The BOOMTOWN RATS	Diamond Smiles *The Fine Art of Surfacing* (Ensign)
David BOWIE	Wild is the Wind *Station to Station* (RCA)
	Fill Your Heart *Hunky Dory* (RCA)
	Quicksand *Hunky Dory* (RCA)
Kate BUSH	Oh England My Lionheart *Lionheart* (EMI)
	Room for the Life *The Kick Inside* (EMI)
	Watching You without Me *Hounds of Love* (EMI)
Tracy CHAPMAN	For You *Tracy Chapman* (Elektra)
	All that you have is your Soul *Crossroads* (Elektra)
Toni CHILDS	Heaven's Gate *House of Hope* (A & M)
	The Dead are Dancing *House of Hope* (A & M)
COWBOY JUNKIES	Blue Moon Revisited (Song for Elvis) *The Trinity Sessions* (Cooking Vinyl)
	To Love is to Bury *The Trinity Sessions* (Cooking Vinyl)
Bob DYLAN	If not for You *New Morning* (CBS)
	Forever Young *Planet Waves* (CBS)
	I shall be Released *Basement Tapes* (CBS)
	Every Grain of Sand *Shot of Love* (CBS)
	Blowin' in the Wind *The Freewheelin' Bob Dylan* (CBS)
EVERYTHING BUT THE GIRL	Come on Home *Baby The Stars Shine Bright* (Blanco y Negro)

Brian FERRY	Carrickfergus *The Bride Stripped Bare* (Island)
Ella FITZGERALD	*They can't take that away from me* (Polygram)
Nanci GRIFFITH	Heaven *Late Night Grande Hotel* (MCA)
Elton JOHN	Song for Guy *A Single Man* (Rocket) Candle in the Wind *Goodbye Yellow Brick Road* (DJM)
Rickie Lee JONES	Stewart's Coat *Traffic from Paradise* (Geffen) Company *Rickie Lee Jones* (Warner)
Carole KING	So Far Away *Tapestry* (Epic)
MADONNA	Promise to Try *Like a Virgin* (Sire)
Joni MITCHELL	Song to a Seagull *Joni Mitchell* (Reprise)
Van MORRISON	Memories *Enlightenment* (Polydor)
The ROLLING STONES	You Can't Always get what You Want *Let It Bleed* (Decca) Sleep Tonight *Dirty Work* (Rolling Stones Records)
SIMON AND GARFUNKEL	Bridge over Troubled Water *Bridge over Troubled Water* (CBS) The Sounds of Silence *Sounds of Silence* (CBS)
Bruce SPRINGSTEEN	If I should fall behind *Lucky Town* (Columbia)
TEARDROP EXPLODES	Tiny Children *Wilder* (Mercury)
THIS MORTAL COIL	With Tomorrow *Blood* (4AD)
THROWING MUSES	Two Step *The Real Ramona* (4AD)
Neil YOUNG	The Thrasher *Rust Never Sleeps* (Reprise)
Tom WAITS	Yesterday is Here *Frank's Wild Years* (Island)

Other favourites are *Amazing Grace* (many recordings; the words can be found in *Hymns and Psalms*, no. 215); Paul Anka's *My Way* sung by Frank Sinatra; *Autumn Leaves; Morning has Broken*; Jelly Roll Morton's *Didn't he Ramble*; Bette Midler, *Wind beneath my Wings*; Sinead O'Connor, *Sacrifice*; *Pie Jesu* from Andrew Lloyd-Webber's Requiem; Carly Simon, *Life is Eternal*; Linda Ronstadt, *Goodbye my Friend*; Nina Simone, *Everything must Change*.

Indexes

Index 1 and Index 2 are self-explanatory, but Index 3 needs some explanation. If you look up Celebration, *you will find* **[373-421]** *followed by three* more *numbers. This is because the readings chosen for* Celebration and Thanks *express these as their main attitudes to death. However, other readings* not *in the Celebration and Thanks section also express this attitude, and so you may explore in this book* beyond *the indications given by the section headings.*

INDEX 1

Who has died ?

Actor **210, 237**
Angler **371, 393**
Artist **370, 384, 444**
Brother **407, 410, 457**
Child **30, 39, 46, 105, 229, 259, 260, 305, 314, 334, 377, 427, 430, 439, 447,** Stillborn **326,** Unborn **453**
Craftsman **143, 400, 413, 440, 444**
Cricketer **376, 381, 389**
Dancer **391, 399**
Daughter **200, 379, 459**
Father **167, 217, 336, 407, 410, 416,**
Flyer **188, 196, 411**
Friend **230, 234, 281, 309, 328, 330, 361, 366, 385, 431, 446, 454, 457, 458, 494**

Gardener **382**
Golfer **406**
Husband/male partner **248, 291, 319, 322, 323, 329, 368, 370, 407, 428, 452, 454, 466**
Mother **218, 242, 255, 271, 374, 417, 461**
Motorist **363**
Musician **370, 383, 419, 444, 470**
Public person **141, 372, 375, 420**
Sailor **325, 488, 506**
Son **447, 448**
Wife/female partner **97, 175, 257, 311, 319, 322, 323, 329, 365, 369, 379, 418, 428,**
Writer **370, 375, 444**
Young person **132, 273, 287, 334, 379, 430, 437, 459**

Index of Authors

Numbers in bold refer to the numbered prayers, psalms, passages from the Bible and readings. Ordinary numbers refer to page numbers. The numbers for each entry in this index are given in the order in which the references appear.

Index of First Lines

Acknowledgements

While every effort has been made to contact owners of copyright material, there are some who have not been traced, and the authors and publishers, who gratefully acknowledge the following copyright owners whose material appears in this book with their permission, would welcome information that will enable them to put matters right when this book is reprinted.

Afterwards and *Regret Not Me* by Thomas Hardy Reprinted with permission of Simon & Schuster from *The Complete Poems of Thomas Hardy*, edited by James Gibson (New York: Macmillan, 1978); *An Exequy* by Peter Porter, from Peter Porter's *Collected Poems* (Oxford University Press, 1993) Copyright © Peter Porter, 1983, reprinted by permission of Oxford University Press; *An Irish Airman Foresees His Death, He Wishes for the Cloths of Heaven* and extracts from *The Song of the Wandering Aengus, The New Faces, The Tower* and *Death* by W. B. Yeats Reprinted with permission of Simon & Schuster from *The Poems of W. B. Yeats: a New Edition*, edited by Richard J. Finneran, Copyright 1919, 1928, 1933 by Macmillan Publishing Company, renewed 1947, 1956, 1961 by Bertha Georgie Yeats; Andrew Best for permission to publish *To Angelica* Copyright © Andrew Best, 1994; Angus & Robertson, a Division of HarperCollins Publishers (Australia) Pty Limited for permission to reprint *The Existence of Love* by Marjorie Pizer from *To You the Living* Copyright © Marjorie Pizer 1992; Associated University Presses for *For These Once Mine* from *Complete Poems of George Santayana* and for a one-line quotation from *War Shrines, Soliloquies in England 1922* from *Complete Poems of George Santayana* Ed. Holzberger; Bantam Doubleday Dell Publishing Group, Inc. as the publishers for courtesy with regard to *The Children's Song, Glory of the Garden* and *When Earth's Last Picture is Painted* by Rudyard Kiping; 'Because of you we will be glad and pray' by Maurice Baring Permission granted by A. P. Watt Ltd. on behalf of The Trustees of the Maurice Baring Will Trust; Cruse – Bereavement Care and Darton, Longman & Todd for permission to reprint an extract from a Cruse Annual Report reprinted in *All in the End is Harvest* (Darton, Longman & Todd in association with Cruse); 'Days' from COLLECTED POEMS by Philip Larkin. Copyright © 1988, 1989 by the Estate of Philip Larkin. Reprinted by permission of Farrar, Straus & Giroux, Inc.; *Do Not Go Gentle Into That Good Night* and extracts from *The Force that through the Green Fuse Drives the Flower* and from *And Death Shall Have No Dominion* by Dylan Thomas from his *Collected Poems* published by J. M. Dent Reprinted by permission of David Higham Associates; Excerpts from "East Coker" and "Little Gidding" in FOUR QUARTETS, copyright 1943 by T.S. Eliot and renewed 1971 by Esme Valerie Eliot, reprinted by permission of Harcourt Brace & Company; Excerpts from *Tree at My Window, Stopping by Woods on a Snowy Evening, Birches, The Lesson for Today* and *Forgive, O Lord . . .* from THE POETRY OF ROBERT FROST edited by Edward

The Life of Noël Coward, Alfred A. Knopf, Inc., 1976; *Remembered Laughter: The Life of Noël Coward*, Random House of Canada Limited, 1976 (Copyright © Cole Lesley, 1976). *Noël Coward Diaries* Copyright 1982 The Estate of Noël Coward. By arrangement with Michael Imison Playwrights Ltd 28 Almeida Street London N1 1TD. From *The Noël Coward Diaries* Ed. Graham Payn & Sheridan Morley (Weidenfeld & Nicolson); For extracts from 'Elegy' and 'Requiem for a Friend' from SELECTED POEMS OF RAINER MARIA RILKE by Stephen Mitchell Copyright © 1982 by Stephen Mitchell. Reprinted by permission of Random House, Inc.; 'For those who have the power' from *A Time to Dance* from THE COMPLETE POEMS OF C. DAY-LEWIS (Sinclair-Stevenson, 1992) Copyright © 1992 The Estate of C. Day-Lewis. Used by permission; From THE PROPHET by Kahlil Gibran Copyright 1923 by Kahlil Gibran and renewed 1951 by Administrators C.T.A. of Kahlil Gibran Estate and Mary G. Gibran Reprinted by permission of Alfred A. Knopf Inc.; Harvard University Press for *Hope is a strange invention*, *To venerate the simple days*, and part of *Behind me – dips Eternity* by Emily Dickinson Reprinted by permission of the publishers and the Trustees of Amherst College from THE POEMS OF EMILY DICKINSON, Thomas H. Johnson, ed., Cambridge, Mass.: The Belknap Press of Harvard University Press, Copyright © 1951, 1955, 1979, 1983 by the President and Fellows of Harvard College; permission to reprint an extract from *After the Death of her daughter in childbirth* by Izumi Shikibu, trans. Edwin A. Cranston Reprinted by permission; *'I am'* and the last two verses from *An Invite to Eternity* by John Clare from *Selected Poems and Prose of John Clare* edited by Eric Robinson and Geoffrey Summerfield (Oxford University Press, 1967) Copyright © Eric Robinson 1967, reproduced by permission of Curtis Brown Group Ltd, London; International Music Publications Limited for an extract from THE SONG IS ENDED Words and Music by IRVING BERLIN © Irving Berlin, USA Warner Chappell Music Ltd, London W1Y 3FA; J. M. Dent & Sons Ltd for permission to reprint an extract from *Letter to a Younger Son* by Christopher Leach; James MacGibbon as sole Literary Executor and New Directions Publishing Corporation for *Man aspires* and *I knew and shall know again* (extracts) from *Collected Poems of Stevie Smith* Copyright © 1972 by Stevie Smith (Penguin 20th Century Classics), Reprinted by permission of New Directions Publishing Corp.; John Murray (Publishers) Ltd for permission to reprint *Seaside Golf* and for an extract from *House of Rest* by John Betjeman from his *Collected Poems*; King's College, Cambridge and the Society of Authors as the literary representatives of the E. M. Forster Estate for an extract from *Howard's End* by E. M. Forster and assorted brief quotations from other works by E. M. Forster; Longman Group Limited for permission to reprint an extract from *Sacred and Secular* by Arthur Michael Ramsey; Mrs Gwen Watkins for *The Healing of the Leper* by Vernon Watkins from *The Lady with the Unicorn* (Faber and Faber), © Gwen Watkins; 'My Lord God, I have no idea where I am going' by Thomas Merton from *The Collected Poems of Thomas Merton*. Copyright © 1977 by The trustees of the Merton Legacy Trust. Reprinted by permission of New Directions Publishing Corporation and Laurence Pollinger Ltd.; *Parta Quies* by A. E. Housman from THE COLLECTED POEMS OF A. E. HOUSMAN Copyright 1936 by Barclays Bank Ltd. Copyright © 1964 by Robert E. Symons. Reprinted by permission of

(1968) by Sir George Trevelyan; The author and Carcanet Press for permission to reprint *For the Unknown Seamen of the 1939-45 War Buried in Iona Churchyard* by Iain Crichton Smith; The author and Carcanet Press for permission to reprint *Time Passing, Beloved* and an extract from *G. M. B.* by Donald Davie; The author for permission to reprint an extract from *Another Nigger Dead* by Taban Lo Liyong (Heinemann, 1972); The author and Fr Jude McHugo CJ for permission to print an extract from *Loss* by Dan Bovington; The author and Gerald Duckworth and Company Ltd for permission to reprint *To Joshua* by Alice Thomas Ellis; The author and HarperCollins Publishers Limited for permission to reprint *The Sparrow's Prayer* and a one-line quotation from *A Sparrow's Flight: Memoirs* by Lord Hailsham; The author and Macmillan London Ltd. for *For a Child Born Dead* from Selected Poems by Elizabeth Jennings, reprinted by permission of David Higham Associates.; The author and Macmillan London Ltd. for permission to reprint extracts from the works of Rabindranath Tagore; The author for permission to reprint a prayer by Majorie Bereza; The author and Watson, Little Limited licensing agent for permission to reprint *In Cemeteries, On the Death of a Child* and *Guest* from *Collected Poems* 1987 (Oxford Poets) by D. J. Enright; The author and William Heinemann Ltd for permission to reprint an extract from *Letters of an Indian Judge to an English Gentlewoman* Reprinted by permission of David Higham Associates; The author for permission to print *Canticle of Joy* Copyright © Maurice O'Connor 1994, originally broadcast on Irish Radio; The author for permission to reprint an extract from *Under the Breath* by Laurence Whistler from *Audible Silence* (Rupert Hart-Davis, 1961) and for a three-line quotation; The author for permission to reprint *Envoi* by Kathleen Raine; The author for permission to reprint *Love doesn't end with dying* by John Addey; The author for permission to reprint *Prayer* by Gavin Ewart; The author for permission to reprint *To My Friend* by Vivienne Prescott; The author for permission to reprint *War-Pilot 1940, War-flying, 1940*, and an extract from *Death in the Aircrew Mess* from *The Poetry of a Fighter Pilot* by J. R. A. Bailey (Images Publishing, 1993) Copyright © J.R.A. Bailey 1993 and for permission to reprint the Preface to *The Sky Suspended* by Jim Bailey (Images Publishing, 1994) Copyright © Jim Bailey, 1964; The author for permission to reprint an extract from *Problems: An open way of Psychotherapy and Counselling* by Carol Jeffrey (forthcoming); The author for permisson to reprint *Cricket at Brighton* from *Blindfold Games* by Alan Ross (Collins Harvill, 1986); The Central Board of Finance of the Church of England for material from *The Alternative Service Book 1980* and *The Prayer Book as Proposed in 1928*; The Estate of John Cowper Powys and Laurence Pollinger Limited for permission to reprint an extract from *A Philosophy of Solitude* by John Cowper Powys; The Frances Horovitz Estate and Bloodaxe Books for permission to reprint an extract from *In Painswick Churchyard* from *Frances Horovitz: Collected Poems* edited by Roger Garfitt (Bloodaxe Books, 1985); The Literary Trustees of Walter de la Mare, and the Society of Authors as their representative for permission to reprint *Fare Well* by Walter de la Mare; The Malvern Publishing Company Limited for permission to reprint extracts from *Lyrics from the Chinese* by Helen Waddell (Malvern, 1987); The Society of Authors as the literary representative of the Estate of John Masefield for permission to reprint *Sea Fever* by John Masefield and three extracts from the works of

John Masefield; The Society of Authors for 'They shall grow not old...' and for an extract from *The Burning of the Leaves* by Laurence Binyon, by permission of Mrs Nicolette Grey and The Society of Authors, on behalf of the Laurence Binyon Estate; The stanzas from "my father moved through dooms of love" are reprinted from COMPLETE POEMS, 1904-1962, by E. E. Cummings, edited by George J. Firmage, by the permission of W. W. Norton & Company and of Liveright Publishing Corporation. Copyright © 1940, 1968, 1991 by the Trustees for the E. E. Cummings Trust; Timothy Arlott for permission to reprint an extract from *To Sir Jack Hobbs on his 70th Birthday* by John Arlott; Two extracts from *Healing into Life and Death* by Stephen Levine. Copyright © 1987 by Stephen Levine and one extract from *Who Dies?* by Stephen Levine. Copyright © 1982 by Stephen Levine. All used by permission of Doubleday, a division of Bantam Doubleday Dell Publishing Group, Inc. and Gateway Books Ltd; Virago for permission to reprint an extract from TESTAMENT OF FRIENDSHIP Copyright © Paul Berry (The Literary Executor of Vera Brittain) 1970, and an extract from TESTAMENT OF YOUTH by Vera Brittain Copyright © Paul Berry (The Literary Executor of Vera Brittain) 1971.; Weidenfeld & Nicolson Ltd and Random House, Inc. for permission to reprint short quotations from the works of Vladimir Nabokov.